ACCOUNTABILITY AND CONTROL IN EDUCATIONAL SETTINGS

Edited by David Scott

CASSELL

Cassell

Villiers House   387 Park Avenue South
41/47 Strand   New York
London WC2N 5JE   NY 10016-8810

First published 1994

British Library Cataloguing-in-Publication Data
A catalogue record for this book is available from the British Library

ISBN 0-304-32913-4 (hardback)
     0-304-32915-0 (paperback)

Library of Congress Cataloging-in-Publication Data
Accountability and control in educational settings/edited by David
     Scott.
          p.   cm. — (Education management series)
     Includes bibliographical references and index.
     ISBN 0-304-32913-4. — ISBN 0-304-32915-0 (pbk.)
     1. Educational accountability—Great Britain.   2. School
management and organization—Great Britain.   3. Education and state—
Great Britain.   I. Scott, David, 1951–   .   II. Series.
LB2806.22.A24   1994   93-44084
379.1'54'0941—dc20   CIP

Typeset by Litho Link Ltd, Welshpool, Powys, Wales
Printed and bound in Great Britain by Redwood Books, Trowbridge, Wiltshire

Contents

Notes on contributors

Robert Burgess is Director of CEDAR (Centre for Educational Development, Appraisal and Research) and Professor of Sociology at the University of Warwick. He has written ethnographic studies of secondary schools and is currently working on case studies of secondary schools and higher education. His main publications include: *Experiencing Comprehensive Education* (Methuen, 1983); *In the Field: An Introduction to Field Research* (Allen & Unwin, 1984); *Sociology, Education and Schools* (Batsford, 1985), together with fourteen edited volumes on qualitative methods and education. He is a past President of the British Sociological Association, and is currently President of the Association for the Teaching of the Social Sciences.

Clyde Chitty is a Lecturer in the School of Education at the University of Birmingham, having previously been a member of the Curriculum Studies Department at the Institute of Education, University of London. His main publications include *Towards a New Education System: The Victory of the New Right* (Falmer Press, 1989) and a number of edited volumes. He is co-editor of the journals *Forum* and *Comprehensive Education*, and a member of the Hillcole Group of socialist and Marxist educationalists.

Rosemary Deem, having lectured in Sociology and Education at North Staffordshire Polytechnic and the Open University, was in 1991 appointed to a Chair in Educational Research at Lancaster University. She has researched and published extensively in the areas of gender, education and leisure. Currently she is co-directing an ESRC-funded project on the reform of school governing bodies in England, and she has been a school governor, chairing the governing body of a large comprehensive school (Stantonbury Campus) from 1986 to 1991.

John Evans has recently been appointed to a Chair at Loughborough University, having been a Senior Lecturer in the Faculty of Educational Studies at the University of Southampton. He has published extensively in the fields of physical education, the sociology of education and policy studies, in particular *Teaching in Transition: The Challenge of Mixed-Ability Teaching* (Open University Press, 1985). He is currently directing two research projects (funded by ESRC and Leverhulme) on the implementation of the National Curriculum for Physical Education.

John Fitz was formerly Senior Lecturer in Policy and Provision in Education at the University of the West of England, Bristol, and now works at the University of Wales, Cardiff. He has undertaken research on schoolchildren and their employment, relations between state and private education and the professional education of health educators. He is currently co-director of an ESRC-supported study of grant-maintained schools.

Mark Halstead is Principal Lecturer in Education at Rolle Faculty of Education, University of Plymouth, and Director of the Centre for Research into Moral, Spiritual and Cultural Understanding and Education (RIMSCUE Centre). He is author of *The Case for Muslim Voluntary-Aided Schools* (Islamic Academy, 1986) and *Education, Justice and Cultural Diversity* (Falmer Press, 1988), and editor of *Parental Choice and Education* (Kogan Page, 1994). He has also written numerous articles on religious and multi-cultural education. He is currently working on a book on liberal values and the education of Muslim children, and editing various collections of papers on spiritual and moral education.

John Lee is Principal Lecturer in Primary Education in the Faculty of Education at the University of the West of England, Bristol. His academic and research interests include curriculum, pedagogy and classroom organization in primary schools, multi-cultural education, and linguistic diversity, and he has published extensively in many of these fields. With John Fitz he has recently been researching HMI practice.

Jon Nixon is a Lecturer within the Division of Education at the University of Sheffield. He has written widely on issues relating to whole-school organization and change and to the professional development of teachers within a range of educational settings. His recent publications include *Evaluating the Whole Curriculum* (Open University Press, 1992); *Dimensions of Discipline* with David Gillborn and Jean Rudduck) (HMSO, 1993); and *Encouraging Learning in Secondary Schools* (Open University Press, 1994). He is currently collaborating with colleagues at the Universities of Birmingham and Ulster on a study of new forms of educational management as part of the ESRC Local Government Programme.

Dawn Penney graduated from Bedford College of Physical Education and then worked as a Sports Development Officer. In 1990 she was successful in applying for a research scholarship funded by the Sports Council to examine the impact of the Education Reform Act on provision for physical education and sport in schools. With John Evans, she has published in a number of professional and academic journals including the *British Journal of Physical Education*, *Physical Education Review* and BERA dialogues.

Jean Rudduck is Director of Research at Homerton College, Cambridge University. She was, until recently, Professor of Education at the University of Sheffield and before that a member of the Centre for Applied Research in Education at the University of East Anglia, Norwich. She is interested in teachers' and pupils' experiences of change and in the quality of teaching and learning. Recent books include *Developing a Gender Policy in Secondary Schools: Individuals and Institutions* (Open University Press, 1994); *Dimensions of Discipline* (HMSO, 1993), (with David Gillborn and Jon Nixon); and *Innovation and Change* (Open University Press, 1991). She was also responsible, with Dr Helen Cowie, for a series of books, published by BP, on co-operative group work in secondary schools.

David Scott is a Lecturer in the School of Education at the University of Southampton. Previously he was a Research Fellow in CEDAR (Centre for Educational Development, Appraisal and Research) at the University of Warwick where he worked on a number of projects: Coursework and Coursework Assessment in the GCSE, Language Teaching in Higher Education, Models of INSET, and Library Use in the Primary School. He has published on assessment in journals such as *Forum, Curriculum, Journal of Policy Studies* and *Research Papers in Education*, in edited books and in the CEDAR Report Series.

Alison Sealey holds a joint post with CEDAR and the Department of Arts Education at the University of Warwick. She was previously the primary advisory teacher for the project Language in the National Curriculum (LINC) with Birmingham Education Authority. She is co-author of *Where It Really Matters: Developing Anti-racist Education in Predominantly White Primary Schools* (Birmingham DEC, 1990), and has also written *Language in Context: Supporting Authenticity with Computers* (NCERT, 1991). Her current research is into young children's understanding of language as a social and cultural phenomenon.

Geoffrey Walford is Senior Lecturer in Sociology and Education Policy at Aston Business School, Aston University, Birmingham. He has researched and published widely, mainly on topics concerned with private education, research methods and higher education. He is the author of *Life in Public Schools* (Methuen, 1985), *Restructuring Universities: Politics and Power in the Management of Change* (Croom Helm, 1987), *Privatization and Privilege in Education* (Routledge, 1990), *City Technology College* (Open University Press, 1991) (with Henry Miller) and a number of edited volumes. His most recent book is *Choice and Equity in Education* (Cassell, 1994).

Foreword by the series editor

During a period of increasing regulation by central government, decreasing administration by local authorities, and apparent control by 'quango' or franchise, the understanding and unravelling of approaches to accountability is vital for the education service.

David Scott has selected some striking and revealing case studies, and has brought them into a valuable interpretation of different models, practices and policies of accountability, which at the same time enables readers to make their own interpretation of the confused episode of the last decade.

In this series, there are strong connections with Mike Bottery on values – and Mark Halstead's chapter here is particularly helpful; with Ian Lawrence on power and politics; with Patricia Leighton on contract and the quasi-employer role of governing bodies; and also with the professional responsibility which is the emphasis of my book on governance. The forthcoming volume *Education Tomorrow* can serve together with David Scott's selection as a tool to demystify the ideologies that recently have damaged policy and threatened good practice in the management of schools and services.

The unique contribution of this book is to show the effects of sometimes conflicting applications of accountability and control not only on the management of organizations but on research, curriculum development, advice and inspection, and to measure these against carefully considered criteria. Those managing any part or project of the education service have the task of understanding and negotiating appropriate modes of accountability and not allowing them to replace the prime purpose of providing a service for a learning society. This is a book which will help us all in that task.

John Sayer

Acknowledgements

The editor would like to thank Falmer Press for sponsoring the original CEDAR (Centre for Educational Development, Appraisal and Research) International Conference – Warwick University, 10 to 12 April 1992 – at which these and fifty-six other papers were given. The ten papers included here have been updated, with a specially written Introduction and Afterword. Acknowledgement should also be made to two journals, *Education Policy* and *Research Papers in Education*, for permission to base two chapters (6 and 8) on articles that had previously appeared in those journals. Finally, thanks are due to Hazel Paul and Jackie Belenger for their help in preparing this manuscript.

Abbreviations

CATE	Council for the Accreditation of Teacher Education
CCT	compulsory competitive tendering
CEDAR	Centre for Educational Development, Appraisal and Research, University of Warwick
CEO	chief education officer
CLEA	Council of Local Education Authorities
CPC	Conservative Political Centre
CPRS	Central Policy Review Staff
CPS	Centre for Policy Studies
CTC	city technology college
DES	Department of Education and Science
DfE	Department for Education
DPAC	Drummond Parents' Action Committee
ERA	Education Reform Act
ESRC	Economic and Social Research Council
FEVER	Friends of the Education Voucher Experiment in Representative Regions
GCSE	General Certificate of Secondary Education
GMS	grant-maintained status
HMI	Her Majesty's Inspectorate; Her Majesty's Inspector
IEA	Institute of Economic Affairs
ITT	initial teacher training
LEA	local education authority
LINC	Language in the National Curriculum
LMS	local management of schools
NCC	National Curriculum Council
NCES	National Council for Educational Standards
NCPE	National Curriculum for physical education
OECD	Organisation for Economic Co-operation and Development
OFSTED	Office for Standards in Education
SAT	standard assessment task
SCAA	School Curriculum and Assessment Authority
SEAC	School Examinations and Assessment Council
SSRC	Social Sciences Research Council
TGAT	Task Group on Assessment and Testing
TQM	total quality management
TVEI	Technical and Vocational Education Initiative

Chapter 1

Introduction

David Scott

Issues of control and accountability are central to understanding how education systems work. The notion of accountability is not an easy concept to come to terms with for a number of reasons: first, a plethora of models and frameworks have been developed by those with an interest in education (see Kogan, 1986). Second, notions of power and control are at the heart of all these models, since the latter cannot be reduced to the accountable body giving an account of its activities without expectation that it will be subject to some form of constraint or sanction should the account prove to be unsatisfactory. An accountable relationship is between two parties (local education authority and headteacher or teacher and colleagues, for example), with the one potentially able to modify the actions of the other. Third, advocates of these different models may share similar views about the purposes of education but disagree about the means to achieve these ends. On the other hand, there may be little agreement about ends, with some understanding education as being the means by which suitably trained individuals are recruited to ensure the efficient workings of the industrial and economic system, and others espousing traditional purposes with their emphasis on personal development and growth.

Kogan (1986) identifies three models. The first is the public or state-control model. This is characterized by hierarchy, clear and understood lines of control, one-way information flows and bureaucratized school and system organizations. It is understood that the central body, having been legitimized by democratic means, has the right, in the last resort, to impose its views on schools. The second model he identifies is that of professional control, either by teachers or professional administrators. Within this he suggests an important variant, namely self-reporting evaluation. Here schools are expected to respond to the demands of external review, while at the same time extending and protecting their professional autonomy. Control remains firmly with the school. Finally there are consumerist models. These may take the form of partnership relationships or operate through market mechanisms. Each of these models proposes different partners for the accountability relationship, different criteria by which that account is judged, and different ways by which one partner exercises control over the other.

In the light of this, this volume discusses and debates answers to three questions in relation to schools, other educational institutions and systems. Who are the appropriate partners in accountability relationships? How should the one exercise control over the other? And how do these models operate in practice?

1

Because the government of the day chose to answer these questions in new and radical ways, the 1988 Education Reform Act (ERA) in England and Wales, has come to be seen as a watershed in the history of education in this country, formally breaking the party political consensus that had existed since the Second World War. Certainly the two governing parties were agreed about the need to implement the 1944 Education Act, with both uncritically accepting fixed notions of ability and differentiated forms of schooling (Bash, Coulby and Jones, 1985). The major challenge to this occurred in the 1970s with the Labour government's espousal of comprehensive schools and systems; though it is interesting to note in these times of legislative impulsion that the courts upheld Tameside LEA's legal challenge to the government's chosen means of introducing this major educational reform, and that thereafter control by 'circular' would become redundant. The courts were thus implicitly endorsing the existing boundaries and areas of control between local and central government, with the inevitable consequence that some authorities were able to resist the clear intention of the government and retain their grammar schools. Henceforth a Conservative government would legislate to change both curricular and assessment arrangements in schools and, more significantly, those relationships between the different parts of the system that had been maintained since the Second World War.

The Education Reform Act and subsequent legislation have therefore changed the framework for debate about educational matters in this country. The Act itself can be seen as one of the outcomes of discussions on the responsibilities of the state that have taken place within right-wing pressure groups in this country over the past thirty years; but it was not until the 1970s that radical right-wing ideas acquired 'respectability', and not until the 1980s that they became a dominant influence on the education agenda of the Conservative Party itself. The success of this right-wing project can be traced back to the collapse of the post-war welfare capitalist consensus in the mid-1970s, but the actual form and content of the 1988 Act was the result of policy-making discussions which took place, in Downing Street and elsewhere, in the months leading up to the 1987 general election. Clyde Chitty, in Chapter 2 of this volume,[1] argues that, despite this, it would be wrong to see the Act as representing a coherent and fully worked-out philosophy; and that the contradictions within right-wing thinking have become ever more apparent as policy formation has given way to implementation.

These contradictions can be traced back to arguments between those who advocated traditional concerns such as the preservation of culture and the maintenance of standards *and* those who advanced neo-liberal ideas about market forces and consumer choice (Whitty, 1990). This paradox is most faithfully represented in the centralizing mechanisms (a national curriculum and a national assessment scheme) and the decentralizing mechanisms (local management of schools and increased powers for governors) implicit in the Act. Westoby (1989), on the other hand, argues that there is no real contradiction between the two because a market model that is designed to encourage consumer freedom, but which by necessity excludes price competition, needs a standardizing mechanism to enable parents to judge between suppliers. Again, these tensions or contradictions may be understood as debates about means rather than ends, with both sides impelled by élitist ideologies which they see as having their ultimate expression in differentiated types of schooling for different types of children.

Chitty concentrates on the antecedents to the Education Reform Act and characterizes that part of the policy process as a contested activity between a diverse range of beliefs and opinions. Indeed, as Graham (1993) shows in his discussion of the National Curriculum history syllabus, policy processes are better characterized as compromises, bargainings and exchanges between participants than as coherent problem-solving exercises. We should of course remember that the frameworks for debates such as these have already been set, with key figures excluded (by election processes as much as anything else) and voices muted by micropolitical and other means. Dawn Penney and John Evans in their discussion of National Curriculum physical education in Chapter 3 provide schemata for understanding the policy process which make full reference to the various sites where policy may be changed and amended. They argue that 'state policy', especially with regard to the National Curriculum, may be 'mediated, adapted, adopted and contested' at different places and moments within the education system. The policy flow is thus not unidirectional, and is subject to a diverse range of influences and interests. This suggests that the gap between policy creation and implementation may be wide and growing, though this model also allows for reassertion of control from the centre at different moments in the process.

David Scott, in a complementary chapter, uses a similar conceptual framework to trace the evolution of the assessment arrangements for the National Curriculum. He identifies two conflicting agendas within ERA policy texts. These roughly correspond to formative and summative modes of assessment, and he shows how each incorporates a different notion of accountability. What both Penney/Evans and Scott emphasize is the gap between initial policy-making and implementation, and between political rhetoric and reality with the consequence that implementors'/ teachers' practice is fragmented. In the case of assessment this means that though the political rhetoric is able to suggest that summative and decontextualized assessments can be made at the end of the various key stages, and that they benefit the taught curriculum, provide useful information for teachers and are integrated productively into learning programmes, in reality this is not the case.

Whitty (1990) has further characterized the Education Reform Act as representing a fourfold attack (open enrolment, local management of schools, testing and publication of results, changes in the composition and powers of governing bodies) on the partnership between teachers, central government and local education authorities that governed education for four decades. Rosemary Deem, in Chapter 5, explores the last of these in her discussion of governing bodies and their extensive reshaping. She examines, as previous authors have done, the gap between the political rhetoric behind these reforms and what has actually happened. She argues that this rhetoric suggests that a widening of the powers of lay governors will add to schools' efficiency and market orientation, increase local parental, business and community involvement in schooling and sharpen public accountability while ensuring that the actions of professional teachers and heads are overseen by lay people. This substitutes a different and conflicting notion of accountability, and is intended in part to change teaching and learning arrangements in schools in line with more formal approaches (this desire has also found expression in a number of recent curriculum documents and initiatives – see Alexander, Rose and Woodhead,

1992). Deem, in fact, identifies two distinct agendas: collective concern ideologies which focus on the public good, and consumer interest ideologies which emphasize markets, competition, consumer rights and private interests. She concludes that the latter may indeed be in the ascendancy with consequent losses in democratic accountability.

The main intention behind the government's reforms has been to give parents a greater say in choice of schools. The justification for this change has been the belief that the workings of the market, and the linked greater direct local accountability to parents, are more likely to lead to improvements in educational standards than any changes that could be made in a planned way by local government. In addition the government has sought by various means to break the monopoly that local government enjoyed over educational matters: implementing the assisted places scheme, introducing city technology colleges, setting up grant-maintained schools and more importantly devolving funds to schools. Other research has cast doubt on the success of some of these initiatives. The assisted places scheme, for instance, was designed to allow children from poorer sections of the community to attend private schools, yet Edwards, Fitz and Whitty (1989) have shown that a considerable proportion of entrants to this scheme have come from middle-class homes. Geoffrey Walford in Chapter 6 examines the consequences of these reforms with particular reference to the first city technology college, and argues that, far from creating greater equality between the educational experiences offered to children from different backgrounds, the opposite may be the case.

So far this volume has examined a number of structural and organizational rearrangements legislated for in the 1988 Education Reform Act. Three important themes running through the discussion have been: changing notions of accountability; an increased emphasis on the sanctioning of 'differences' between pupils; and differential allocations of resources to different parts of the system. The first of these can best be illustrated by reference to the introduction of a national curriculum and national system of assessment with consequent increases in the amount of control exercised by government in these fields, and the setting up of markets to give parents more power. Both signal a move away from professional and collegial forms of accountability. The second theme has been the stress on difference. Again, this is best illustrated by reference to the new assessment arrangements, which, though in a state of flux, emphasize evaluative and summative functions at the expense of formative and diagnostic ones, with differentiated examination papers and formal testing procedures chosen as the preferred means of data collection. We have also seen recently the first tentative moves towards the reintroduction of selective schools. This trend, it needs to be stressed, is as yet far from established. The third theme relates to differential provision between the different parts of the education system. Scott and Morrison (1993), for instance, found that local devolution of funds to schools has, in its short time of operation, meant that schools have been compelled to look for alternative sources of funding for areas such as books for the library. Schools in affluent areas have found it easier to raise money for this purpose than schools in less affluent neighbourhoods.

Accountability and its associated notion of control have in the past been exercised by the local inspectorate on behalf of the local education authority and by HMI on behalf of the central government. Recent reforms, the establishment of

OFSTED (the Office for Standards in Education) for example, have in part brought these two closer together. Most OFSTED teams of inspectors have been constituted from previous LEA inspectorate/adviser teams, though control over their activities has now been centralized. John Fitz and John Lee, in Chapter 7, unravel HMI notions of good practice which until recently have been implicit rather than explicit. In Chapter 8 Jon Nixon and Jean Rudduck, concentrating on LEA advisers/inspectors, unpack and explore the kinds of criteria which LEA inspectors routinely used, often intuitively, when making judgements about schools, and the way in which those criteria were being articulated and sometimes negotiated across schools and LEAs. OFSTED's approach veers towards the explicit rather than the implicit, though we have yet to see how published criteria for judgement impact upon actual school practice, and whether the procedures OFSTED inspection teams adopt are adequate for collecting useful and valid information. If the account given of a school by the Inspectorate is inaccurate, far from enhancing accountability, it weakens it. If further action is to be taken by outside bodies (see the 1993 Education Act) to remedy such perceived failings, it would seem sensible for this process to be grounded in actual rather than imagined practice.

This applies equally well to media representations of school practice. Alison Sealey in Chapter 9 examines the press coverage of a specific conflict between the Department of Education and Science (now the Department for Education) and an education project. The conflict concerned the decision by Ministers not to publish materials for teachers' professional development in the area of knowledge about language. These materials were commissioned by the DES and developed by the project LINC (Language in the National Curriculum). Sealey summarizes the events which led up to the press reporting of the decision to ban the materials and explores some of the reasons why teaching about English language in this country should be so controversial. More importantly, she addresses the way a number of newspaper articles reported the controversy and the kinds of discourse they used.

While Sealey focuses on media texts, Robert Burgess in this volume examines academic texts, paying particular attention to social, political and methodological issues arising from different forms of educational research and evaluation. At a time when members of the research community have become increasingly worried about the types of control exercised by the Department for Education and other government bodies over research projects (Gipps, 1993; Simons, 1993), it is pertinent to suggest that professional models of accountability in this field are more facilitative than models which emphasize sponsor control of data-collection methods, analytical techniques, conclusions and means of dissemination.

Throughout this volume the various chapters have concentrated on specific areas as they relate to changing arrangements for education, in part but not wholly in response to the Education Reform Act 1988, and in particular to issues of control and accountability. Mark Halstead in Chapter 11 discusses these last two issues with particular reference to related concepts such as power, responsibility, rights, professional autonomy and entitlement. In common with Kogan (1986) he advances the argument that ideas about accountability are essentially value laden and incorporate complementary notions about particular models of government, definitions of feelings and epistemologies. Kogan writes as follows:

For example the belief in the professional control of schools carries with it assumptions, often implicit and unclarified, about the nature of democracy and participation. It entails assumptions about the purposes of education and schooling and about the feelings, or affect, which are aroused by particular forms of power relationships between teachers, the larger political system, and client groups such as parents and pupils. The professional model of accountability rests on assumptions too, about how knowledge is generated, how it is communicated, and the ways in which different forms of the curriculum lend themselves to external control.

(1986, p. 16)

Halstead identifies six models of accountability and shows how all of them were relevant to what has come to be known as the Honeyford affair, in which a headteacher of a school in Bradford was eventually forced to resign his post after he had published a provocative article in the *Salisbury Review*.

At the end of this volume David Scott discusses and analyses these various accounts of control and accountability as they relate to particular aspects of educational activity.

This volume examines the different models of educational accountability; the different roles politicians, teachers, governors, parents, advisers/inspectors, the media and the academic community play in educational decision-making; the relationship between formulation and implementation of policy texts; and policy and practice in relation to the 1988 Education Reform Act. It draws on a range of theoretical positions as contributors use evidence from empirical research, policy analysis and philosophical review. It does not, however, provide instant answers to questions relating to appropriate relationships between the different parts of the education system in this country, though it does seek to discuss and debate the issues that are relevant to this area, to allow us a better understanding of the relationship between policy and practice.

NOTE

1. The 11 papers in this volume constitute a selection from the 65 papers presented at the Centre for Educational Development, Appraisal and Research (CEDAR) International Conference on 'Accountability and Control in Educational Settings' held at Warwick University between 10 and 12 April 1992.

REFERENCES

Alexander, R., Rose, J. and Woodhead, C. (1992) *Curriculum Organization and Classroom Practice in Primary Schools*. London: Department of Education and Science.

Bash, L., Coulby, D. and Jones, C. (1985) *Urban Schooling: Theory and Practice*. London: Cassell.

Edwards, T., Fitz, J. and Whitty, G. (1989) *The State and Private Education: An Evaluation of the Assisted Places Scheme*. London: Falmer Press.

Gipps, C. (1993) The profession of educational research. *British Educational Research Journal* 19 (1), 3–16.

Graham, D. with Tytler, D. (1993) *A Lesson for Us All*. London and New York: Routledge.

Kogan, M. (1986) *Educational Accountability: An Analytical Overview*. London: Hutchinson.

Scott, D. and Morrison, M. (1993) *Libraries for Learning: Approaches to Book Resources in Primary Schools*. London: British Library.

Simons, H. (1993) The politics and ethics of educational research in England. Paper presented to the American Educational Research Association's Annual Conference, Atlanta, Georgia, April.

Westoby, A. (1989) Parental choice and voice under the 1988 Education Reform Act. In Glatter, R. (ed.) *Educational Institutions and Their Environments: Managing the Boundaries*. Milton Keynes: Open University Press.

Whitty, G. (1990) The New Right and the National Curriculum: state control or market forces. In Flude, M. and Hammer, M. (eds) *The Education Reform Act: 1988*. Lewes: Falmer Press.

Chapter 2

Consensus to conflict: the structure of educational decision-making transformed

Clyde Chitty

THE WELFARE CAPITALIST CONSENSUS

For nearly half a century, the education system of this country was dominated by the provisions of the 1944 Education Act. This Act owed much to a recognition of the importance of education to economic advance and social welfare, and came to be regarded by many as a cornerstone of the post-war welfare state.[1] It was the product of at least three years' consultation with a variety of interested bodies, and was piloted through Parliament by a wartime coalition government which felt obliged to take account of a number of different viewpoints. It was characterized by Timothy Raison in 1976 as 'a Rolls-Royce among statutes' (Raison, 1976, p. 76); and according to Professor H.C. Dent: 'it is a very great Act, which makes – and, in fact, has made – possible as important and substantial an advance in public education as this country has ever known' (Dent, 1968, p. 1). While such praise might now seem a little excessive, it remains true that the Act established secondary education for all pupils as an integral part of an education system which was to be seen as a continuous process – ranging from the primary sector through to further or higher education. And it was able to provide, in the words of Keith Evans, 'a fairly satisfactory legislative framework for the unprecedented expansion and development of the statutory system of education over the next thirty years' (Evans, 1985, p. 109).

Administratively, the 1944 Act set up what is often referred to as 'a national system, locally administered'. What this amounted to was a tripartite 'partnership' between central government, local government and the individual schools and colleges.[2] According to Vernon Bogdanor (1979), the 'efficient secret' of the system was that no *one* individual participant should enjoy a monopoly of power in the decision-making process so that:

> Power over the distribution of resources, over the organisation and over the content of education was to be diffused amongst the different elements and no one of them was to be given a controlling voice. . . . Such a structure . . . offered clear and obvious advantages not only for the administrator concerned with the efficient working of the system, but also for the liberal, anxious to avoid the concentration of power and the pluralist, insistent that different interests are properly represented. For parallel to the formal relationships between central and local government,

embodied in statute and convention, there grew up a network of professional communities whose role it was to soften the political antagonisms which might otherwise render the system unworkable. ... The diffused structure of decision-making led, it could be argued, to better decisions because it ensured a wide basis of agreement before changes were made.

(pp. 157–8)

For at least thirty years after the end of the Second World War, both major parties shared a basic commitment to the underlying principles of the welfare state: a set of tacit assumptions that Tony Benn (1987) has described as 'the welfare capitalist consensus'. This involved a threefold commitment to full employment, to the welfare state and to the coexistence of large public and private sectors in the economy. As far as education was concerned, the general emphasis was on expansion, with a remarkable increase in the number of schools and teachers and of students in higher education. Although the Conservative governments of the 1950s were generally hostile to local experiments in comprehensive reorganization, there is much truth in Dale's assertion (1983, p. 234) that from 1954, when Sir David Eccles was appointed Minister of Education, until the 1964 general election, when the Conservatives were defeated, government education policy was essentially non-partisan, and even, when Sir Edward Boyle was Minister of Education (1962–4), almost bipartisan.

A number of factors contributed to the prevailing mood of optimism and consensus. The relative absence of damaging political conflict in the 1950s and early 1960s was greatly helped not only by the general climate of expansion, but also by the availability of sufficient financial resources to ensure the successful implementation of expansionist policies. At the same time, this was a period when the number of powerful interest groups was fairly small and it was comparatively easy to secure consensus among a cosily restricted network. As Bogdanor (1979, p. 161) has observed:

The system of consultation worked best when only a small number of interests were involved whose rank and file were content to defer to elites, and could, therefore, be relied upon to act 'sensibly'. This process of elite accommodation reached its apogee during the post-war period when, or so it was believed, many policy decisions in education were taken over lunch at the National Liberal Club by a troika consisting of Sir William Alexander, Secretary of the Association of Education Committees, Sir Ronald Gould, the General Secretary of the National Union of Teachers, and the Permanent Secretary of the Department of Education. If these three agreed on some item of educational policy, it would, more often than not, be implemented. Such at least was the general belief; and even if it was a caricature, it is at least significant that it was widely held.

The spirit of co-operation and compromise was not broken, at least to begin with, by the Labour government's use of Circular 10/65 to promote the cause of comprehensive schooling in July 1965.[3] A number of pioneering local education

9

authorities – including Conservative ones – had already introduced comprehensive schools in their areas in the preceding twenty years; so that by the time the Labour government was returned to power in 1964, such schools were already educating nearly 10 per cent of secondary-school pupils in England and Wales (Benn and Simon, 1972, p. 102). As Fenwick (1976, p. 158) has commented:

> With the advent of a Labour government, national and local policies come largely into line, and Circular 10/65 seemed an acceptable progression of policy to many in education who were not ardent supporters of reorganisation.

Furthermore, the educational philosophy of Sir Edward Boyle was an important factor in facilitating change. As Minister of Education from 1962 to 1964, he made it clear that he was broadly sympathetic to the case for comprehensive schools and prepared to accept practical proposals for change; but his party's record on education and the opposition of a significant group of Conservative backbenchers made it impossible for him to seize the initiative. Nevertheless, he made it clear in the Conservative pamphlet *Educational Opportunity*, published in 1963, that:

> None of us believes in pre-war terms that children can be sharply differentiated into various types or levels of ability; and I certainly would not wish to advance the view that the tripartite system, as it is often called, should be regarded as the right and normal way of organising secondary education, compared with which everything else must be stigmatised as experimental.
>
> (quoted in Fenwick, 1976, p. 118)

The Foreword to the 1963 Newsom Report, *Half Our Future* (Ministry of Education, 1963), shows that Boyle accepted one of the crucial arguments against a rigid system of selection at 11-plus: that so-called intelligence could be 'acquired' and was not therefore a fixed quantity impervious to any educational influence. In Boyle's words 'The essential point is that all children should have an equal opportunity of acquiring intelligence, and of developing their talents and abilities to the full' (ibid., p. iv).

These sentiments were somehow typical of the radical and progressive spirit of the 1960s, a spirit which, initially at least, cut across party divisions. The decade saw a vigorous expansion of parent interest in education which expressed itself in the creation of a number of influential campaigning pressure groups. The removal of the 11-plus straitjacket resulted in a new excitement in many primary schools which brought people from all parts of the world to look at 'progressive' primary practice. And between 1960 and 1970 the number of comprehensive schools grew from 130 to 1,145, catering by the end of the decade for over 30 per cent of maintained-sector pupils. As Maurice Plaskow has observed, for those who believed in a genuine extension of educational opportunity, 'it was the best of times':

> It is fashionable to deride the 1960s as culturally aberrant and wildly idealist. Healthy idealism may be preferable to entrenched ideology

parading as pragmatism. Many of us who were active in education in the 1960s look back on a time of optimism, a spirit of shared concerns, and the beginnings of an articulation (in every sense) of an education system which would offer the greatest possible opportunities to everyone as an entitlement, not a privilege.

(1990, p. 90)[4]

Yet as the 1960s progressed, the uneasy cross-party alliance on a number of welfare issues fell apart, leaving little trace of that benign consensus which was the basis of the organizational implementation of the comprehensive reform. This was due, in large measure, to increasing evidence of the exposed nature of Boyle's position on the 'liberal' wing of the Conservative Party – a position which eventually became untenable as large groups of right-wing backbenchers and constituency activists mobilized against the beleaguered shadow Education Minister (see Knight, 1990, pp. 22–60). It was now widely held within the Party that the Conservative government had been defeated in 1964 not simply because of internal dissensions nor because the public had become bored with it (though there was seen to be truth in both assertions), but because it had espoused economic and social policies which were a diluted version of its opponents' ideas. Nowhere did this appear to be more true than in the area of education policy – and Boyle was seen to be the main culprit. At any rate, he was a convenient scapegoat. Matters came to a head at the 1968 Conservative Party Conference, where Boyle was challenged to acknowledge that the Party was hopelessly divided on such issues as secondary education, the grammar schools and reorganization, and where he made a passionate plea for modernization and consensus:

I will join with you willingly and wholeheartedly in the fight against Socialist dogmatism wherever it rears its head. But do not ask me to oppose it with an equal and opposite Conservative dogmatism, because in education, it is dogmatism itself which is wrong.

(quoted in Corbett, 1969)

The plea was unsuccessful and the official motion on education was defeated.

By 1969, when Boyle relinquished the post of shadow Education Minister, it was obvious that his largely non-partisan or even bipartisan approach had lost the support of grass-roots activists in the Party – and that it was simply no longer possible to paper over the cracks. Writing in *New Society* in May 1969, Ann Corbett argued that: 'However you express it – left versus right, consensus versus backlash, collectivists versus radicals, or just the informed versus the ignorant – the Tory Party in parliament and in the country is divided on education' (p. 785). But at that time, according to Corbett, the views of Boyle's many critics did not add up to a 'coherent rival philosophy'. Above all, there was a very real split on the right of the Party between the 'preservationists' who simply wanted to defend the grammar schools, and the so-called 'voucher men' who wanted to experiment with new and untried ways of organizing education.

It was the 'preservationists' who dominated right-wing thinking until at least the mid-1970s. The first three Black Papers published in 1969 and 1970 (Cox and

11

Dyson, 1969a, b, 1970) were a vehicle for those Conservatives who wanted to put back the clock: to the days of formal teaching in the primary schools, of high academic standards associated with a grammar-school education and of well-motivated, hard-working and essentially conservative university students. It was only in the last two Black Papers published in 1975 and 1977 (Cox and Boyson, 1975, 1977) that support was given to the introduction of educational vouchers and the idea of much greater scope for parental choice of schools. By the mid-1970s, the politics of *reaction* had been replaced by the politics of *reconstruction*. The ground was being prepared for a more bitter ideological struggle between the main political parties.

It was the economic recession of 1973–5 that fundamentally altered the map of British politics in the mid-1970s and provided the necessary conditions for the widespread dissemination of right-wing ideas. The OPEC oil crisis exposed all the underlying weaknesses of Keynesian social democracy; and Heath, Wilson and Callaghan all failed to breathe new life into the old system. The post-war welfare capitalist consensus relied on an increasing prosperity for any success it might have had in creating a semblance of social unity; and when that prosperity disintegrated, so, too, did the consensus together with the false consciousness it generated.[5] As David Marquand has argued, the Keynesian approach to the management of capitalism, with its tacit rejection of the reality of class conflict, simply could not cope with the economic shocks and adjustment problems of the 1970s:

> The post-war consensus finally collapsed under the Wilson–Callaghan Government of 1974–79 amid mounting inflation, swelling balance of payments deficits, unprecedented currency depreciation, rising unemployment, bitter industrial conflicts and what seemed to many to be ebbing governability. The Conservative leadership turned towards a new version of the classical market liberalism of the nineteenth century. Though the Labour leadership stuck to the tacit 'revisionism' of the 1950s and 1960s, large sections of the rank and file turned towards a more inchoate mixture of neo-Marxism and the 'fundamentalist' socialism of the 1920s and 1930s.
>
> (1988, p. 3)

It is interesting to note that while both major parties contained groups with radical ideas about the future direction of society, it was only in the Conservative Party – at least after the defeat of Edward Heath as leader and his replacement by Margaret Thatcher in February 1975 – that such groups enjoyed easy access to the leadership. Indeed, it has been suggested (Young, 1993) that the events of the mid-1970s 'put paid to an entire tradition of British Conservatism'.

NEW TRENDS IN DECISION-MAKING

As far as educational policy-making is concerned, the last twenty years have been notable for the existence of two powerful and related trends: the growth on the right of a number of enterprising think-tanks anxious to redefine Conservatism and to influence policy-making on a wide range of social issues and, running parallel with this, the tendency of governments to rule out the need for wide consultation and rely for advice on a select group of committed ideologues. We will consider each of these in turn.

REVERSING THE LEFT-WING RATCHET

It was Sir Keith Joseph (now Lord Joseph) who, following the Conservative defeats in the two 1974 elections, set out to articulate the views and aspirations of the new right-wing radicals within the Party, and to persuade its new leader to move away from the 'middle ground' in politics.[6] In an important speech to the Oxford Union in December 1975, Sir Keith argued that the major task facing the Conservative Party in opposition was to reverse what he described as 'the left-wing ratchet'. As far as he was concerned, the 'middle ground' was 'a guarantee of a left-wing ratchet' and had therefore to be abandoned:

> The middle ground is not rooted in the way of life, thought and work of the British people, not related to any vision of society, or attitude of mind, or philosophy of political action. It is simply the lowest common denominator obtained from a calculus of assumed electoral expediency, defined not by reference to popular feeling, but by splitting the difference between Labour's position and that of the Conservatives! But Labour's position, as we know, is itself arrived at by splitting the difference between their left and their centre. So the middle ground, at any given time, is fixed in relation to the Labour left and the Conservative centre. In other words, it is dictated by the extremists of the left.
>
> (Joseph, 1976, p. 21)

Joseph went on to argue that in the 1960s the 'middle ground' moved continually to the left by its own internal dynamic – a process that had disastrous consequences for both the economy and society:

> It created not prosperity but crisis. Far from saving the private sector, it has gone a long way towards destroying it. Far from achieving social harmony and strengthening the centre, it has created resentments and conflict, has moved the centre of gravity of the whole labour movement to the left, strengthening the left-wing, the irreconcilables, the revolutionaries. Because we Conservatives became identified with the shifting middle ground, we were inhibited from fighting a vigorous battle of ideas; we became identified with an unworkable *status quo*; we therefore allowed the crisis of British socialism to be presented as the crisis of capitalism by default.
>
> (Ibid., p. 25)

In the 1970s, reversing the 'left-wing ratchet' meant reversing the *ideological* ratchet, and a number of groups had an important role to play in this process. In August 1974 Margaret Thatcher and Sir Keith Joseph were instrumental in the setting up of the Centre for Policy Studies (CPS), an organization intended to be a think-tank to rival the essentially moderate Conservative Research Department. It soon established a variety of study groups – among them the Education Research Group – whose aim was to develop radical solutions to current problems. In the same year, Marjorie Seldon presented a motion in favour of experimental education vouchers at the Annual Conference of the National Council for Women, which led to

13

the setting up in December 1974 of FEVER – Friends of the Education Voucher Experiment in Representative Regions. And throughout the 1970s, the Institute of Economic Affairs (established in 1955) worked tirelessly to persuade the Conservative Party to abandon the corporatist consensus and adopt policies based on nineteenth-century free-market anti-statism. It is significant that a few months after becoming Prime Minister, Mrs Thatcher felt obliged to write to the IEA's founder to express her appreciation of the Institute's 'magnificent work' in helping to create a new intellectual climate:

> I am delighted to underline my admiration for all that the IEA has done over the years for better understanding of the requirements for a free society. The Institute's publications have not only enabled us to make a start in developing sound economic policies; they have also helped create the intellectual climate within which these policies have commanded increasingly wide acceptance in the universities and the media. I wish you every success in your efforts to advance the principles in which we all believe. I am one of your strongest supporters.
>
> (quoted in Knight, 1990, p. 144)

As we have already noted, the last two Black Papers, published in 1975 and 1977, went further than ever before in delineating a distinctive right-wing agenda for education. The new emphasis was on choice and competition and parental control of schools. Progress towards privatization of the system could be achieved by the gradual introduction of the educational voucher, a device for establishing consumer sovereignty in education based on the simple principle that all parents should be issued with a free basic coupon, fixed at the average cost of schools in the local authority area. In 1975, the Black Paper editors were urging the introduction of the educational voucher in at least two trial areas (Cox and Boyson, 1975, p. 4); and the pamphlet included a special essay by Dr Rhodes Boyson, former headteacher and now a prominent Conservative Member of Parliament, on 'The developing case for the educational voucher' (ibid., pp. 27–8). Support for the voucher was then reiterated in the editorial introduction to *Black Paper 1977*, which took the form of a 'Letter to Members of Parliament':

> The possibilities for parental choice of secondary (and primary) schools should be improved via the introduction of the educational voucher or some other method. Schools that few wish to attend should be closed and their staff dispersed.
>
> (Cox and Boyson, 1977, p. 9)

Rhodes Boyson was indeed a key figure in the bid to translate right-wing educational ideas into practical policy options. He was a leading member of the National Council for Educational Standards (NCES), established in 1972 to campaign against 'progressive' teaching methods. With his ability to command the attention of the media, he acted as an important link between the Black Papers and NCES on the one hand and Conservative Party activists on the other, publishing *Battle Lines for Education* (1973) and *Parental Choice* (1975) through the

Conservative Political Centre (CPC). Also in 1975 he published *The Crisis in Education*, in which he outlined some of the themes that were to become familiar in the 1980s:

> The malaise in schools in Britain has followed from a breakdown in accepted curriculum and traditional values. There was little concern about either political control or parental choice so long as there was an 'understood' curriculum, which was followed by every school. Schools may have differed in efficiency, but their common values or curriculum were broadly acceptable. The present disillusionment of parents arises from their resentment that their children's education now depends upon the lottery of the school to which they are directed. Standards decline because both measurement and comparisons are impossible when aims and curriculum become widely divergent. . . . These problems can be solved only by making schools again accountable to some authority outside them. The necessary sanction is either a nationally enforced curriculum or parental choice or a combination of both.
>
> (Boyson, 1975b, p. 141)

The Labour Party was thrown on to the defensive by the ferocity and scale of the right-wing attack on its policies. The leadership appeared to be acutely embarrassed by the association of the Party in the eyes of the public with so-called progressive education, characterized as it often was by a child-centred approach to teaching, informal pedagogic and assessment methods and a general antipathy to hierarchy and inequality. There was, therefore, some justification for Dr Boyson's triumphant claim at a meeting of the National Council for Education Standards, held in London in May 1976: 'The forces of the Right in education are on the offensive. The blood is flowing from the other side now' (reported in *The Times Educational Supplement*, 21 May 1976).

What is quite remarkable is the extent to which the right has been successful in seeing its ideas translated into legislation. This success tells us a good deal about changing patterns of decision-making since the mid-1970s.

For crucial to the right's success in the 1980s has been the existence of the Downing Street Policy Unit, a body of prime-ministerial advisers whose influence can be said to have accelerated the trend away from *collective* towards *presidential* government. It is to the origins of this body that we must now turn.

REDEFINING THE CONSULTATION PROCESS

The Downing Street Policy Unit was not, in fact, an innovation of the Thatcher years but had been created by Harold Wilson in March 1974 shortly after the Conservative defeat in the first of the two 1974 elections. Under the leadership of Dr Bernard (now Lord) Donoughue in the first five years of its existence, it soon became, in Peter Hennessy's phrase, 'a prime-ministerial cabinet in all but name' (Hennessy, 1986, p. 82). According to the press release issued from Downing Street in 1974, it was intended that the new unit would 'assist in the development of the whole range of policies contained in the government's programme, especially those arising in the short and medium term'. This was an attempt to distinguish it from the Central

Policy Review Staff (CPRS), created by Edward Heath in 1970, which was more, although not exclusively, orientated to longer-term policy horizons. Bernard Donoughue himself was well aware of the potential role of his unit as 'the eyes and ears' of the Prime Minister (which was probably Harold Wilson's own concept):

> The Policy Unit was the newest part of the Downing Street machine. Previous Prime Ministers had employed individual advisers. However, until Harold Wilson created the Policy Unit in 1974, there was no systematic policy analysis separate from the regular civil service machine and working solely for the Prime Minister. These are the three characteristics which distinguished the Policy Unit from what had existed before: it was systematic, it was separate from the Whitehall machine and it was solely working for the Prime Minister.
>
> (Donoughue, 1987, p. 20)

It was Donoughue who argued that the Labour government had to respond to the Conservative accusation of declining standards in schools. By the mid-1970s, the government was looking perilously vulnerable on this issue, and there was little evidence of a genuine concern to allay public disquiet. The Policy Unit had soon acquired a generally low opinion of the DES, which found itself accused in a 1975 OECD report of secrecy, passivity and conservatism and of being held back by 'the inertial power of the historically enshrined goals' of the civil service (OECD, 1975, p. 30).[7] And few had anything positive to say about the hapless Fred Mulley, Education Secretary from June 1975 until September 1976, with one leading journal summing up his first twelve months in office with the following observations:

> When he was appointed, nobody expected much of him, so perhaps nobody is too disappointed . . . What the education service needed was an obvious enthusiast who could breathe life into hope deferred. What it got was Mr Mulley – a parliamentary Eeyore.
>
> (*Times Educational Supplement*, 11 June 1976)[8]

Harold Wilson's resignation as Prime Minister in March 1976 and his replacement the following month by James Callaghan gave Donoughue the opportunity he needed to seek to make education an issue of major government concern. He accordingly sent Callaghan a lengthy memorandum in April suggesting, among other things, that it would be appropriate, given the widespread anxiety being expressed, for the new Prime Minister to make the raising of educational standards an important feature of his public pronouncements. In Donoughue's view, this was an area where the Prime Minister might well convey his personal concern and commitment:

> I suggested that although it was undesirable for a Prime Minister to meddle in every department's affairs, it would be no bad thing if he were to identify a few areas of policy of genuine interest to himself where he could try to make an impact, and I put forward education as a leading candidate.
>
> (1987, p. 111)

With this initiative, the Policy Unit was, in effect, seeking to enlist the support of the Prime Minister in the cause of forcing the DES to adopt a more interventionist role in educational policy-making. Donoughue clearly disliked the cosily restricted network of powerful interest groups which had been such a marked feature of the so-called partnership years. In his view, much of the blame for the current malaise in the education system lay with the malign influence of the teachers' unions in general and the National Union of Teachers in particular:

> Education policy was conducted by the local authorities and the teachers' unions with the Department of Education ... being little more than a post-box between the two. A further problem was that each Minister was burdened with party policy commitments which were based on the assumption that all education problems would be solved by simply throwing money at them or, to be more precise, giving the cash to the teachers' unions. But in fact the latter, and especially the National Union of Teachers, had become a major part of the problem. In all my many dealings with the NUT ... I never once heard mention of education or children. The Union's prime objective appeared to be to secure ever decreasing responsibilities and hours of work for its members; and it seemed to me that the ideal NUT world would be one where teachers and children never entered a school at all – and the executive of the NUT would be in a permanent conference session at a comfortable seaside hotel.
>
> (Ibid., pp. 109–10)

In Donoughue's view, the teachers' unions had allowed themselves to be taken over by militants and progressives with little real concern for developing pupils' abilities. At the same time, young people were not being trained in the skills necessary to find useful employment in industry and commerce. The solution was for the government to take the lead in forcing teachers to be more accountable to politicians, employers and parents. And this might well involve a degree of central involvement in matters relating to the school curriculum.

Callaghan seems to have accepted the Donoughue analysis of the problems facing education, and he welcomed the idea of making an important speech on the state of the service at the earliest opportunity. With few new ideas emanating from Fred Mulley's DES, he was clearly prepared to make effective use of the think-tank inherited from his predecessor. In his words: 'its thinking was unorthodox and refreshing, and it had considerable influence when I launched the so-called Great Debate on education' (Callaghan, 1987, p. 405).

It was the Policy Unit which secured the replacement of Sir William Pile by James Hamilton (at that time working in the Cabinet Office) as Permanent Secretary at the DES in June 1976;[9] which drafted the questions to be asked of Fred Mulley by the Prime Minister at an important interview which took place in Downing Street in May of that year (Callaghan, 1987, p. 409); and which co-ordinated the various drafts of the speech on educational standards that was eventually delivered by Callaghan at a foundation-stone-laying ceremony at Ruskin College, Oxford in the middle of October. As indicated in the Callaghan recollection quoted above, it was the Policy

17

Unit which was influential in promoting the idea of staging a Great Debate on education, even though the resulting 1977 Green Paper (DES, 1977) was not to be as challenging and assertive in its final form as Donoughue himself would personally have wished (Donoughue, 1987, pp. 112–13).

In all of this frenetic activity in 1976–7, Donoughue had a willing ally in James Hamilton. The new Permanent Secretary at the DES shared the Policy Unit's concern for a stronger government voice in educational matters in general and curriculum matters in particular, and was to be described years later by Stuart Maclure, in a valedictory article in *The Times Education Supplement* (29 April 1983), as 'an unrepentant centralist'.[10] While at the Cabinet Office, Hamilton had joined forces with Donoughue in suggesting to the Prime Minister that Fred Mulley should be asked in the May interview to prepare a lengthy memorandum on matters causing concern in the educational system. Hamilton then arrived at the DES to find his civil servants engaged in the feverish activity which produced the 63-page confidential document to be known as the Yellow Book. In Maclure's words: 'having helped to set the exam paper, Hamilton then moved to the DES to answer it, or at any rate to take final responsibility for the Department's response' (ibid.).

The Yellow Book expressed concern at the alleged failure of large numbers of secondary schools to prepare their pupils adequately to enter the world of work, and saw the long lists of subject options presented to pupils in Years 4 and 5 as a particular 'source of worry'. It argued that 'the time has probably come to try to establish generally accepted principles for the composition of the secondary curriculum for all pupils' (DES, 1976, p. 11); and further suggested that there was a need 'to explore and promote further experiment with courses of a higher level of vocational relevance likely to appeal to a significant number of 14- and 15-year-olds' (ibid., p. 22). The general tone of the Yellow Book fitted well with the message that Donoughue was hoping to get across in the Ruskin College speech, and it was considered 'appropriate' to 'leak' sections of it to *The Guardian* and *The Times Educational Supplement* in the middle of October, as a means of 'testing the water' prior to the Prime Minister's visit to Oxford (see Chitty, 1989, pp. 81–6).[11]

Both James Callaghan and Bernard Donoughue had clear ideas about the purposes that the Ruskin speech was meant to serve. According to Callaghan:

> My general guidance for the Speech was that it should begin a debate about existing educational trends and should ask some controversial questions. It should avoid blandness and bring out the criticisms I had heard, whilst explaining the value of the teachers' work and the need for parents to be closely associated with their children's schools. It should ask why industry's status was so low in young people's choice of careers and seek the reasons for the shortage of mathematics and science teachers.

> (1987, p. 410)

For Donoughue, it was particularly important that the speech should concern itself with, among other things, the need to improve standards and the concept of teacher accountability:

In the Speech, I included all the feelings which I shared with the Prime Minister on the need for more rigorous educational standards, for greater monitoring and accountability of teachers, for greater concentration on the basic skills of literacy and numeracy, and for giving greater priority to technical, vocational and practical education.

(1987, p. 111)

The Ruskin speech was indeed an important development – both for what it chose to highlight and expand upon and on account of its peculiar origins. If this highly publicized event, together with the Great Debate which followed, are seen as important Policy Unit initiatives, it seems clear that the early months of the 1976–9 Callaghan administration can be recognized as the first occasion when a body of influential advisers operating *outside* the normal policy-making networks played a major role in determining the future direction of government education policy. By the spring of 1976 Donoughue was anxious to circumvent the teachers' unions, the local authorities and, above all, the civil servants of the DES. Callaghan's new concern with value for money and his fear of the populist appeal of the opposition campaign on standards meant that he was not prepared to rely solely on the DES for strategic advice. According to Christopher Price, Parliamentary Private Secretary to Fred Mulley in 1976:

The whole educational establishment was coming under siege in 1976. Mr Callaghan was surreptitiously ordering his Ruskin Speech to be prepared – outside the suspect Department of Education – because he felt the education card was rapidly slipping from Labour's hands.

(Price, 1985, p. 170)

It can, of course, be argued that once Hamilton was installed at the DES, the political viewpoint and the bureaucratic viewpoint coincided. With the deepening economic crisis associated with balance of payments difficulties and spiralling domestic inflation, the DES was prompted to re-examine the bases of centre–local relationships in order to clarify and redefine points of control. Under James Hamilton, civil servants developed a new interest in policy, efficiency and the need to make effective use of limited resources. At the same time, in the view of both politicians and civil servants, there now had to be greater control of education in general, and of the secondary curriculum in particular, in order to ensure a measurable improvement in standards and wide acceptance of the view that teachers had to play their part in improving relations between education and industry. What we find in 1976 is the attempt to create a new educational consensus – built around more central control of the curriculum, greater teacher accountability and the more direct subordination of secondary education to the perceived needs of the economy. It was after 1976 that *partnership* was, in fact, replaced by *accountability* as the dominant metaphor in discussions about the distribution of power in the education system.

The period from 1976 to 1979 was, then, one of considerable importance in the evolution of the Downing Street Policy Unit as a form of prime-ministerial cabinet. Yet its influence appeared to be threatened by the change of occupant of 10 Downing

Street in May 1979. Somewhat surprisingly in the light of later developments, when Margaret Thatcher became Prime Minister for the first time, her initial inclination was to rely for political advice on her Ministers and, by implication, for policy advice on their departments. She accordingly cut down the number and seniority of her political aides at Number 10 and reduced the size of the Policy Unit. For the next three years, while it was headed by Sir John Hoskyns, the unit appeared to have a much reduced role in policy formulation.[12]

It was the experience of working with a predominantly cautious set of Ministers (see King, 1985, pp. 101–7) that caused Mrs Thatcher to revise her earlier judgement where the Policy Unit was concerned. By the time of the 1983 general election she had clearly decided to rely for advice, encouragement and a steady supply of radical new ideas on a growing number of young, committed right-wing analysts who would henceforth occupy all the key positions in the Policy Unit. The growth of her assistance at Number 10 counterbalanced her elimination of the Central Policy Review Staff (CPRS). The demise of Edward Heath's 1970 creation came immediately after the 1983 election, and could be said to be one element in a significant shift towards presidential government. For it has been pointed out (Jones, 1985, p. 93) that the CPRS had provided policy advice for the cabinet *as a whole* and had been an important feature of collective government. While Mrs Thatcher was now strengthening her own personal staff resources, she was weakening those at the disposal of her cabinet colleagues for the performance of their collective deliberations. With the removal of the CPRS, the stage was now set for the most important phase in the Policy Unit's short history. As far as education was concerned, it was also to be a period which marked the effective end of the partnership years and the passing of the constitutional settlement drawn up in 1944.

THE IMPORTANCE OF BEING ONE OF US
Jonathan Rosenhead has argued that both the abolition of the CPRS in 1983 and the accompanying expansion in the size and scope of the Prime Minister's Policy Unit contributed massively to 'the disarray of British policy-making' in the 1980s. For Professor Rosenhead, the Thatcher government's style of policy-making could be said to be indicative of: 'a negative attitude ... to policy choice based on evidence and argument rather than on principles and gut reaction' (1992, p. 297). The politics of 'the gut reaction' has certainly embraced a large number of enterprises, prominent among them the attempt to overturn the organizing principles of the education system. Rosenhead believes that it suited Mrs Thatcher's purpose for important policies to be formulated without the 'inconvenience' of wide-ranging discussion and debate. She welcomed the development of her Policy Unit into what Hennessy has called 'a shadow Whitehall' (1986, p. 194), with each of its enthusiastic young members covering a clutch of subject areas – a distinct change from the free-ranging approach of the unit's early days. It could be relied upon to challenge existing orthodoxies; and after Professor Brian Griffiths took over its day-to-day running in October 1985 it became particularly influential in matters relating to education and health where the early years of the Thatcher administration had not been notable for radical developments.[13]

A revealing account of how the Policy Unit worked in the mid-1980s has been provided by a former member, David Willetts – now a Conservative MP (Willetts,

1987).[14] Unlike the CPRS, the Policy Unit did not undertake long-term, large-scale studies. One of its functions was to offer policy advice on matters of current concern, working to a timetable 'determined by that night's box, the weekend box, or a meeting planned several days in advance' (ibid., p. 443). It was very much a part of the Prime Minister's own machine in Downing Street: the advice it offered did *not* go to Cabinet where it could be rebutted by hostile or unsympathetic departmental Ministers. It expected to receive copies of all papers sent to the Prime Minister concerning domestic policy: according to Willetts, 'members of the Unit must be prepared to stay late and to brief at short notice, so that departments don't believe they can escape Policy Unit scrutiny simply by sending in a paper after 6 p.m., with a reply needed the following morning' (ibid., p. 448). Not that the unit's work was determined simply, or indeed largely, by the actions of government departments. Members of the unit were 'always on the lookout for new policy ideas, the fresh angle, the new policy proposal worth putting before the Prime Minister' (ibid., p. 450). The unit saw one of its main tasks as being to help the Prime Minister roll back 'the frontiers of the politically impossible'. According to Willetts: 'the Policy Unit, because it is directly subordinated to the most senior and astute politician of the lot, is not afraid of putting forward what might initially appear to be politically far-fetched' (ibid., p. 452).

Under Professor Brian Griffiths, the Policy Unit conspired with the Prime Minister to secure implementation of favoured policies – without the time-wasting involvement of civil servants and Ministers. Professor Rosenhead has provided us with his own concise version of Mrs Thatcher's idiosyncratic style of policy-making:

> the Policy Unit supplies the Prime Minister with a radically new policy consistent with her principles and instincts. She then announces this policy in a glare of publicity, thereby establishing a political *fait accompli.* The debate having thus been finessed and forestalled, the relevant Department is left with the job of trying to make the innovation work. As the policy is commonly only in outline form and has not been subject to the filter of critical scrutiny, this task has been known to present some difficulties.
>
> (Rosenhead, 1992, pp. 297–8)[15]

It is, of course, fair to point out that few of these new policies *originated* in the Number 10 Policy Unit itself. After Brian Griffiths became Head of the Unit in 1985, it began to act as a conduit between a number of increasingly influential right-wing pressure groups, particularly the Centre for Policy Studies, and the Prime Minister herself (see Gow, 1988).[16] By the time of the 1987 general election, these groups had devised a number of radical policies for overturning the so-called dependency culture of the consensus years. Their controversial proposals attracted widespread publicity in the media; and 'the drip-effect of their insistent promotion of market-based policies' can be said to have secured 'palpable shifts' in what was perceived as the accepted wisdom (Rosenhead, 1992, p. 298).

As far as education was concerned, the Centre for Policy Studies, in existence since 1974, was one of three groups which were now beginning to exert a powerful influence on the formulation of policy, the other two being the Institute of Economic

Affairs, which established its own Education Unit with Stuart Sexton as Director in 1986,[17] and the Hillgate Group, comprising Caroline Cox, Jessica Douglas-Home, John Marks, Lawrence Norcross and Roger Scruton, which began publishing manifestos and pamphlets at the end of 1986. It is difficult to be precise about *which* of these groups was responsible for particular elements of the government's new education programme, but variations of the ideas which eventually found their way into the 1987 Education Bill can be discovered in, for example: *The Riddle of the Voucher*, published by the Institute of Economic Affairs in February 1986; *Our Schools – A Radical Policy*, written by Stuart Sexton and published by the IEA's Education Unit in March 1987; and *Whose Schools? A Radical Manifesto*, issued by the newly formed Hillgate Group in December 1986. After a meeting with the Centre for Policy Studies Education Study Group, held in the House of Lords in spring 1987, Education Secretary Kenneth Baker told his chief political adviser: 'these are the people who are setting the educational agenda' (quoted in Wilby and Midgley, 1987, p. 11). Baker well understood when he was offered the education portfolio in May 1986 that the CPS, the IEA and the Hillgate Group were the *real* policy-makers as far as the Prime Minister was concerned.

These groups are just three examples – though possibly the most prestigious and influential – of an extraordinary array of right-wing organizations and education study groups which sprang up in the 1970s and 1980s and which boasted impressive titles and interlocking memberships (see Griggs, 1989, pp. 116–17). With the prospect of an imminent general election serving to concentrate their thinking, what these groups all agreed on in early 1987 was the need both to undermine the powers of the local education authorities and to establish something resembling a free market in education. They also placed tremendous emphasis on their role as Mrs Thatcher's leading intellectual supporters. According to Professor Roger Scruton:

> The Conservative Party for many years tried to limp along without having an attendant halo of intellect – unlike the Labour Party which has always been able to draw on people who have been saying things more radical and more explicit than itself. . . . I think a political party very much needs people who are saying things not because they are politically possible, but because they think they are true, which will then define the issues and give them the language with which to discuss them. . . . In so far as people like myself and Caroline Cox and so on have any influence, that's the sort of influence it is . . . writing things – which give a certain language and tone to the debate, define ultimate goals and give analysis of the situation, which I should imagine the Conservative Party can then pick and choose a bit from.
>
> (quoted in Wilby and Midgley, 1987, p. 11)

With their easy access to Brian Griffiths and the Downing Street Policy Unit, Professor Scruton and his allies were in an ideal position to influence the policy-making process.

A number of educational planning meetings were held in Downing Street in 1986 and 1987 and, to begin with at least, the chief concern of the discussions was to devise practical ways of both breaking up the comprehensive system of secondary schooling and, at the same time, overturning the concept of a 'national system, locally administered'. For the members of the Hillgate Group the ultimate objective was a system where *all* schools would be owned by individual trusts, their survival depending on their ability to satisfy their customers (see Hillgate Group, 1986, p. 7). But it was accepted that it would be difficult to move *directly* towards this privatized system of schooling, and it was therefore important to find ways of gradually reaching this goal over the lifetime of another parliament. In his IEA pamphlet *Our Schools – A Radical Policy*, published in 1987, Stuart Sexton admitted that the far right had tried to move too quickly in recent years:

> In pursuit of the 'privatization' of management, if not of ownership also, the mistake has been to assume that we can get from where we are now to where we want to be in one giant stride, and all in a couple of years. . . . After a hundred years of state-managed education, it will take more time to accommodate the schools, the teachers, and, above all, the parents themselves, to a system of 'free choice': from a producer-led system to a consumer-led system, which is what it ought to be. . . . Vouchers, or 'education credits' to use a better term, available for every child and usable at any registered school, should be the ultimate objective. That would probably take five years to achieve if a series of measures began to be introduced now, each being a positive constructive step towards that ultimate objective.
>
> (Sexton, 1987, p. 10)[18]

These measures would include the creation of new types of school at the secondary level and the introduction of a system of per capita (that is: per pupil) funding as stage one of a *phased* introduction of the education credit.

The one issue on which the various groups failed to reach agreement concerned the desirability or otherwise of a centrally imposed National Curriculum. This source of conflict could be said to reflect a major paradox within Thatcherism itself. For, as has often been pointed out (see, for example: Belsey, 1986; Gamble, 1988; Chitty, 1989; Jones, 1989), what makes New Right philosophy special is a unique combination of a traditional *liberal* defence of the free economy with a traditional *conservative* defence of state authority. This combination of potentially opposing doctrines means that the New Right can appear by turns libertarian and authoritarian, populist and élitist. For neo-liberals the emphasis is always on freedom of choice, the individual, the market, minimal government and *laissez-faire*; while neo-conservatism prioritizes notions of social authoritarianism, the disciplined society, hierarchy and subordination, the nation and strong government. For Andrew Gamble, the phrase that best summarizes the doctrine of the New Right and the hegemonic project it has inspired is: 'free economy/strong state'. The liberal tendency argues the case for a freer, more open, and more competitive economy, while the conservative tendency is more interested in the restoration of social and political authority throughout society. Keith Joseph, Stuart Sexton and Alfred Sherman could be said to be leading figures on the neo-liberal wing of the movement; while the leading exponent of neo-conservatism is probably Roger Scruton. In *The Meaning of Conservatism*, published in 1980, Scruton described the philosophy of liberalism, particularly when it is applied to non-economic issues, as 'the principal enemy of conservatism', and denounced all 'liberal' notions of 'individual autonomy' and the 'natural rights of man'. In his view, a genuine conservative attitude is one which:

> seeks above all for government, and regards no citizen as possessed of a natural right that transcends his obligation to be ruled. Even democracy – which corresponds neither to the natural nor to the supernatural yearnings of the normal citizen – can be discarded without detriment to the civil well-being, as the Conservative conceives it.
>
> (Scruton, 1980, p. 16)

As far as education was concerned, it was the Hillgate Group, of which Roger Scruton was a leading member, which urged the introduction of a detailed national curriculum for all pupils. Such a curriculum would, in their scheme of things, uphold the values of a traditional education and instil respect for the family, the church, private property and all those bodies charged with maintaining the authority of the bourgeois state. It would preach the moral virtue of free enterprise and the pursuit of profit – a concept designed to appeal to the IEA *and* the Prime Minister herself. Yet in the course of heated discussions even this aspect of the proposed curriculum framework failed to win the support of the neo-liberals. Talking on a BBC Television *Panorama* programme, broadcast in November 1987, of the planning which had taken place in Downing Street earlier in the year, Stuart Sexton made it clear that he and others had remained totally opposed to the idea of a government-imposed curriculum. There was general support for the Hillgate Group's special emphasis on morality and social order; but it was felt that a return to traditional values could be achieved quite easily by the imposition of a fairly limited compulsory core. On one occasion, according to Sexton, Prime Minister Margaret Thatcher said her chief concern was 'the teaching of the 6Rs: reading, writing, arithmetic, religious education and right and wrong'. This would constitute her *limited* compulsory core curriculum for both primary and secondary schools.

It was largely the new Education Secretary, Kenneth Baker, and a number of influential DES civil servants who found a way of winning the support of some at least of the neo-liberals for the concept of central control of the curriculum (see Cordingley and Wilby, 1987, p. 8; Chitty, 1989, p. 218). It was possible to argue that in one major respect, a national curriculum was not necessarily incompatible with the furtherance of free-market principles. It would, after all, act as justification for a massive programme of national testing at important stages in a child's school career, thereby providing crucial evidence to parents of the desirability or otherwise of individual schools. In other words, additional consumer information provided by the test results would actually *help* a market system to operate more effectively.

This, then, was the intellectual background to the framing of the 1988 Education Reform Act. And it can be argued that the Conservative Party's decision to make educational change an important part of its programme for a third term in government was based on the realization that comparatively little had been done in the previous eight years to shake up the educational establishment. This was one of those areas where Thatcherite principles had not so far been actively applied; and the right-wing think-tanks were determined to ensure that this time the revolution they sought should not be undermined. As Stuart Maclure has expressed it:

> What eventually emerged in the 1987 election manifesto – and therefore ultimately in the 1988 Act – was assembled in secret in the nine months before the 1987 General Election. There was a determined effort *not* to consult either the DES or the civil servants or chief education officers or local politicians. Under the discreet eye of Professor Brian Griffiths, the Head of the Prime Minister's Policy Unit, the outline of a radical reform was set down in bold lines from which there was no going back.
>
> (1988, p. 166)

POSTSCRIPT: THE DES/DFE STRIKES BACK?

Thatcherism did *not* come to a sudden end with the replacement of Mrs Thatcher by John Major as Prime Minister in November 1990. As far as education is concerned (and the same is true of other areas of social policy), it can be argued that the Thatcherite agenda has been carried out with unswerving devotion over the past three years. The Major government seems determined to create new types of school at the secondary level, to speed up the process by which schools can opt out of local authority control, and to increase the power of the Secretary of State for Education. In all this, it has continued to listen to a few strident voices on the far right of the Conservative Party. As former Senior Chief Inspector of Schools Eric Bolton argued in a speech delivered to the Annual Conference of the Council of Local Education Authorities (CLEA) in Liverpool in July 1992:

> There is no crime in listening to your political friends. But a wise government listens more widely than that, and especially to those with no political axe to grind. . . . It is as damaging, and as nonsensical, to turn a deaf ear to the professionals in education as it is to believe that the professional is the only voice that should be heard. It is lacking in wisdom not to listen to the views of those long involved in administering and governing education at the local level. It is shortsighted and ultimately counterproductive to believe, or appear to believe, that anybody who is not with us is against us.
>
> (Bolton, 1993, pp. 14–15)

Yet there is evidence to suggest that the civil servants at the DfE may now be starting to assert themselves against the politicians. John Patten has not apparently had an easy ride at the Department, where he has suffered a number of defeats. For example Sir Ron Dearing, Head of the new School Curriculum and Assessment Authority (SCAA), is seen very much as the appointment of Sir Geoffrey Holland, Permanent Secretary at the DfE from January 1993 to April 1994; and the review of the National Curriculum has not been carried out along lines approved of by the IEA and the Centre for Policy Studies. Members of the right have felt themselves excluded from the process, and believe that the hated education establishment has begun to reassert its influence. In the words of Nick Seaton, spokesperson for the Campaign for Real Education: 'We are concerned that Sir Ron Dearing is too busy listening to the trade unions to take on board what we on the Right have to say. I am not very optimistic about the outcome of all this' (quoted in *The Times Educational Supplement*, 16 July 1993).

We may be in a period of transition where the outcome is indeed uncertain. For if we are right to view modern education systems as an area of conflict where the vested interests of different classes and groups meet and clash, then it is always hard to be dogmatic about future developments – particularly at a time when ideas which have held sway for a considerable period are seen to have such limited appeal.

NOTES

1. The 1944 Education Act is often referred to as the Butler Act, since R.A. Butler had been President of the Board of Education since July 1941. In his book of memoirs, *The Art of the Possible*, published in 1971, Butler talked in terms of being excited to have the opportunity to 'harness to the educational system the wartime urge for social reform and greater equality' (Butler, 1971, p. 86).

2. The *third* element in the partnership is sometimes referred to as the organized teaching profession (see, for example, Manzer, 1970; Dale, 1983).

3. This circular (DES, 1965) asked local authorities to submit schemes for secondary reorganization, based on six existing LEA patterns.

4. Maurice Plaskow was a curriculum officer at the Schools Council until he took early retirement on the closure of the Council in 1984. He was the editor of *Life and Death of the Schools Council* (1985).

5. Karl Marx was very clear about the harmful illusions created by a transient prosperity. In his *Critique of the Gotha Programme*, written in 1875 and first published in 1891, he pointed out that social democrats liked to believe that it was possible to produce a fairer distribution of social resources for citizenship in a privately owned economy. In Marx's view, such an assumption involved ideological distortion:

> In a class-based society, class interests are antithetical and while in periods of prosperity, it may be possible for there to be a veneer of agreement between the classes, this always embodies false consciousness: the reality of class division and domination is still there and will reappear in periods of recession when the apparent gains in terms of citizenship and social and economic rights will be eroded and cut back.
>
> (see Plant, 1990, p. 34)

6. According to Hugo Young, the Joseph speeches of the mid-1970s contained 'everything that is distinctive about the economic and political philosophy which later became known as Thatcherism'. Mrs Thatcher herself, on the other hand, was not, in Young's view, an accomplished theoretician, and never had 'an original view'. 'She dealt in simple convictions, which had survived in some fashion even while, as an education minister, she was doing, and watching others do, exactly the opposite of where those convictions ought to have pointed' (Young, 1989, pp. 100, 103).

7. Similar criticisms of the DES were made in the tenth report of the House of Commons Expenditure Committee, Session 1975–76, entitled *Policy Making in the DES* and published in September 1976. This all-party group was severely critical of

the DES for being too secretive and too slow to give a lead. It made *four* major recommendations: that the Secretary of State should take part in shaping the curriculum (but should *not* try to control it); that the DES should make more documents available to the public and should encourage wider debate; that the government should set up a Standing Education Commission comprising employers, trade unionists and academics; and that DES planning should consider broad, long-term issues – not just the allocation of resources.

8. When Fred Mulley left the DES in September 1976, all that Janet Fookes (Chairperson of the Expenditure Committee investigating the Department) could say of him was that 'he was totally blinkered and too preoccupied with providing resources to be able to look ahead' (quoted in *The Times Educational Supplement*, 24 September 1976).

9. According to Bernard Donoughue (1987, p. 110): 'Downing Street intervened, with the full support of the Cabinet Secretary, to secure a change at the top of the Department of Education. The existing Permanent Secretary was transferred to a more appropriate department and was replaced by James Hamilton, who had a background in science and engineering and whom I had previously found encouragingly positive on Cabinet Office Committees.' This version of events has been challenged by Ian Lawrence (1992, p. 74). He argues that since the appointment of all permanent and deputy secretaries was handled by the head of the civil service, and the Prime Minister, and *not* by the Cabinet Secretary, the grounds for Donoughue's interpretation seem uncertain.

10. Shortly after moving to the DES, James Hamilton made an important speech at the Annual Conference of the Association of Education Committees meeting in Scarborough, in which he warned that, in future, the Department would be taking 'a much closer interest' in what was being taught in the nation's schools. According to Hamilton, teachers had traditionally reserved the right to decide what was taught in schools, but now the key to 'the secret garden of the curriculum' had to be found and turned (report in *The Times Educational Supplement*, 2 July 1976).

11. The leaking of the Yellow Book a few days before the delivery of the Ruskin speech led some commentators to conclude – erroneously – that the speech *must* be based solely or largely on the DES confidential memorandum. While it is true that *some* of the ideas in the Yellow Book found their way into the speech, it has to be stressed that Callaghan's Oxford address had an altogether separate provenance.

12. Significantly, while Sir John Hoskyns was its Head (1979–82), the Policy Unit had no remit to discuss or formulate education policy (see Knight, 1990, pp. 141, 148).

13. When Brian Griffiths became Head of the Policy Unit in 1985, he was already known for having a keen interest in educational matters. A former Dean of the City University Business School, he was also a Director of the Bank of England and Chairman of Christian Responsibility in Public. As Lord Griffiths of Fforestfach, he later replaced Philip Halsey as the Chair of SEAC (School Examination and Assessment Council). He has been described (Judd and Crequer, 1992) as 'the invisible overlord of education policy'.

14. David Willetts worked in the Prime Minister's Policy Unit from April 1984 to December 1986, specializing in DHSS and Treasury issues. At the time of writing his paper for *Public Administration*, adapted from his prize-winning entry to the 1986

Haldane essay competition, he was Director of Studies at the Centre for Policy Studies. Since April 1992 he has been Conservative MP for Havant.

15. The Policy Unit's determination – with the connivance of the Prime Minister – to forestall discussion and criticism has been compared with the traditional civil service attitude towards policy-making described by Blackstone and Plowden in their 1988 book, *Into the Think Tank*. Here they outlined a strategy, known as 'the bounce', employed, or so it is said, by experienced civil servants. This consisted of the presentation to the Cabinet of a departmental paper urging a particular course of action – at the last minute and on a topic on which delay could be said to be 'highly damaging'. The intention, and often the result, was to secure instant and unreflective action, involving, not surprisingly, total commitment to the particular course of action proposed. Assessment of the downside effects, and awareness of possible alternative strategies, was thereby effectively excluded (see Rosenhead, 1992, p. 297).

16. David Gow relates (for example in Gow, 1988), that the CPS pamphlet *Correct Core*, prepared by Sheila Lawlor, was 'compulsory bedtime reading' for the Prime Minister in March 1988.

17. Having been a member of Croydon Education Committee in the 1970s, Stuart Sexton was Education Adviser to both Mark Carlisle and Sir Keith (now Lord) Joseph between 1979 and 1986. He lost the job when Kenneth Baker arrived at the DES in May 1986 and in the October was appointed the first Director of the Education Unit of the IEA.

18. Stuart Sexton is here remembering that Sir Keith Joseph found it impossible, for financial and administrative reasons, to implement a nationwide system of education vouchers – one of Mrs Thatcher's pet projects – in the period 1981–3.

REFERENCES

Belsey, A. (1986) The New Right, social order and civil liberties. In Levitas, R. (ed.) *The Ideology of the New Right*. Cambridge: Polity Press.

Benn, C. and Simon, B. (1972) *Half Way There: Report on the British Comprehensive School Reform*, 2nd edition. Harmondsworth: Penguin.

Benn, T. (1987) British politics, 1945–1987: a perspective. In Hennessy, P. and Seldon, A. (eds) *Ruling Performance: British Governments from Attlee to Thatcher*. Oxford: Basil Blackwell, pp. 301–8.

Blackstone, T. and Plowden, W. (1988) *Into the Think Tank: Advising the Cabinet 1971–1983*. London: Heinemann.

Bogdanor, V. (1979) Power and participation. *Oxford Review of Education* 5 (2), 157–68.

Bolton, E. (1993) Imaginary gardens with real toads. In Chitty, C. and Simon, B. (eds) *Education Answers Back: Critical Responses to Government Policy*. London: Lawrence & Wishart, pp. 3–16.

Boyson, R. (1973) *Battle Lines for Education*. London: Conservative Political Centre (December).

Boyson, R. (1975a) *Parental Choice*. London: Conservative Political Centre (January).

Boyson, R. (1975b) *The Crisis in Education*. London: Woburn Press.

Butler, R. (1971) *The Art of the Possible*. London: Hamish Hamilton.

Callaghan, J. (1987) *Time and Chance*. London: Collins.

Chitty, C. (1989) *Towards a New Education System: The Victory of the New Right?* Lewes: Falmer Press.

Conservative Party (1963) *Educational Opportunity*. London: Conservative Research Department Library.

Corbett, A. (1969) The Tory educators. *New Society* 22 May, 785–7.

Cordingley, P. and Wilby, P. (1987) *Opting Out of Mr Baker's Proposals* (Ginger Paper 1). London: Education Reform Group.

Cox, C.B. and Boyson, R. (eds) (1975) *Black Paper 1975: The Fight for Education*. London: Dent.

Cox, C.B. and Boyson, R. (eds) (1977) *Black Paper 1977*. London: Maurice Temple Smith.

Cox, C.B. and Dyson, A.E. (eds) (1969a) *Fight for Education – A Black Paper*. London: Critical Quarterly Society.

Cox, C.B. and Dyson, A.E. (eds) (1969b) *Black Paper Two: The Crisis in Education*. London: Critical Quarterly Society.

Cox, C.B. and Dyson, A.E. (eds) (1970) *Black Paper Three: Goodbye Mr Short*. London: Critical Quarterly Society.

Dale, R. (1983) Thatcherism and education. In Ahier, J. and Flude, M. (eds) *Contemporary Education Policy*. London: Croom Helm, pp. 223–55.

Dent, H.C. (1968) *The Education Act, 1944*, 12th edition. London: University of London Press.

DES (Department of Education and Science) (1965) *The Organisation of Secondary Education* (Circular 10/65). London: HMSO (July).

DES (1976) *School Education in England: Problems and Initiatives*. London: HMSO (July).

DES (1977) *Education in Schools: A Consultative Document* (Cmnd 6869), (Green Paper). London: HMSO (July).

Donoughue, B. (1987) *Prime Minister: The Conduct of Policy under Harold Wilson and James Callaghan*. London: Jonathan Cape.

Evans, K. (1985) *The Development and Structure of the English School System*. Sevenoaks: Hodder & Stoughton.

Fenwick, I.G.K. (1976) *The Comprehensive School 1944–1970: The Politics of Secondary School Reorganisation*. London: Methuen.

Gamble, A. (1988) *The Free Economy and the Strong State: The Politics of Thatcherism*. London: Macmillan.

Gow, D. (1988) Why the test is far from child's play. *The Guardian*, 29 March.

Griggs, C. (1989) The New Right and English secondary education. In Lowe, R. (ed.) *The Changing Secondary School*. Lewes: Falmer Press, pp. 99–128.

Hennessy, P. (1986) *Cabinet*. Oxford: Basil Blackwell.

Hillgate Group (1986) *Whose Schools? A Radical Manifesto*. London: Hillgate Group (December).

House of Commons (1976) *Tenth Report of the Expenditure Committee, Session 1975–76, Policy Making in the DES* (The Fookes Report). London: HMSO (September).

Jones, G.W. (1985) The Prime Minister's aides. In King, A. (ed.) *The British Prime Minister*, 2nd edition. London: Macmillan, pp. 72–95.

Jones, K. (1989) *Right Turn: The Conservative Revolution in Education.* London: Hutchinson Radius.

Joseph, K. (1976) *Stranded in the Middle Ground? Reflections on Circumstances and Policies.* London: Centre for Policy Studies.

Judd, J. and Crequer, N. (1992) The right tightens its grip on education. *The Independent on Sunday*, 2 August.

King, A. (1985) Margaret Thatcher: the style of a prime minister. In King, A. (ed.) *The British Prime Minister*, 2nd edition. London: Macmillan, pp. 96–140.

Knight, C. (1990) *The Making of Tory Education Policy in Post-war Britain, 1950–1986.* Lewes: Falmer Press.

Lawlor, S. (1988) *Correct Core: Simple Curricula for English, Maths and Science.* London: Centre for Policy Studies (March).

Lawrence, I. (1992) *Power and Politics at the Department of Education and Science.* London: Cassell.

Maclure, S. (1988) *Education Re-formed: A Guide to the Education Reform Act 1988.* Sevenoaks: Hodder & Stoughton.

Manzer, R.A. (1970) *Teachers and Politics: The Role of the National Union of Teachers in the Making of National Educational Policy in England and Wales since 1944.* Manchester: Manchester University Press.

Marquand, D. (1988) *The Unprincipled Society: New Demands and Old Politics.* London: Jonathan Cape.

Marx, K. (1875) Critique of the Gotha Programme. In Fernbach, D. (ed.) (1974) *The First International and After: Political Writings*, Vol. 3. Harmondsworth: Penguin, pp. 339–59.

Ministry of Education (1963) *Half Our Future* (The Newsom Report). London: HMSO.

OECD (Organisation for Economic Co-operation and Development) (1975) *Review of National Policies for Education: Educational Development Strategy in England and Wales.* Paris: OECD.

Plant, R. (1990) Citizenship, empowerment and welfare. In Pimlott, B., Wright, A. and Flower, D. (eds) *The Alternative: Politics for a Change.* London: W.H. Allen, pp. 33–42.

Plaskow, M. (ed.) (1985) *Life and Death of the Schools Council.* Lewes: Falmer Press.

Plaskow, M. (1990) It was the best of times. *Education* 176 (5), 90.

Price, C. (1985) The politician's view. In Plaskow, M. (ed.) *Life and Death of the Schools Council.* Lewes: Falmer Press.

Raison, T. (1976) *The Act and the Partnership: An Essay on Educational Administration in England.* London: Centre for Studies in Social Policy/ Bedford Square Press.

Rosenhead, J. (1992) Into the swamp: the analysis of social issues. *Journal of the Operational Research Society* 43 (4), 293–305.

Scruton, R. (1980) *The Meaning of Conservatism.* London: Macmillan.

Seldon, A. (1986) *The Riddle of the Voucher: An Inquiry into the Obstacles to Introducing Choice and Competition into State Schools* (Hobart Paper No. 21). London: IEA.

Sexton, S. (1987) *Our Schools – A Radical Policy.* London: Institute of Economic Affairs Education Unit (March).

Wilby, P. and Midgley, S. (1987) As the new right wields its power. *The Independent,* 23 July.

Willetts, D. (1987) The role of the Prime Minister's Policy Unit. *Public Administration* 65, 443–54.

Young, H. (1989) *One of Us: A Biography of Margaret Thatcher.* London: Macmillan.

Young, H. (1993) Times long gone. *The Guardian,* 6 July.

Chapter 3

From 'policy' to 'practice': the development and implementation of the National Curriculum for Physical Education

Dawn Penney and John Evans

Educational policies are never free of interests or ideological intent, and this is as true of the Education Reform Act (ERA) 1988 as of previous legislation. Indeed, ERA asserts that the state education system can function more efficiently on free-market principles and that the creation of a social market in education, through the mechanisms of a national curriculum and system of testing, and the devolution of financial responsibilities from local education authorities to schools, will raise education standards (DES, 1987). Faith, hope but all too little (fiscal) charity have been very obvious features of ERA's text and prose. The curricula of state schools have, of course, always been contested domains (Chitty, 1989, and Chapter 2 in this volume), with the debates over what is to count as physical education (PE) among the most emotional and vitriolic to have occurred in recent years. In the last decade, media figures and politicians alike have variously charged 'progressive' physical educationalists with prompting the nation's moral, physical and economic decline while bringing PE and sport into disrepute (Evans, 1990).

The development of the National Curriculum for Physical Education (NCPE) has highlighted these struggles and demonstrated that the 'making' of state education policy is a complex social and political process in which vested interests and values are expressed. It has also revealed both the range and the limits of the central state's power to determine the thinking of educationalists and to control the constitution of the curriculum of schools in England and Wales. Furthermore the creation of a National Curriculum text is not the only 'point' at which contestation occurs. There are good grounds for believing that conflicts and contestation over the form and content of PE will continue after the publication of the final order for the NCPE (DES, 1992). Struggles in these terms are likely to feature throughout its 'implementation' in schools as the NCPE is recursively made and remade in very different circumstances of resourcing and educational work. The claim made by the DES (1987) that offering clear NC statements of objectives, programmes of study, attainment levels and regular assessment of the levels of attainment, *will* entitle pupils in all schools to the same opportunities and a curriculum that is 'balanced and broadly based' (DES, 1989, para. 2.1), is therefore no guarantee that this is either what schools can or will deliver or what children will receive.

These concerns, which lie at the heart of our research,[1] have highlighted the importance of examining not only what curriculum is being provided and for whom in state schools in England and Wales, but also how and why provision takes on particular forms. Accordingly, we have adopted a qualitative methodology and utilized both quantitative and qualitative techniques in our investigations (see Evans and Penney, 1992). It is increasingly apparent that both the form and content of education 'policy' and 'practice' cannot be divorced from their national and local political, economic, social and organizational contexts.

Kelly (1990) has argued that whatever the rhetoric of politicians, the thrust of most of the major initiatives in the development of the state-maintained education system has tended to be economic rather than educational. The ERA and the NC are no exceptions to this rule. Certainly, political and economic rather than educational concerns have driven the development of the NCPE. At times it has been very difficult to find any educational intent in the discourse of politicians as it has touched on the interests of PE in school. The working group established by the government (in July 1990) to construct the NCPE was consistently reminded of the 'resource implications' of its recommendations. In his response to the groups' interim report the Secretary of State for Education assiduously underlined the need to consider the economic 'feasibility' of the proposals and implored the group to ensure that the recommendations in their final report were realistically related to the general level of school funding which can reasonably be expected to be available (DES, 1991a). Effectively the group was being 'asked' to construct a curriculum with respect to its economic viability rather than its educational desirability (see Evans, Penney and Bryant, 1993b; Evans, Penney with Davies, 1993).

In this respect the development of the NCPE has vividly illustrated not only the tension between stated educational intentions (namely that the curriculum should be 'broad and balanced' and 'available to all children') and harsh economic realities (the limits of economic resources), but also that the policy process is inevitably political. A period of recession exacerbates this tension, 'precisely because more education and not less is seen as a means of tackling its causes and consequences' (McPherson and Raab, 1988, p. 484). Central government is presented with an acute dilemma: how to provide more education for less investment. In this context a key concept, 'flexibility', emerged in the government's political discourse on curriculum provision as the principal means of resolving the problem.

The importance of this concept as a rhetorical device cannot be overstated. It was used systematically not only to reduce the level of prescription in the NCPE throughout its various stages of development, but also to obscure the limited commitments of the state to PE, and shift the onus of responsibility for the provision of this curriculum from central government to schools (see Evans and Penney with Bryant, 1993a, b). For example, the NC recommendations for the PE curriculum for pupils at Key Stages 3 (ages 11–14) and 4 (ages 14–16) underwent significant changes in the course of their development. In the interim report the working group recommended that, in order to experience a broad and balanced curriculum, at Key Stage 3 pupils should experience physical activities from six areas of physical activity,[2] and at Key Stage 4 experience from at least three activities including one game and either gymnastics or dance (DES, 1991a). The final report, however, anticipating and expressing pressure from central government, reduced the number of areas of activity at Key Stages 3 and 4 to five. It recommended that during Key Stage 3 pupils should experience all areas, but in any one year at least four, including games and either gymnastics or dance. In Key Stage 4 pupils should experience two activities from the same or different areas (DES, 1991b). Subsequently, the National Curriculum Council (NCC) and the Secretaries of State endorsed the recommendations for Key Stage 4, but deemed those for Key Stage 3 to be 'too prescriptive' (NCC, 1991). In the interest of 'greater flexibility', the NCC recommended that pupils should experience a minimum of four of the five activities by the end of Key Stage 3, with games being the only compulsory activity in each year (NCC, 1991, p. 14). The final report of the working group also insisted that swimming should be compulsory in the National Curriculum. The NCC, however, advocated a delay in the introduction of swimming until it was 'practicable' (NCC, 1991). The socio-cultural implications of these changes have been discussed elsewhere (Evans and Penney with Davies, 1993).

On the surface, ascribing 'flexibility' to a subject area does (and no doubt was intended to) sound like good news. However, in a highly differentiated state school system and in organizational contexts of competition for limited resources, this ascription can be equated neither with freedom from constraint nor with unlimited possibilities for curriculum development. Although in a liberal discourse this concept does signify possibility, in reality schools and teachers are being given opportunity without statutory support for their initiatives; responsibility without power. Their capacity to act upon such 'freedom' is inevitably dependent upon existing levels of resourcing, and this may vary considerably between schools and across the subject areas of the curriculum within them. It has to be noted that in the making of the National Curriculum the lower the status imputed to a curriculum subject by the Secretaries of State the greater the 'flexibility' it was afforded. For example, few references to 'flexibility' are to be found in recent debates accompanying the (re)making of the English National Curriculum. Needless to say, the status imputed to a subject (even when expressed as levels of prescription which are unwelcome) tends to have an important bearing on whether it is privileged or disadvantaged in the acquisition of resources. The low status historically imputed to PE in the school curriculum, a position endorsed and hardened by the political culture and educational outlook of the conservative 'New Right' in recent years (Kirk, 1992), therefore potentially has very serious implications for the future of PE. The struggles and conflicts evident throughout the development of the NCPE are likely to be equally apparent in its implementation in schools. Within LEAs and schools, issues of resourcing are likely to continue to dominate discussions of the future provision of PE. In a context of scarce resources, 'entitlement' and 'flexibility' may be fundamentally incompatible. Armed with the latter rhetorical device, schools may free themselves from the task of delivering a PE curriculum that is 'broad and balanced' (Thomas, 1993).

Our interest in how and why the NCPE is constructed as policy text and practice in schools has led us to interrogate both policy-making and policy implementation, and to ask, 'Who is influential in these processes?', 'How are decisions made concerning future provision?' and 'How do policy actions help produce, reproduce or contest inequalities and inequities in schools?'

We share Hill's view that policy is a complex social process, in which 'making' and 'implementation' are very difficult to divide. As Hill states,

It is hard to identify a dividing line at which making can be said to be completed and implementation to start. There is also a considerable amount of feedback from implementation which influences further policy making and many policies are so skeletal that their real impact depends upon the way they are interpreted at the implementation stage.

(1980, p. 44)

In this view, policy is not an event or an action undertaken only by powerful 'others' who operate 'somewhere', either outside schools or in the upper echelons of an institution's hierarchy, and hand policy on for others – their subordinates – to implement. As others have pointed out (Hill, 1980; Ball, 1990) policies are always and inevitably interpreted, and in the process they may be adapted, adopted, contested and resisted at various 'sites' of educational practice before being put into practice. Bowe and Ball with Gold (1992) have illustrated how policies are 'made' at all sites in the education system. They are not just a 'legislative moment'. Policy making is a continual process of engagement, interpretation and struggle (Bowe and Ball with Gold, 1992). Although we endorse this view we also stress that policies are not always made in conditions of the agents' own making. In our view, the policy process, like all other forms of human endeavour, has to be viewed as a 'relational activity' (see Penney and Evans, 1991), a process in which the actions of individuals not only help shape, create and/or re-create the social and organizational contexts in which they are located, but are also shaped by those contexts and the political, social and cultural influences or constraints which are found within them. In Giddens's terms, we have to acknowledge the fundamentally recursive character of social life, in this case the policy process, and the way in which this expresses the mutual dependence of structure and agency (Giddens, 1979, p. 68).

Our attempts to capture and conceptualize the complexity of this process have centred on four concepts: *mechanism, content, context* and *structure*. An understanding of each of these phenomena *and* the relationships between them is, we contend, a prerequisite to understanding the way in which policy is made, expressed and articulated as practice.

The concept of *structure*, much debated and contested in the discourse of social theory, directs our attention to the influence of both the 'system as a whole', and (Giddens, 1979) the rules and resources which are recursively implicated in its production and reproduction. We take the concept of 'system' to refer to 'the reproduced relations between actors or collectivities, organised as regular social practices'; and 'structure' to the rules and resources organized as properties of the social system (Giddens, 1979, p. 66). The latter concept commands both the description and interrogation of the 'arrangements' for 'carrying' policy, the direction and strength of influences, and the way in which social rules and power relations are both expressed and carried within and by such arrangements. We share Hill's view that the arrangements for policy-making will in many cases have a fundamental impact upon the character of the policy and may thus be deemed to be part of the policy. As Hill points out, arrangements and administrative procedures for policy implementation may be explicitly designed to affect impact and may constitute a constraint: 'The simplest form of constraint here is, of course, the failure to provide the means in money and staff, to enable policy to be implemented properly' (Hill,

1980, p. 88). Needless to say, it is economic constraints that are at the forefront of debate over how the NCPE is to be implemented and, therefore, determine what provision will be made.

By *mechanism* we refer to the nature of the 'relay' (Bernstein, 1990) of policy texts in the education system. At *all* sites in the education system interpretation occurs, and policy is thus recursively made and remade. Practice resulting from the interpretation of policy is, invariably, the creation of 'new' policies within a site. These policies may reflect, or contrast with (in varying degrees), the original policy and may then themselves be interpreted and once again adapted, adopted, contested or resisted before producing practices and discourse within that site.[3] The creation of any form of policy need not involve the production of a written text. The creation of a new policy may involve 'only' a mental recontextualization which is acted upon. For example, having received a policy document from the Department for Education, officers within an LEA may not necessarily draft their own written policy document on the subject, but will read and interpret the DfE document. In doing so they will produce another text, their own 'mental map' of the policy. This map forms the reference point for their subsequent action. This action or 'practice' may in fact be the creation of policies or guidelines for the 'next site'. Thus a modified form of the original is passed on to the next site in the process, and there the sequence of interpretation leading to policy creation, itself interpreted to produce practices and discourse, occurs again. Policy implementation can therefore be seen as involving the creation and transmission of hybrid policies.

Hill's 'chain' image partly captures the processes which we have observed in studying the making and implementation of the NCPE. The DfE, NCC (now part of SCAA), LEAs, governing bodies, headteachers, heads of department and teachers may be regarded as comprising a series of links in this process. However, as Hill acknowledges, the chain image is not entirely appropriate, 'since varying responsibilities and degrees of autonomy are involved, and individuals in the chain may be bypassed' (Hill, 1980, p. 83). The varying degrees of autonomy mean that different sites have different degrees of influence in the process. Variations in the strength and direction of influence at different points in the policy process and at different times draw our attention to issues of power and the apparent influence of different sites at different historical moments. Furthermore, the policy process is not unidirectional, as the chain image and the notion of policy being 'handed down' from government to schools implies. Individuals or groups may often play a role in decisions made 'above' them, either within a site, or in a different site. The consultation process accompanying various stages in the production and modification of the NCPE, with LEAs, schools and teachers being invited to comment on proposals, is at least surface evidence of the scope for 'upward flow' in the system. In his letter to the NCPE working group concerning their interim report, the Secretary of State indicated that responses to this report would be critical in determining subsequent recommendations (DES, 1991a). The flow of policy is undoubtedly both complex and uneven. Invariably it involves (at least) a two-way flow of text and discourse, within and between sites of practice. In our view the mechanisms of policy-making and implementation cannot be conceptualized as distinct stages. Rather, they may be seen as constituting overlapping steps inherent in which there is a recursive flow of intentional activity involving different forms of policy.

As indicated earlier, much of the *content* of the NCPE is not highly specific; it allows LEAs and schools some freedom to decide on their own policies for the provision of PE. For example, the time required to 'deliver' the NCPE, and what constitutes a 'broad and balanced curriculum' in terms of both the activities included in the curriculum and the time given to each, are matters that remain unspecified, and variations in interpretation and implementation of policy are to be expected. Our case-study LEA has produced guidelines for the allocation of timetable time in Key Stage 3, identifying 240 hours as the recommended amount to be allocated to PE (Hampshire County Council Education, 1991). The PE inspectors within the authority are then likely to make further specific policy recommendations or guidelines relating to the NCPE, relating to this total allocation for PE and the time that should be devoted to different areas of activity within the NCPE. These recommendations will be passed on to schools, whose governing bodies and headteachers will decide on school policies for the provision of PE in the National Curriculum. In turn, the Head of PE will have the job of putting the policy into practice. Even then, however, the implementation process is not complete. Each member of the PE department will have their own interpretation of how this curriculum is to be put into practice, and this interpretation will direct their subsequent practices and discourse.

This highlights the potential complexity of the policy process and the many points at which interests, values and ideologies can come into play. Even though power may not be evenly distributed among individuals, policy 'making' and 'implementation' will invariably occur at each site. Individuals interpret the policy they receive, 'make' their own policy, and use this as a reference point for action within that site.

Interpretation and action are, of course, influenced by their political, economic and social *contexts*. Policy decisions are rarely straightforward. At all sites of educational practice, policies will be formed in the knowledge of past and present policy action. In schools, decisions will be taken in the light of the existing curriculum, past and present policies and practices and the parallel implementation of other policies. For example, the staffing and funding implications of local management of schools (LMS) may have an important bearing on the future of PE. Equally, past provision will be an important reference point for what will be incorporated within the NCPE in any school. Additionally, extant policies and practices of other sites will be influential. Those of the LEA may 'set the frame' for the implementation of the NCPE in schools. In both their own policy statements and/ or guidance on the NCPE and in apparently 'separate' policies (most notably LMS schemes) LEAs clearly have the capacity effectively to create or restrict opportunities for the provision of PE and sport in schools.

The complex interrelationships between policies generated within and at different sites have been outlined by Hill, who claims that 'even policies with little direct impact upon each other [can] be "rivals" for scarce resources' (1980, p. 106). Resolving differences and incompatibilities in this process may not only give rise to inter-policy issues and conflicts, but also to inter-agency issues. As Hill explains, 'This means that policy implementation may require bargaining and dealing between agencies, and that therefore considerations may be brought into the inter-policy relationship that are very much wider than the ones that appear to be at stake'

(1980, p. 106). At a glance the compulsory competitive tendering (CCT) of local authority leisure centres appears an issue unrelated to the implementation of the NCPE in schools. However, CCT is likely to have a strong bearing on whether or not centres will continue to subsidize school use of facilities, and so will help determine the future content of the PE curriculum in schools. With the introduction of LMS, schools may not have the economic wherewithal to cover any increases in leisure centre charges. The implementation process thus involves both multiple policies and multiple agencies, and the flow of decision-making is neither so neat nor so patterned as ours and other models describe. The structure and context of policy-making and implementation (and the rules and resources inherent in each) combine to establish the limits and possibilities for 'acceptable' policy content (see Evans, Penney and Bryant, 1993b).

However, as our discussion has indicated, the social and political contexts of implementation are not the sole determinants of the 'scope', or 'freedom for action' at different educational sites. The form in which a policy is expressed will also be determined by the text itself and the discourses it expresses. The form and *content* of policy will frame, if not determine, practice. Irrespective of its level of prescription, policy content will undoubtedly also have more subtle influences. The discourses expressed through and privileged in policy texts will influence interpretation, practice and policy creation. The production of the NCPE has highlighted that the discourses of physical educationalists are neither homogeneous nor unified. The PE profession does not speak and has never spoken with one voice (Kirk, 1992; Evans, Penney and Bryant, 1993b). Intra-professional micro-political struggles to privilege or sustain particular versions of PE in schools have been very evident in the development of the NCPE and will continue to be a feature of its implementation. Games are privileged as the central feature of a PE curriculum in the text of the NCC consultation report on the NCPE (NCC, 1991). This is the only compulsory area of activity in each year of Key Stage 3, which, the NCC stated, 'has the advantage of perpetuating the best of English traditions and cultural heritage' (1991, p. 14). Whether individuals can and will want to resist, adopt or contest policy initiatives such as this will depend not only on their beliefs and values but also on the nature of their resources (money, opportunity, status, authority), and their power to contest or engage with the means by which policies are both produced and reproduced in schools.

Our attempts to conceptualize the policy process reflect its complexity. The boundaries between the concepts presented are blurred. We stress the need to address not only each of the concepts, but also the relationships between them if we are fully to appreciate the complexity and the consequences of policy-making and implementation. In our view it is the combined effects of the mechanisms, context, content and structure that explain the intended and unintended outcomes of educational policy and the gap so often reported between policy and practice. At present we know very little of where key policies arise, how they do so, or who the key decision-makers are. Investigating the process in these terms may improve our understanding of how and why particular outcomes and differences in practice arise and thereby better place us to play a part in and influence future policies *and* practices in education. Our concepts are in need of much further development. However, the ongoing development of models of the social world is in keeping with our commitments to qualitative research principles (see Evans and Penney, 1991). The presentation of concepts at this stage is intended only to help us clarify and develop our own thoughts and highlight certain issues. In our view the making of the NCPE (like other curriculum subjects; see Bowe and Ball with Gold, 1991) highlights 'the politics of knowledge' and the nature of the struggle over what is to count as a valid educational experience for children and young people in all state schools. It also brings into focus the nature of the relationships both between educational practice and the state, and between human agency and structure. What we witness in the particular case of PE, we claim, are the limits to any single interest group (for example the 'cultural restorationists' of the New Right; see Ball, 1990; Evans and Penney with Davies, 1993) either controlling or determining a policy text, even when its actions are supported by the authority of the central state, because of the complexity of the policy process. In this respect, we claim (Evans and Penney with Davies, 1993), it may be more accurate to view the struggle to define policy texts not as a politics of the possible but rather as a politics of the probable, the outcomes of which define what is thinkable among teachers in schools and among educationalists at other sites of educational practice. Arguably, this is authority and power in their most subtle and invidious forms defining what 'consciousness', what ideological representations, are now legitimized in the practice of education and PE (ibid.). Only time, and detailed studies of the processes highlighted in the discussion above, will tell whether all children in state schools are receiving the quality of education and physical education they both need and deserve.

NOTES

1. This discussion emerges from the research project, 'The impact of the Education Reform Act on the provision of sport and PE in schools', sponsored by the ESRC (project R000233629) and the Sports Council. We are grateful for their support.
2. 'Areas of activity' is the terminology of the NCPE referring to categories of physical activities (see DES, 1991a, b; NCC, 1991).
3. Another example of this process is documented in Chapter 4.

REFERENCES

Ball, S. (1990) *Politics and Policy Making in Education.* London and New York: Routledge.

Bernstein, B. (1990) *The Structuring of Pedagogic Discourse.* Volume 4, *Class, Codes and Control.* London: Routledge.

Bowe, R. and Ball, S.J., with Gold, A. (1992) *Reforming Education and Changing Schools: Case Studies in Policy Sociology.* London: Routledge.

Chitty, C. (1989) *Towards a New Educational System: The Victory of the New Right?* Lewes: Falmer Press.

Department of Education and Science (DES) (1987) *The National Curriculum 5–16: A Consultation Document.* London: HMSO.

DES (1989) *National Curriculum: From Policy to Practice.* London: HMSO.

DES (1991a) *National Curriculum Physical Education Working Group: Interim Report.* London: HMSO.

DES (1991b) *Physical Education for Ages 5–16: Proposals of the Secretary of State for Education and Science and the Secretary of State for Wales.* London: HMSO.

DES (1992) *Physical Education in the National Curriculum.* London: HMSO.

Evans, J. (1990) Defining a subject: the rise and rise of the new PE? *British Journal of Sociology of Education* 11 (2), 155–69.

Evans, J. and Penney, D. (1992) Investigating ERA: qualitative methods and policy orientated research. (Research Supplement), *British Journal of Physical Education Research Supplement* 11, Summer, 2–6.

Evans, J. and Penney, D., with Bryant, A. (1993a) Education policy, PE and the National Curriculum. In McFee, G. and Tomlinson, A. (eds) *Cultural and Curricular Issues in Education, Sport and Leisure: Controversies and Critiques.* Chelsea School Research Centre (Topic Report 3), Brighton Polytechnic, pp. 9–36.

Evans, J., Penney, D. and Bryant, A. (1993b) Theorising implementation: a preliminary comment on power and process in policy research. *Physical Education Review*, 16 (1), Spring, 5–22.

Evans, J. and Penney, D., with Davies, B. (1993) Policy, pedagogy and the politics of the body. Paper presented at the 'New Directions in Education Policy Sociology' Conference, Southampton, 30–31 March.

Giddens, A. (1979) *Central Problems in Social Theory.* London: Macmillan.

Hampshire County Council Education (1991) The use of time in secondary schools – timetabling the secondary curriculum. Unpublished paper, Hampshire County Council Education. Winchester: The Castle.

Hill, M. (1980) *Understanding Social Policy.* Oxford: Basil Blackwell.

Kelly, A.V. (1990) *The National Curriculum.* London: Paul Chapman.

Kirk, D. (1992) *Defining Physical Education.* London: Falmer Press.

McPherson, A. and Raab, C.D. (1988) *Governing Education.* Edinburgh: Edinburgh University Press.

National Curriculum Council (1991) *Physical Education in the National Curriculum. A Report to the Secretary of State for Education and Science on the Statutory Consultation for the Attainment Target and Programmes of Study in Physical Education.* York: NCC.

Penney, D. and Evans, J. (1991) The impact of the Education Reform Act (ERA) on the provision of physical education and sport in the 5–16 curriculum of state schools. *British Journal of Physical Education* 22 (1), 38–42.

Thomas, S. (1993) Education reform: juggling the concepts of equality and elitism. In Evans, J. (ed.) *Equality, Education and Physical Education.* Lewes: Falmer Press, pp. 105–25.

Chapter 4

Making schools accountable: assessment policy and the Education Reform Act

David Scott

The recently completed interim review of the National Curriculum for England and Wales (Dearing, 1993) proposes a number of changes to the arrangements for assessment. At Key Stage 1 they include: limiting the number of areas which must be assessed to the core subjects; reducing the amount of time that pupils spend on formal testing in English and mathematics, even replacing the science tests with statutory teacher assessments; and giving equal status to teacher assessments and test results. At Key Stage 2 they include: reworking the timetable for introduction; reducing the amount of formal testing; and substituting a simpler marking scheme. At Key Stage 3 Dearing suggests similar processes of streamlining, simplifying and clarifying.

This episode in the evolving saga of National Curriculum assessment arrangements points to the complexity of the policy process. Policy, it will be argued, is not made at one site and implemented at another, but is better understood as a disjointed two-way flow between different sites at different moments (see Penney and Evans, Chapter 3 in this volume). The policy flow is therefore not unidirectional and is subject to a diverse range of influences and interests. In contrast to state control models of curriculum change, this suggests that the gap between policy creation and implementation may be wide and widening, though the model also allows for reassertion of control from the centre at different moments in the process. Indeed it suggests that those 'site' influences are not equally important and that participants at these 'sites' are not equally empowered, as is evidenced by the Secretary of State's recent modifications to the GCSE coursework arrangements. This policy change will have two main effects, one of them systemic: first, curriculum and assessment arrangements for students will be reordered; second, relations between the different parts of the system will change, with teachers experiencing significant amounts of disempowerment.

But it is important not to infer from this example that the privileged position enjoyed by the government always guarantees successful and unamended implementation of its policies. This is so for two reasons: first, the 'official' text still has to be interpreted at different moments and places, and second, the central authority is both an amalgam of competing ideas and impulsions and subject to a diverse range of influences. Collectivities of agents are able to exert a significant influence on policy decision-making and text production. The 'Dearing Proposals' are in part a reaction to the boycott of assessment arrangements at Key Stages 1 and 3 orchestrated by the teacher unions in the summer of 1993.

The first part of this chapter elaborates on this model of policy processes. The second part relates the theoretical model to the way assessment arrangements for the National Curriculum have evolved since the 1988 Education Reform Act was passed. We begin with a discussion of the role policy texts play in the process.

READING TEXTS

National Curriculum documents such as the Dearing Report (1993) are examples of purposive texts designed to change curriculum, pedagogic and assessment practices in schools. Reading texts, though, is necessarily an act of re-creation (Eco, 1984; Crossman, 1980); and thus, within temporal and spatial contexts, these texts allow multiple readings. They are also interpreted and reinterpreted at different moments of use, as meanings and outcomes are contested (Bowe and Ball with Gold, 1992; Scott, 1991). This allows for the possibility of 'resistance' (Giroux, 1983) to the original aims or purposes embedded in those documents. Understanding the relationship between intended outcomes and realization therefore always involves making sense of competing sets of meanings situated within specific events in the lifetimes of institutions and systems.

Textual reading is only part of the process – a process that involves textual construction (the initial writing of the text), textual reconstruction (formulations and reformulations of sets of meanings by practitioners), and implementation (teacher strategies influenced by textual readings). As Bowe and Ball with Gold make clear: 'Policy texts are not closed, their meanings are neither fixed nor clear, and the "carry over" of meanings from one policy arena and one educational site to another is subject to interpretational slippage and contestation' (1992, p. 83). Indeed the policy process is not one-way. Decision-making at the various sites impacts backwards and forwards along the chain, causing policy texts to be rewritten and then repositioned in the policy arena. Penney and Evans (Chapter 3 in this volume) argue that, as a result, the ' "flow" of policy is undoubtedly both complex and uneven', both because there is this 'two-way flow of text and discourse', and because actors at different sites in the policy process have different degrees of influence and autonomy. Indeed actors make decisions in contexts not of their own making, though the decisions they make impact upon future contexts and arenas of decision-making. The composition, length and direction of each relay (Bernstein, 1985) will vary with each episode of meaning transfer.

Texts are differently constituted. In Barthes's (1975) words, aspects of these 'official' texts are 'readerly'. The textual meaning is unequivocal, not subject to interpretation, non-writerly and therefore prescriptive. The text compels certain forms of action and proscribes others. On the other hand, texts such as these are not unidimensional: any text is likely to contain 'readerly' as well as 'writerly' aspects. In the latter case the text is so constructed that the reader is allowed interpretative space. His or her options are not foreclosed by the text.

Paradoxically, Barthes's dichotomized view of reading ignores the reader. As Cherryholmes argues, 'prior understandings, experiences, codes, beliefs and knowledge brought to a text necessarily condition and mediate what one makes of it' (1988, p. 12). So the degree to which such passivity or industry resides in the text itself or in the decoder of that text can be determined only by addressing each particular case. What is certain is that the relationship between reader and text lies somewhere on a continuum between active interpretation and passive reception. Texts, therefore, have properties which allow creative interpretation to a greater or lesser extent. They allow multiple readings, and contain contradictions and disjunctions. The result is that the practitioner who works within the textual framework has to choose between these different meanings, because he or she cannot accommodate them all.

These meanings compete with other sources of meaning, which support or deny particular interpretations. They compete with other textual meanings gathered from, for example, school and LEA documents, academic commentaries, newspaper reports and so forth, and they compete with other texts which bear indirectly on the matter in hand – other educational texts and non-educational books and pamphlets. Meanings held by individual teachers are influenced by spoken as well as written sources, and the everyday interactive processes that teachers go through confirm, deny, enrich, impoverish and certainly may change meanings which in turn will influence actions. This is to place textual reading within its proper context, and to argue that full understandings of endogenous and exogenous influences on actual practice cannot be achieved by textual analysis alone. Teachers do more than simply read official documents.

The implementation of a new policy in schools has to be understood as a complex social process, within which meanings and actions are fragmented at different sites during the passage of ideas from policy-making to realization. It would be misleading to conceive of the policy process as a linear chain with strategies and technologies made at one site and implemented at another. Texts and their subsequent reconstructions are read differently at different moments of use.

READING CONTEXTS

It is important to place these different readings in context, and in doing so give full weight to the respective roles played by agency and structure in the policy process. Giddens (1984), for instance, has attempted through his structuration approach to reconcile the two, so that human beings are neither the 'unwitting dupes' of structural forces beyond their control, nor free, unconstrained agents neither controlled nor influenced by those sets of relations and conjunctions which constitute society. For Giddens, actors continually draw upon sets of 'rules and resources' which, once substantiated, allow social life to continue as they become routinized. Archer adopts a similar approach with her morphogenetic perspective, though she disputes the necessity of tying structure and agency so closely together: 'Structuration, by contrast, treats the ligatures binding structure, practice and system as indissoluble, hence the necessity of duality and the need to gain a more indirect analytical purchase on the elements involved' (1982, p. 458). She also questions whether every human action, every facet of the particular human being, is involved in the ongoing moulding and remoulding of society that is implied by both structuration and morphogenetic cycles. She writes: 'there are a good many things about human beings and their doings (things biological, psychological and spiritual) which have a precious independence from society's moulding and may have precious little to do with re-modelling society' (ibid., p. 455). Both Archer and Giddens argue that human beings play an active and intentional role in the construction of their world, though that building activity is subject to structural constraints. Human beings make their world in the context of previous attempts, and at the same time transform those structures and change the conditions which influence subsequent moves to make the world. It is also important to recognize that whilst agency is responsible for structural transformation, in the process it simultaneously transforms itself (Archer, 1982).

Teachers' initial textual readings or their initial confrontation with the ideas implicit in the new text draw upon both those internalized rules which actors reproduce in their day-to-day working lives and those structural resources which position actors within set frameworks. Those elements of structure that are relevant to the matter in hand condition, but do not determine, actors' responses (Archer, 1982). Initial textual readings give way to subsequent interpretations and reinterpretations of assessment processes, and all the various readings are implicated in the implementation and reimplementation of assessment and pedagogic strategies. The dialectical interplay of structure and agency is transformed into new forms of structure and agency, and produces, in Archer's word, 'elaboration'; that is, both elaborated structure and transformed agency. This cycle of activity at different moments and in different guises influences actual implementation of processes.

STRUCTURAL AND INTERACTIONAL INFLUENCES

In short, textual readings are transformed at different moments and places within schools as teachers construct and reconstruct meanings. This fragmentation is only realizable because, as Whitty puts it, there is within educational contexts a high degree of 'tenuousness, dysfunction, interruption and possibility' (1985, p. 45). These meanings, moreover, are in competition with meanings conveyed by other texts and by other discursive forms. They are tested in formal and informal forums in schools, and they are formulated and reformulated within situationally constraining and enabling contexts which may or may not be fully understood by participants. These rules and resources (Giddens, 1984) structure and condition these sets of ideas and subsequent actions.

In the context of the implementation of a new assessment system in schools, policy is determined in three ways: by agents' bodies and biographies; by agents operating in settings which are not of their own making but upon which they leave their mark; and within interactional arenas which draw together agents and settings, and promote change (see Figure 4.1). These result in both intended and unintended consequences (that is, unintended both by individual, and collectivities of, agents), and produce conformations and configurations of policy processes.

Biographical factors provide one type of context; material and structural factors another. Examples of the latter are differential allocations of persons to functions and roles (Bhaskar, 1979); external constraints – examination technologies, for example; teacher culture – subject hierarchies (cf. Goodson, 1985); professional codes and ideologies (Ball, 1982); conditions of work – arrangements of resources, pupil 'resistance' (Spradberry, 1976; Willis, 1977); and institutional properties – devolved or centralized systems of decision-making (Ball, 1987).

Material, biographical and structural arrangements therefore constitute the

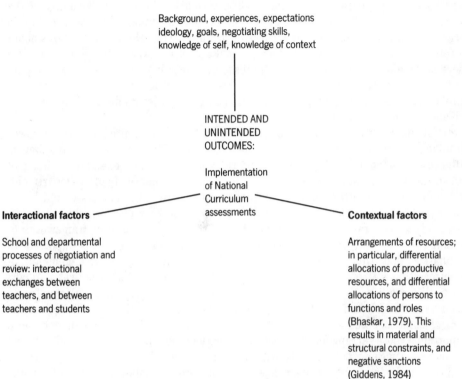

Biographical factors

Background, experiences, expectations
ideology, goals, negotiating skills,
knowledge of self, knowledge of context

INTENDED AND
UNINTENDED
OUTCOMES:

Implementation
of National
Curriculum
assessments

Interactional factors

School and departmental
processes of negotiation and
review: interactional
exchanges between
teachers, and between
teachers and students

Contextual factors

Arrangements of resources;
in particular, differential
allocations of productive
resources, and differential
allocations of persons to
functions and roles
(Bhaskar, 1979). This
results in material and
structural constraints, and
negative sanctions
(Giddens, 1984)

Figure 4.1 Biographical, interactional and contextual factors in decision-making.

settings in which agents make decisions and formulate strategies. We have already suggested that structures (whether defined as patterned behaviours or as the arrangements of rules and resources) have fleeting material existences, though, in Giddens's words, they do exist as 'memory traces' and as instantiations 'in social practices' (1984, p. 25). This is because structure exists as both media and outcome of decisions made by agents who could have acted in other ways. Archer (1982) argues that structures provide agents with good reasons for acting in the way they do, but not overwhelmingly necessary ones. Thus the over-determination of much sociological theorizing is avoided.

There are then two senses in which structure is used by sociologists. The first is the sense which Giddens gives to the term; that is, arrangements of 'rules and resources'. Within schools there are both human and material resources. In the first place we have a group of differently resourced agents who interact in various ways. Their capacity to respond to externally initiated change such as the introduction of a new assessment system in schools has both an internal element (biographical factors) and an external element (interactional and contextual factors). Though the two are separated here, this separation is artificial, because capacity is determined both by what actually is – arrangements of resources and rules at that precise

45

moment and place – and how the agent perceives the situation. The actual balance of the two is an empirical matter and is determined by the knowledgeability of the agent. Agents, though, perceive of themselves and act upon those perceptions in terms of publicly negotiated frameworks of meaning. Thus the teacher who is about to retire may be marginalized in decision-making arenas within the school because there is a feeling (whether publicly expressed or not) that the school needs to plan for the future. Within a situation in which actors have different degrees of power and autonomy, the amount and type of power and autonomy they do have is dependent on the amount and type held by others.

But this is not a zero-sum game, in which a finite and limited amount of power circulates between actors in particular social settings. First, the same actors may be differently related to each other in different situations. For example, a Head of House speaks with more authority on pastoral matters than a Head of Department, and conversely the latter has more influence over curriculum matters within his or her department than the Pastoral Head, who may also be a class teacher. What, of course, is a pastoral matter is as much a part of the negotiated frameworks of meaning that operate within institutions as any other matter; but it is important to emphasize that this process of negotiation is structured by arrangements of resources that we referred to earlier. Meanings are not negotiated between equals, but by differently resourced agents operating in differently arranged settings. In the last resort this form of constraint derives its force from 'punitive responses on the part of some people towards others' (Giddens, 1984, p. 176). Second, and more important, those arrangements have implications for the amount and type of autonomy experienced by agents within their institutions. Third, some externally initiated projects empower some agents, while others empower different agents. Government reforms to do with decentralizing resource allocations empower headteachers; but reforms to the public examination system through the intro-duction of coursework empower individual teachers.

Material resources exert significant influences on human actions. Giddens's characterization of context operating as a form of constraint on human agents includes 'the character of the material world and ... the physical qualities of the body' (1984, p. 176). Human agents cannot be in more than one place at any one time. The environment of the institution, its physical qualities, is the setting in which actors make decisions. Classes of students are allocated. Rooms operate to limit movement. The availability of books and other paper resources influences and restricts possible teaching approaches. In short, the arrangement of such resources is the context within which actors devise and implement teaching strategies.

Giddens's third type of constraint deriving from 'the contextuality of action, i.e. from the "given" character of structural properties vis-à-vis situated actors' (ibid., p. 176), refers to the more generally used notion of structure: that is, patterned behaviour that exists over time. These patterned behaviours are the outcome of a multitude of human actions which by virtue of their sameness have been constituted as structural properties. They do not, and cannot, cause actors to behave in any particular ways. Indeed, if Giddens intends to characterize them as forms of constraint, which directly impact upon interactional arenas in which agents make decisions, and if he intends them to operate in the same way as his other two forms of constraint – material impediments and negative sanctions – then he has to show how those patterns of behaviour developed. Halsey makes a similar point:

> A theory which explains educational achievement as the outcome of a set of individual attributes has lost the meaning of those structural forces which we know as class. An adequate theory must also attend to those structural inequalities of resource allocation which are integral to a class society.
>
> (1975, p. 17)

In other words, material impediments and negative sanctions are in part responsible for human agents behaving in similar ways, and thus allow patterned behaviours. An example would be gendered relations in schools impacting on and restricting learning programmes for girls. It is the rules and arrangements of resources which operate in particular schools and generally in the school system which constitute the setting; and which provide good reasons for actors within those settings to behave in the way they do.

Finally, we need to examine those decision-making arenas in schools. They can be characterized by degrees of formality: staff and departmental meetings, individual face-to-face contacts, teachers reading texts of various sorts on their own. We have already suggested a number of features. First, they are made up of a number of differently resourced agents. Second, organizational arrangements determine that some interactional arenas are more important than others. Third, it is the topic under discussion that influences the degree of impact of any interactional exchange. Fourth, the type (especially with regard to time, place and agenda) of interaction influences outcomes. Fifth, transactions between different parts of education systems (usually, but not always, expressed as policy texts) influence the way a new initiative is received in schools.

STATE CONTROL

Within this framework, there is scope for the central authority to reassert control in three ways. First, those policy texts which convey messages from one part of the system to another can be rewritten. In extreme cases this could involve legislative action. Thus the text can be changed or amended, so that readers are more or less constrained than they were before. This rewriting may also involve a repositioning if the new text changes the rules by which it is read. Future transactions between the different parts of the system are now carried out from a different base, with some parts acquiring greater leverage and influence and others having less. The textual messages concerning devolution of some funding decisions to schools (local financial management) had the effect of repositioning the financial text as LEA powers in this field declined. The changes to coursework arrangements in the GCSE involved a rewriting of the text, and a repositioning of that amended text, which now has greater relevance to, and bestows greater powers on, examination boards, with consequent diminutions of relevance and powers for teachers.

The second way for the central authority to reassert control is directly through legislative action to change the relationship between the different parts of the system, and thus to redistribute abilities and capabilities to influence events. Deem (Chapter 5 in this volume) discusses the way legislation passed in 1986 (No. 2

Education Act), 1988 (Education Reform Act) and 1993 (Education Act) have progressively reshaped the composition, duties and, more importantly, powers of school governing bodies. The introduction of the National Curriculum and a national system of assessment (legislated for in the 1988 Education Reform Act) has had, and continues to have, a considerable impact on relationships between the different parts of the system, and on their respective spheres of influence.

The third way that the centre can reassert control over the periphery is by changing the arrangements for resource allocation in the system. We have already referred to the context – biographical, material and structural – within which practitioners make decisions and formulate strategies; a context, moreover, that is forever evolving as agents work within it. That context can be changed by decisions made by the central authority, which operate as constraints on action at a local level. In short, teachers operate in terms of these contexts, and their powers to devise their own teaching and learning strategies are restricted by them. Evolving arrangements for National Curriculum assessments provide us with a case study of these policy processes.

NATIONAL CURRICULUM ASSESSMENTS

In the context of the introduction of the National Curriculum, four assessment phases can be identified. The first, which found its fullest expression in the TGAT Report (DES, 1988a), emphasized the central place of teacher assessments in pedagogic processes. It recommended a system of terminal and summative assessments at the end of each Key Stage to ensure the comparability and reliability of those teacher assessments. Proposing a ten-level system to encourage progression with the average pupil expected to change levels every two years, it adopted a criterion-referenced framework so that pupils' achievements were assessed against written statements. The report was fundamentally opposed to assessments being made which were separate from, and not connected to, curricula, and suggested that results at the end of three of the Key Stages should be published without being adjusted for the socio-economic background of the individuals and schools concerned.

In the second phase a number of significant changes to the original model were made. These downgraded the importance of teacher assessment, with consequent losses in the ability of teachers to make formative assessments. Henceforth, end of Key Stage summative assessments were to be the principal method used. Teacher assessments would cover those Attainment Targets which could not be covered by standard assessment tasks (SATs), and more significantly, would be the mechanism by which it was decided at which level of SATs pupils would be entered.

The third phase, which coincided with the appointment of a new Secretary of State, was in effect a continuation of the trend established in phase two. Instead of SATs, which were long, interactive, had formative potential, and were closely connected to curricula, the development agencies were instructed to deliver 'paper and pencil', summative, easily managed and simpler-to-process end of Key Stage tests. At the same time coursework components in the GCSE (Key Stage 4) were to be statutorily reduced, and publication of 'raw' tests scores was endorsed by the 1992 Education Act.

The final phase (the Dearing Report), which has yet to be properly fleshed out, separates formative and summative purposes of assessment, repositions on an equal basis teacher assessments and SATs, questions the need for a ten-level system and suggests replacing it by four separate reporting stages, and proposes a slimming down both of curricula and assessment.

PHASE ONE – MIXED MESSAGES

The Task Group on Assessment and Testing (TGAT) published its report in 1988 (DES, 1988a), followed by three supplements (DES, 1988b) a few months later. TGAT argued that a fully integrated system of assessment can and should be formative and summative:

> Promoting children's learning is the principal aim of school. Assessment lies at the heart of this process. It can provide a framework in which educational objectives may be set and pupils' progress charted and expressed. It can yield a basis for planning the next educational steps in response to children's needs. By facilitating dialogue between teachers, it can enhance professional skills and help the school as a whole to strengthen learning across the curriculum and throughout its age range.
>
> (DES, 1988a, para. 3)

Later changes to the assessment arrangements have concentrated on unpicking this apparent conflation within the same system of these two purposes (either by downgrading one at the expense of the other, such as in phase three; or clearly separating the different purposes, as Dearing (1993) suggests in phase four). The problem is both conceptual and organizational. Formative and summative (and therefore evaluative) modes of assessment are, it is argued, fundamentally opposed, though the latter can provide useful but limited diagnostic information.

Formative aspects of assessment are most closely associated with the process of teaching itself, but it is the results of summative assessment which are most public and visible. Formative assessment sets out to provide information for the teacher about the way pupils complete particular tasks. The information produced is intended to feed directly into the teaching process, so the focus is on how pupils tackle those tasks and how they proceed with them, as well as what results they achieve. The context in which assessment is undertaken does not need to be standardized for formative purposes, although it may be noted as relevant. From formative assessment the teacher draws conclusions about how to move the pupils' learning forward, and thus plans can be made for the next stage of the teaching.

Summative assessment is concerned with determining whether pupils have mastered particular elements of the curriculum. Summative assessments aim to be reliable and valid, and homogeneity of context is important so that comparability is possible and so that no pupil is disadvantaged. A summative assessment marks some point in the otherwise potentially 'organic' teaching–learning process at which it is decided to stop teaching and give full attention to assessment. The stage at which it is most appropriate and desirable to carry out this kind of assessment is often determined by factors other than those arising from learning goals, such as predetermined times in the school year, or a requirement to report to other interested parties.

TGAT further argued that assessments should be connected with, not separated from, curricula (Goldstein, 1989):

> The assessment system being proposed differs from most of the standardised testing that is now used in many primary schools and some secondary schools. Those tests are not related closely to what children are being taught, and when they identify children likely to have difficulties they give little indication of the nature of problems. Their purpose is to compare children with each other and with samples of children with whom the tests were originally developed, often many years ago.
>
> (DES, 1988a, para. 76)

Assessments may be more or less closely integrated with the teaching programmes that pupils follow. Some kinds of assessment are not actually designed to measure the pupils' learning (or the results of the teachers' teaching), in which case they are often associated with measures of qualities supposedly inherent in the pupil, such as 'intelligence'. Assessment which is placed at the 'integrated' end of the continuum is likely to be more informal than formal, more formative than summative, process- as well as product-orientated, and to be frequent or continuous rather than taking place on one predetermined occasion at the end of the course.

TGAT advocated a criterion-referenced system of assessment

> in which an award or grade is made on the basis of the quality of the performance of the pupil, irrespective of the performance of other pupils ... [so] that teachers and pupils [can] be given clear descriptions of the performances being sought.
>
> (DES, 1988a, para. 76)

Though norm-referenced systems of assessment have become discredited, criterion-referenced systems are not without their problems. First, they are much easier to operate with a simple pass–fail mechanism such as a driving test than to apply to complex multi-level systems such as the National Curriculum. Criteria are relatively easy to identify for the purposes of testing a performance like driving proficiency, but much harder to associate precisely with the range of levels related to learning as envisaged in the National Curriculum. Second, criterion-referenced systems conflate logical hierarchies of skills and content with developmental approaches to learning employed by pupils. Third, there is a conceptual anomaly, in that the process of establishing criteria appropriate to the various levels involves some notion of an 'average student', which means that a normative component is involved.

The fourth element of the assessment scheme proposed by TGAT was the reporting arrangements. The task force recommended that there should be no requirement of a school or LEA to publish information about the results of the assessments made at Key Stage 1. At other stages they suggested that 'raw' data should be published, but:

only if this is done in the context of reports about that school as a whole, so that it can be fair to that school's work and take account so far as possible of socio-economic and other influences.

(DES, 1988a, para. 18)

The arguments against this approach and in favour of 'value-addedness' have been well rehearsed (not least by Dearing, 1993). However, it quickly became policy to publish such information in league or alphabetically arranged tables without reference to the school's socio-economic profile in the form of any general statement.

TGAT thus combined different functions of assessment, incorporated different models of school improvement and supported conflicting notions of accountability. Two models of assessment can be identified. The first of these argues that information gathered during assessments should be used by teachers and students to plan future learning experiences. Assessment as part of school improvement is perceived as *contextualized* – the timing of the assessments, their relationship to the specifics of the course and the conditions under which they were undertaken are all taken into account as teachers and pupils interpret the results; as *ipsative* – the assessments refer only to the teaching and learning of those pupils and their past achievements, and comparisons with other pupils and schools cannot be drawn from them; and as *non-competitive* – this emphasizes a professional commitment to high standards of teaching rather than a competitive incentive to outperform other pupils, teachers or schools. More importantly, this model places a low emphasis on external accountability, whether in the context of free-market consumerist or state control notions of accountability. Accountability may be directly to the pupils, but in the context of professional integrity rather than in response to external pressure.

The alternative model characterizes assessment as *decontextualized* – here a high emphasis is placed on comparability, so that variables pecular to specific pupils, teaching situations or schools are not given the same priority as they are in the first model; and as *competitive* – a teacher's work is judged in relation to the achievements of his or her peers. This model also strongly emphasizes external accountability. Indeed in line with Kogan's (1986) free-market consumerist model of accountability, failure in the context of the public market-place leads to loss of income for the school and of employment for teachers. Aspects of both models featured in the initial TGAT report, though subsequent arrangements made for assessment of the National Curriculum are more in line with our second model. It was hardly surprising that the TGAT Report was read differently by different people, some pointing to progressive features (Brown, 1992; Lawton, 1992), others identifying more regressive elements (Noss, Goldstein and Hoyles, 1989).

PHASE TWO – ADJUSTMENTS BY THE CENTRAL AUTHORITY

TGAT had made a number of recommendations about the role and importance of teacher assessments. The chief purpose of SATs (end of Key Stage tests) was to ensure reliability and comparability, and furthermore it was suggested that these should work at the class and not individual level. If they diverged, the teacher assessment was to be adjusted. The School Examinations and Assessment Council (SEAC, 1989a) proposed in response to the TGAT Report that:

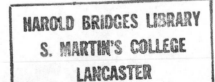

First, teachers would assess pupils on every attainment target ... subject scores would be aggregated and passed onto local moderators in the spring. Second, teachers would administer SATs in the summer to all pupils 'but possibly only for some attainment targets'. Where available, the SAT result would displace the teacher assessment.

SEAC went further at the end of the year in making the following recommendations to the Secretary of State (1989b):

1. By the end of the spring term preceding the end of the key stage there should be a recorded teacher assessment giving the level each pupil had reached in each attainment target.
2. When the SATs have been used in the summer term there will also be a recorded SAT outcome for some attainment targets – probably not all.
3. Where (1) and (2) yield the same outcome for each profile component, that is the end of the matter. The SAT outcome for the attainment, where there is one, should stand.
4. Where (1) and (2) yield a different outcome for any profile component, the SAT outcome may be used for the pupil record if the teacher is content. If the teacher believes (1) should be used, the teacher will be required to make a case for this choice through local moderating arrangements, details of which still await clarification.

These proposals formed part of the final standing orders published in July 1990. They also included complicated rules for aggregating Attainment Target achievements, and aggregating profile achievements into subject achievements. The new orders signalled a radical change of direction. Henceforth, assessment, moderation and reporting would operate at individual Attainment Target level and, more importantly, SATs were to be the main method of assessment, with teacher assessments being marginalized.

Despite this, the Secretary of State at this time (1990), John MacGregor, was still arguing in favour of a number of the principles enshrined in TGAT (see DES, 1988a), namely that assessment should be firmly connected to curricula and that teachers had a central role to play in assessment arrangements:

The tasks themselves have been designed to be indistinguishable from the kinds of work that most seven year old pupils are used to ... Turning to 14 year olds, I have indicated to the School Examinations and Assessment Council that I shall expect the arrangements for assessing technology, history and geography and modern foreign languages to combine both teacher assessment and statutory Standard Assessment Tasks ... both continuous assessment and end of year examinations are much more generally established in secondary schools, so that the new arrangements should be able to grow that much more readily out of existing practice.

(MacGregor, 1990, p. 2)

He was referring to the successful implementation of coursework in the GCSE, a move much derided by the New Right (North, 1987; Marenbon, 1987; Beattie, 1987). O'Hear (1987) for instance argued that the then new examination would be less rigorous, would lead to a downgrading of standards and would not allow 'genuine comparisons' between pupils. Worthen, likewise, writing about teacher assessments, suggested that 'no man should be a judge in his own cause' (1987, p. 30), reflecting a clear distrust of professional and collegial modes of accountability.

Assessment arrangements in this phase were in a state of transition with no clear ideological line as yet forthcoming. Without recourse to legislation, significant amendments were being made on a number of fronts. First, the text was being rewritten with the result that teachers would experience significant amounts of disempowerment. It was becoming more 'readerly' and less 'writerly' (Barthes, 1975). Second, the amended text was being repositioned in the system so that relations between the different parts were being reordered. What was also beginning to emerge was a desire by the central authority to reinforce and augment public or state control modes of accountability. In phase three, the trend became clearer.

PHASE THREE – REASSERTION OF CONTROL

In 1990 a new Secretary of State, Kenneth Clarke, took over. He was determined to reassert the power of the central authority over its constituent bodies. He wanted to limit and circumscribe the power of the individual teacher, 'the professional expert', by reordering relations between the different parts of the system. He inherited a number of problems: the first SATs appeared to be too long, too detailed and difficult to manage. They also demanded considerable input by teachers with the result that doubts began to be expressed about their reliability and comparability. Furthermore it was suggested that standards were being eroded in the GCSE, as the number of candidates obtaining high grades increased year by year. The Secretary of State acted in two ways. First a number of Key Stage 3 SAT development contracts were terminated, and new specifications set out. These asked the Mathematics Development Agency, for instance, to produce, at Key Stage 3, three one-hour tests covering all the content Attainment Targets. Process Attainment Targets were to be assessed by non-statutory SATs, and there was to be a general revision and culling of Attainment Targets. Brown, writing about these new orders, noted that:

> The irony of this decision to revert to short written tests is that they are purported to be in the interest of teachers who, it was assumed – before waiting for evidence to the contrary to become available – would find the KS3 SATs unmanageable and disruptive.
>
> (1992, p. 17)

The effect of this type of testing was problematic: it limited the ability of the assessments to allow formative and diagnostic judgements to be made; it further separated assessment from curricula by restricting and standardizing the way those assessments were to be made (Brown, 1992, for instance, estimated that pupils would be allowed six minutes to demonstrate mastery of each Statement of Attainment); and it downgraded the importance of teacher assessments.

A similar move occurred with the coursework arrangements in the GCSE, the political rhetoric emphasizing reliability, comparability and the maintenance of standards. The Secretary of State argued that:

> Coursework should play an important part in its curriculum, but not all of it is good. SEAC and HMI have constantly identified cases in which there is too much variation in the tasks set, too much diversity in marking and moderation, and too much opportunity for cheating. It may not give a true and honest indication of a pupil's ability.
>
> (Clarke, 1991, p. 1)

From 1994, the maximum amount of coursework allowed will be: English, 40 per cent; mathematics, 20 per cent; science, 30 per cent; technology, 60 per cent; history, 25 per cent; geography, 25 per cent; social sciences, 20 per cent; business studies, 25 per cent; and economics, 20 per cent.

Phase three then represents the clearest expression of what Gipps (1990) calls 'a standards and accountability model'. In particular, this phase saw considerable emphasis on the publishing of league and alphabetically arranged tables of performance, with the unit of currency 'raw' and not adjusted. This and other aspects of the testing arrangements would lead to a boycott by the teacher unions, with few schools completing the Key Stage 3 statutory tests in the summer of 1993, and a significant number of primary and infant schools abandoning Key Stage 1 assessments halfway through. The ability of the central authority to impose its agenda on schools was being challenged. The response of the government was to commission the Dearing Report (1993), with the Chairman of the newly created School Curriculum and Assessment Authority (SCAA) being asked to answer four key questions:

(a) What is the scope for slimming down the curriculum itself?
(b) What is the future of the ten-level scale for graduating children's attainments?
(c) How can the testing arrangements themselves be simplified?
(d) How can central administration of the National Curriculum and testing arrangements be improved?

(Dearing, 1993, pp. 65–6)

PHASE FOUR – COMPROMISE

Dearing, in his interim report, sought to bridge the divide between the competing parties. He proposed a number of significant amendments. First, though he accepted the need to separate teacher assessments from national test results by recommending that they 'should be shown separately in all forms of reporting and in school prospectuses' (1993, p. 52), he also argued for those teacher assessments to be moderated in terms of statutory end of Key Stage tests. Depending on the means used, this could result in two sets of similar results being reported side by side. Despite this, Dearing is attempting here to separate formative and diagnostic purposes of assessment from summative and evaluative ones. This is intended to reinforce the importance of teacher assessments, albeit that they will be moderated by SATs.

He further proposed that the prescribed curricular arrangements as expressed in the published orders should be cut back. The time released would allow the teaching of non-statutory material as defined by SCAA; the teaching of Programmes of Study which go beyond those laid down in the new orders; the teaching of subjects not included in the National Curriculum; and the reinforcing of mastery of basic skills. Though the time left would still be small in proportion to the time spent on the prescribed curriculum, this would significantly affect the ability of teachers to contribute to curriculum-making, and thus to be responsive to the needs of their pupils.

The third significant suggestion that Dearing made was that the ten-level system should be re-evaluated. Though alternatives – Dearing proposes four separate age-related systems – do not meet all the objections made about the operant system, the intention is clear: to simplify and clarify, and thus to make workable, these assessment arrangements. He cites three major problems with the ten-level system: subject knowledge and skills cannot necessarily be organized in linear patterns; pupils do not necessarily learn in simple orderly and linear ways; and 'it is difficult to devise clear, unambiguous, hierarchical criteria except for simple or clearly defined tasks' (Dearing, 1993, p. 40; see also Scott, 1987). Though he makes no recommendation, the suggestion in his report is that the ten-level system integral to TGAT (DES, 1988a) should be either modified or abolished.

Finally he argued that there was still a need to collect and publish summative data about pupils and schools. He is sympathetic, but not yet convinced, about the need to rework the 'raw' data to allow for socio-economic factors; and he rejects the arguments for carefully devised light sampling to judge the system year by year. So while separating formative and summative functions of assessment, he is tying closely together summative and evaluative functions and thus aligning any new model within a standards and accountability framework (Gipps, 1990). The report itself is an interim one,[1] and has yet to be translated into specific orders for schools, but it is further evidence of the tensions between two conflicting models of accountability. The first of these emphasizes professional control over curricula, though teachers would be expected to respond to the demands of external review. The second is a variant on the consumerist model described by Kogan (1986), in which market mechanisms are influential and data are gathered to compare school with school. If those data reflect badly on particular schools, then the market exacts a penalty and the school loses pupils and teachers and may even have to close down.

CONCLUDING REMARKS

This case study of the evolving arrangements made for assessing the National Curriculum illustrates a number of facets of policy processes. First, though the government would seek to impose education policy on schools, it is subject to, and subjects itself to, a number of important limitations or constraints. There are limits to how prescriptive texts can be made, since even the most 'readerly' text can be selectively read. Again, given the stated purposes of the government, to write curricular and assessment orders which exclude active roles for teachers would be self-defeating. Though control over curricula has been centralized, to remove all discretion from those whose task it is to implement such curricula would render that implementation inflexible, inefficient and unproductive. Second, governments and government agencies are composed of individuals with different understandings and different conceptions of policy matters. Policy is always contested at this level and at other moments and places in the system, though, as has been stressed, 'site' influences are not equally important and individuals working at these 'sites' are not equally empowered. Third, individual agents operating in collectivities can exert a significant influence on governments, even if the views they propagate differ radically from those being advocated 'officially'.

But such a view cannot and should not been seen to support pluralist policy models, which seek to suggest that the final outcome of state policy is always an amalgam of, and compromise between, different interests and concerns. Actors in the policy process adopt positions in terms of contexts which are not of their own making, though their activities contribute to new texts and contexts. These position actors unequally and thus differentially allocate resources and roles. Such a view seeks to provide a corrective to both simplistic pluralist *and* state control models of curriculum change.

NOTE

1. Dearing has since (January 1994) published his final report.

REFERENCES

Archer, M. (1982) Morphogenesis versus structuration. *British Journal of Sociology* 33 (4), 455–83.

Ball, S. (1982) Competition and conflict in the teaching of English: a socio-historical analysis. *Journal of Curriculum Studies* 15 (1), 1–28.

Ball, S. (1987) *The Micro-politics of the School.* London: Methuen.

Barthes, R. (1975) *S/Z.* London: Jonathan Cape.

Beattie, A. (1987) *History in Peril.* London: Centre for Policy Studies.

Bernstein, B. (1985) On pedagogic discourse. In *Handbook of Theory and Research in the Sociology of Education.* New York: Greenwood Press.

Bhaskar, R. (1979) *The Possibility of Naturalism.* Brighton: Harvester Press.

Bowe, R. and Ball, S., with Gold, A. (1992) *Reforming Education and Changing Schools.* London: Routledge.

Brown, M. (1992) Elaborate nonsense? The muddled tale of Standard Assessment Tasks in mathematics at Key Stage 3. In Gipps, C. (ed.) *Developing Assessment for the National Curriculum.* London: University of London Institute of Education.

Cherryholmes, C. (1988) An exploration of meaning and the dialogue between textbooks and teaching. *Journal of Curriculum Studies* 20 (1), 1–21.

Clarke, K. (1991) Cited in *Department of Education and Science Bulletin*, 362/91. London: DES.

Crossman, R. (1980) Do readers make meaning? In Sullerman, S. and Crossman, R. (eds) *The Reader in the Text: Essays on Audience and Interpretation.* Princeton, NJ: Princeton University Press.

Dearing, R. (1993) *The National Curriculum and Its Assessment – Interim Report* (The Dearing Report). London and York: School Examinations and Assessment Council and NCC.

Department of Education and Science (DES) (1988a) *Task Group on Assessment and Testing: A Report.* London: HMSO.

DES (1988b) *Three Supplementary Reports to TGAT.* London: HMSO.

Eco, V. (1984) *Semiotics and the Philosophy of Language.* Minneapolis: University of Minnesota Press.

Giddens, A. (1984) *The Constitution of Society.* Cambridge: Polity Press.

Gipps, C. (1990) National assessment: a comparison of English and American trends. In Broadfoot, P., Murphy, R. and Torrance, H. (eds) *Changing Educational Assessment.* London: Routledge.

Giroux, H. (1983) *Theory and Resistance in Education.* London: Heinemann.

Goldstein, H. (1989) Psychometric test theory and educational assessment. In Simons, H. and Elliott, J. (eds) *Rethinking Appraisal and Assessment.* Milton Keynes: Open University Press.

Goodson, I. (ed.) (1985) *Social Histories of the Secondary Curriculum: Subjects for Study.* London: Falmer Press.

Halsey, C. (1975) Sociology and the equality debate. *Oxford Review of Education* 1 (1), 9–23.

Kogan, M. (1986) *Educational Accountability: An Analytical Overview.* London: Hutchinson.

Lawton, D. (1992) Whatever happened to the TGAT Report? In Gipps, C. (ed.) *Developing Assessment for the National Curriculum.* London: University of London Institute of Education.

MacGregor, J. (1990) *Speeches on Education: National Curriculum and Assessment.* London: DES.

Marenbon, J. (1987) *English, Our English.* London: Centre for Policy Studies.

North, J. (1987) *GCSE: An Introduction.* London: Claridge Press.

Noss, R., Goldstein, H. and Hoyles, C. (1989) Graded assessment and learning hierarchies in mathematics. *British Educational Research Journal* 15 (2), 109–20.

O'Hear, A. (1987) The GCSE philosophy of education. In North, J. (ed.) *GCSE: An Introduction.* London: Claridge Press.

School Examinations and Assessment Council (SEAC) (1989a) *National Curriculum Assessment Arrangements (1).* London: SEAC.

SEAC (1989b) *National Curriculum Assessment Arrangements (2).* London: SEAC.

Scott, D. (1987) Problems of knowledge in the assessment of empathy in the GCSE. *Curriculum* 8 (3), 31–6.

Scott, D. (1991) Issues and themes: coursework and coursework assessment in the GCSE. *Research Papers in Education* 6 (1), 3–20.

Spradberry, J. (1976) Conservative pupils? Pupil resistance to curriculum innovation in mathematics. In Whitty, G. and Young, M.F.D. (eds) *Explorations in the Politics of School Knowledge.* Driffield: Nafferton.

Whitty, G. (1985) *Sociology and School Knowledge.* London: Methuen.

Willis, P. (1977) *Learning to Labour.* London: Saxon House.

Worthen, J. (1987) *English.* In North, J. (ed.) *GCSE: An Introduction.* London: Claridge Press, pp. 27–48.

Chapter 5

School governing bodies: public concerns and private interests

Rosemary Deem

This chapter is based partly on data from a longitudinal, multi-site, case study of school governing bodies in two English local education authorities, conducted by myself, Kevin Brehony, Sue Hemmings and Suzanne New between 1988 and 1993. However, the paper also rests on a more speculative analysis of certain elements of the educational policy process in England during the last two decades of the twentieth century. No exaggerated claims are made for the arguments presented, but it is suggested that they provide a possible framework for understanding what is happening to English educational administration at the present time. Since endeavours to offer more power in and over schools to lay people are now occurring in several countries, it is felt that the framework has applicability beyond England (Brehony and Deem, 1992; Deem, 1993).

The chapter examines some of the possible consequences for English state education of the coexistence of two different underlying ideologies about, and hence two different models of, lay participation in educational administration. One ideology stresses the significance of democracy, public accountability and collective concerns. This ideology, which I term *collective concern ideology*, although still current among some parent and governor pressure groups, now appears to be in decline. The other ideology, which I term *consumer interest ideology*, emphasizes markets, competition, consumer rights and private interests. This ideology appears to be in the ascendancy and finds its fullest expression in the idea of grant-maintained schools, where heads and governors fully control all aspects of their school's management and funding is direct from the state rather than through LEAs.

CHANGES IN GOVERNING BODY RESPONSIBILITIES

Recent educational reforms in England, including the 1986 No. 2 Education Act, the 1988 Education Reform Act, and the 1993 Education Act, have attempted extensive reshaping of the composition of individual state school governing bodies and considerable clarification and extension of their responsibilities and duties, as well as enabling outside agencies to step in if problems arise. The extension of governing body powers has included giving governors in LEA schools the responsibility for admission and exclusion of pupils, budget approval, discretionary teacher pay and determination of headteacher salaries (within national parameters), sex education, policy on charging for optional activities, and the hiring and firing of staff (although

LEAs remain the employers). In grant-maintained state schools, governor responsibilities extend even further; governing bodies are the employers of school staff and responsible for the freehold of the premises.

Despite these recent onerous responsibilities and the four-year term of office governors serve, they are volunteers who are not remunerated for their services. Furthermore, their activities are intended to be informed by lay rather than professional concerns, although teacher and headteacher governors clearly have educational expertise, as do some other governors. For the majority of lay governors, however, common sense and a sense of 'active citizenship', rather than educational expertise are seen to characterize their administrative strengths (Brehony, 1992; Brehony and Deem, 1991).

Prior to the legislation of the late 1980s, governing schools was a much less demanding activity. Indeed in the early 1980s, a study by Kogan *et al.* (1984) suggested that governing bodies were largely shaped by the culture, ethos and policies of their local education authorities and that of the schools in which they were located. Prior to 1980, governing bodies were often largely populated by political nominees, though many local education authorities did permit parental representation before the 1980 Education Act required them to. Since 1988, as a result of the 1986 No. 2 Education Act, parents and co-opted governors, including those from business and industry, have achieved numerical dominance on LEA school governing bodies over LEA nominees.

THE REFORM OF SCHOOL GOVERNING BODIES PROJECT

This project was an intensive study of ten school governing bodies in two LEAs, Northshire and Southshire, over four years. The schools covered a range of types of educational establishment, including primary and secondary, working-class and middle-class schools, inner-city and suburban, and included pupils from a range of different ethnic groups. A cross-section was chosen not for the purposes of making broad generalizations but in order to allow the constant comparison which Hammersley, Scarth and Webb (1985) suggest is important for ethnographic case-study research. A more detailed account of our methodology can be found in Deem and Brehony (1992). The two local authorities we used also provided us with significant comparisons. These included contrasting styles of chief education officers, and different approaches to a variety of educational policies, including those affecting school governors. Whereas Northshire adopted a 'hands-on' policy towards its governing bodies, providing clerking and standard agendas as well as extensive briefing papers on important issues for all its schools, in Southshire there was a 'hands-off' approach and schools and governors were very much left to their own devices.

We have used a variety of methods to carry out the research, believing that method triangulation is an important consideration in contentious areas of current educational policy. We have undertaken extensive observation of formal, informal and sub-committee meetings of governing bodies, making very detailed, almost verbatim, notes on the proceedings, attended early governor training sessions, sent questionnaires to governors in 1989 and 1992, and conducted semi-structured interviews with heads, chairs, chairs of sub-groups, teacher governors and business governors during the period of the research. We also held informal discussions with relevant officers from the two LEAs concerned and have collected for analysis a huge amount of documentation from the governing bodies concerned. No claims about typicality are made for the study but we do feel that in-depth, longitudinal research of this kind offers the possibility of reaching a high level of understanding of the processes involved in governing schools and enables the testing of theoretical ideas in ways not easily permitted by a snapshot representative survey.

TWO MODELS OF GOVERNING SCHOOLS

In the 1970s and early 1980s a prominent and extremely prevalent view of governing bodies was one which saw them as a form of democratic lay participation in education and as a means of public accountability for state schools. This *collective concern ideology* was particularly well expressed by the Taylor Report on governing bodies (DES, 1977). Much of the ideology was given practical expression in the organizational form that governing bodies took. The trend from the 1970s onwards was towards having a larger number of governing bodies in each LEA, so that schools had their own or shared one with a sister school on the same site. There was growing representation of parents as well as teachers and LEA nominees, although this was not required by law until after the 1980 Education Act. Governing bodies did not make major policy decisions or shape management policy in their schools but were expected to have an overview of their schools' organization and curriculum and met termly to discuss the school and its activities. After a *cause célèbre* in a London school where managers (as primary governors were called until the 1980 Act) were shown to be unable to deal with a major educational and organizational crisis in the school's leadership (Dale, 1981), it was felt necessary to clarify further the role of governing bodies, and this was one factor in the establishment of the Taylor Committee. The Taylor Report showed itself to be broadly in favour of a structure which would offer equal representation of different groups (teachers, parents, older students, LEAs and community representatives) and which would provide a framework of public accountability within which all state-maintained and state-controlled schools would have to operate (DES, 1977).

Throughout the 1970s the emphasis on collective values and public concerns in the administration of education was very evident. The 1980 Education Act, which secured parental representation as of right on governing bodies, did not depart significantly from this ideological position. Equivalent beliefs and values about the important public accountability and interest role of lay governors are still extant today (Sallis, 1988; Brigley, 1991). The 1984 Education Green Paper *Parental Influence at School* (DES, 1984) and the 1985 White Paper *Better Schools* (DES, 1985) also seemed to reflect similar values, culminating in the 1986 No. 2 Education Act, which clarified and extended governing body powers as well as changing their composition. But the 1986 Act may have been a watershed, for it also placed considerable emphasis on bringing in more governors from business and industry. This was an important change; since then there has been a significant shift in the political rhetoric underlying the rationale for school governing bodies, and in the model of governing bodies thereby adopted. The beliefs and values on which the 1988 Education Reform legislation rests enabled a move to site-based management of schools and formula funding using pupil-weighted units, through either local management of schools (LMS) or grant-maintained status schools (GMS). There was a further widening of the powers of lay governors and a corresponding reduction in the powers of democratically elected LEAs. It was thought by some politicians that these changes would add to schools' efficiency, competitiveness and market orientation, while ensuring that the rights and voices of individual education consumers, rather than those of educational producers, were clearly heard in educational contexts through parental choice of, and influence within, schools (Deem, 1990). The new values emphasized individual rights and interests rather than collective and public ones.

The strength of this new 'consumer interest' ideological view was confirmed by the 1992 Education White Paper, which sought to encourage more schools to opt out of LEA control and offered the promise of even greater financial and other delegation to those schools remaining within LEA control, and the subsequent 1993 Education Act. Alongside measures designed to increase centralization of educational administration, the powers of individual parents and governing bodies were to be strengthened while the powers of LEAs were reduced further. Thus, the appeal is not so much to a collectivity of caring citizens concerned with public good in education as to individual consumers of schooling, whether parents, businesspeople or politicians. These consumers, it is believed, are then able to ensure the preservation and fostering of market rights of users of schools, competition between schools for pupils, high educational standards and the efficient use of resources. In July 1992 the then Secretary of State for Education, John Patten, was quoted as saying that opting out (GMS) was a measure which enabled the depoliticizing of education. The arguments he apparently adduced for this were that more parents voted in opt-out ballots than in local elections and that parents knew better than educationalists what were the needs of their children (Meikle, 1992). Ironically, the further devolution of powers to parents and governors proposed by the White Paper is accompanied, as in the 1988 Act, by a strengthening of the powers of central government and the Secretary of State for Education to intervene in individual schools and/or governing bodies, should problems occur. The notion of depoliticizing education has been a dream of politicians in pursuit of greater centralism for nearly a century (Webb, 1973), and it is this contradiction between devolution and centralization which lies at the heart of the dilemma posed for the administration of universal state education by the education reforms of the 1980s and 1990s.

PUBLIC PARTICIPATION AND CONSUMER ORIENTATION

It is worth saying here that the two ideological stances whose existence I am suggesting, and the two models of participative educational administration which those stances support, differ from other attempts to classify, for the English education system in the 1990s, models of parental empowerment (Woods, 1992), the values of schools (Ball, 1990a) and the models underlying the general strategy of the Education Reform Act (Westoby, 1989). There is, of course, a connection between some of these attempts at classification and my own, although only that of Woods specifically refers to governors. Ball's work is closer to my own interpretation than that of Westoby or Woods. Woods seems to opt for a form of pluralism in which a number of models of consumer empowerment – by which he means only the empowerment of parents, not students or employers – are believed to coexist and overlap. He proposes four models of such empowerment: market, personal consumer control, quality assurance and participation. Admittedly Woods's main concern is with the mechanisms of empowerment rather than the means by which this is achieved, or the outcomes. Westoby (1989), on the other hand, suggests that the Education Reform Act strategy for schooling rests on a broader model than that of parents as consumers purchasing schooling from competing suppliers. The strategy, Westoby claims, 'also has a second "prong", based on the recognition that, in becoming customers of a particular supplier, parents also enter ... into the organization whose customer they become, and can influence what it does' (Westoby, 1989, p. 69). In other words, both consumer choice and participation are seen to be part of the underlying philosophy of the 1988 Reform Act. In one sense this is not in my view an inaccurate description of certain aspects of the Act. But Woods seems to interpret Westoby's statement as meaning that the notion of market customer and participating parent are thereby fully incorporated, in a straightforward and non-contradictory manner, into the ideological notions underlying the 1988 Reform Act.

However, my argument is not about whether both notions (consumer and participant) can or do coexist in the reform legislation. It is rather about their fundamental incompatibility, a view also shared by Ball (1990a, b) and Ball and Bowe with Gold (1992). Ball (1990a) contends that what he terms the market/choice position, in claiming that competition in education will raise standards, 'is an unequivocal abandonment of the objective of a universal or comprehensive form of education for all and its replacement with an entirely different organizing principle; welfare rights in relation to education are replaced by market rights' (Ball, 1990a, p. 6). He subsequently argues that the market notion does not operate 'as a neutral mechanism marked by an absence of values'; rather

> the tensions, dilemmas and ethics, the issues of social justice and social caring that should in my view, be better and more appropriately subject to open, public debate are being displaced into institutional and inter-personal decision making. ... What we see is a privatization of public values.
>
> (Ball, 1990a, p. 8)

Like Ball, I am suggesting that there are two contradictory sets of values at work in the process of English educational reform. However, while Ball's analysis takes in the whole schooling system, I confine mine to saying that these competing values are of particular relevance in shaping the arguments and forms of, and the political processes within, school governing bodies.

Unlike the apparently neutral concept of consumers which is a feature of Woods's research on parental involvement (1992), I do not see parental consumers, or for that matter community or industry consumers, as homogeneous groups. They are classed, gendered subjects who are also influenced by ethnicity and biography. Thus *who* becomes a school governor is, for the purposes of my argument, more important than the fact that it is possible for *some* consumers of education (ironically, *not* pupils) to become involved in the administration of schooling through such reforms as local management of schools or grant-maintained status. Who becomes empowered and what they do with those powers is more crucial than an abstract notion of empowerment regarded as a 'good thing' in itself. To adopt this argument is not to disagree with the idea that parents and members of local communities should have involvement with the administrative affairs of schools. Rather it places emphasis on the social and political conditions which shape that involvement and the consequent effects of those conditions on what can or cannot be achieved.

THE SOCIAL COMPOSITION OF GOVERNING BODIES

As with voluntary work in general, there can be no guarantee that governing schools will not be middle-class dominated (Brehony, 1992). The 1980s legislation was less concerned with representing cross-sections of the population than with getting anyone willing and eligible to take on the task. One parent governor, in this view, is generally much like another, although there was a long-running debate from 1988 to 1992 about whether teachers could also be parent governors (Deem and Brehony, 1991). The desire for co-opted governors to be drawn at least partially from business and industry, as set out in the 1986 Education Act, also assumed a high degree of homogeneity among that community, which is belied by the variety of ways in which schools seem to have interpreted this piece of legislation.

We have found in our research that while governors of middle-class schools do tend to share some characteristics in common with their school's student intake, this is much less the case in working-class schools, especially where there are high numbers of black and Asian pupils. The recent national survey research on governors (Streatfield and Jefferies, 1989; Keys and Fernandes, 1990) indicates that governors tend to be white and in professional or managerial jobs. Forty-four per cent of the Keys and Fernandes sample had a degree or professional qualification. Their study indicates a sharp rise in women governors, from 40 per cent in 1989 to 53 per cent in 1990, mainly explained by the fact that women are most likely to be teacher or parent governors, whereas the highest turnover has been in co-opted governors, who were more likely to be male. However, we should beware of simply reading off, from data on the social composition of governing bodies, assumed attitudes of individual governors towards education. If we do so we might, for example, assume that women governors would be more likely than men governors to support equal opportunities; in our research the reverse has sometimes been the case, with white businessmen making a case for equal opportunities in relation to gender on the basis that women as well as men are now required to play a role in the labour market.

Nevertheless, if some members of the population, including those in low-paid, low-skill jobs, mothers with demanding household responsibilities and those from disadvantaged ethnic minority groups, are constrained from becoming governors, then this does suggest that the notion of schools being publicly accountable to the community as a whole is difficult to achieve. The consumer interest model of governing schools does not require the same degree of cross-sectional membership, since its principal concern is with the representation of individual consumers and their market rights.

CONSUMER INTEREST AND COLLECTIVE CONCERN GOVERNORS

Before the 1988 Act, it is probable that relatively few governors had much interest in seeing schools as markets operating in a competitive way. Certainly Kogan *et al.*'s classic study of governors (Kogan *et al.*, 1984), carried out in the early 1980s, gives no hint, in its categorization of the mediating, the advisory, the supportive and the accountable types of governing body, that there were in existence governors principally concerned only with the success of their school. Undoubtedly, however, schools in areas with falling rolls did compete with each other for pupils and governors are likely to have been involved in this process.

Our own research suggests that rivalry between schools in some areas by far predates the 1988 Education Reform Act. But the absence of formula funding and the opportunities for parents and governors to oppose school closures meant that only very sharp changes in roll had much effect on a school's fortunes. Hence while governors might have been interested in promoting their school, this was not very often likely to be a consuming passion except where closure moves were imminent. But the advent of LMS and GMS has considerably changed the context in which state schools operate, since money now follows the pupil. Even if governors do not show any interest in marketing their school, heads are likely to draw marketing to their attention, and the financial consequences of unpopularity will be evident in the budgets for which governors as well as heads are now responsible, as well as in the requirements and demands made by newly appointed and more established teaching staff for particular salaries. But not only unpopularity leads to deficit budgets. In pre-LMS days many LEAs were able to direct extra resources into schools in deprived areas; with the advent of formula funding this possibility has all but disappeared, leaving dilemmas for governors in schools which are full but have lost this source of extra staff or money.

Of course many governors who were socialized into governing schools in an earlier era remain in post. In our research we found that some of them retained a notion of governorship as public or community service. But the class of the 1970s and early 1980s has been joined by more recently recruited governors, who may or may not share the same values and vision. In all of our case-study governing bodies, there were both collective concern and consumer interest governors (Deem, 1990; Brehony, 1992). However, it is not possible to identify these values via a simple correlation between values and different categories of governor. Despite the 1986 (No. 2) Education Act's intention that schools should have co-opted governors from the business community, and the co-option of such governors in some schools, co-opted governors in our study were no more likely to express consumer interest values than were their LEA or parental counterparts. This was partly because our investigations revealed that relatively few co-opted governors in our case-study bodies were actually from business and industry. For example, several accountants and managers turned out to be working in the public sector rather than the private one. But contrary to the view dominant since the mid-1980s that LEA governors are on the side of the producers of education (Deem, 1990), we found quite a few who did not identify at all with anyone working in education, and several examples of LEA governors who held a firm consumer interest orientation.

The consumer interest governor, with a distinct market orientation, has the potential to alter significantly the nature both of what governing bodies do and of how schools perceive themselves. Underlying the collective concern and consumer interest categorization of types of governor are not just their own values and beliefs but two different value systems which can be used to legitimize the activity of school governance. The broader questions which the consumer interest ideology raises are twofold. First, is the consumer interest model potentially more effective than the collective concern model in ensuring that the education of a nation's children is as good as possible? Second, how well is the consumer interest model actually working in its own terms? Does it have the capacity to produce schools which are market responsive but also serving the requirements of the wider society for a universal education system, in which all state-funded pupils in state-provided schools study the same National Curriculum? First I want to suggest that the consumer interest model and ideology tend to privilege private, individual interests over the wider public interests at the forefront of the collective concern model. This privileging may operate against the interests of those children who are working class, from ethnic minority groups or have special educational needs. Second, the organization and distribution of state schools and state education in our society are such that it is in any case difficult for a market concept to operate. Not all parents do have a real choice of school and no financial exchange takes place if state schooling is used (Ball, 1990a, 1990b). Schools in the state sector in England are not 'real' markets where services are freely bought and sold by all concerned.

PUBLIC CONCERNS AND PRIVATE INTERESTS

Our research evidence suggests that we are beginning to see in some governing bodies a divergence of attitudes and outlook between collective concern and consumer interest governors. Of course we cannot say from our study whether this tendency is widespread, though it is certainly worthy of further exploration. Governing bodies of LEA schools were reconstituted in 1988 and at this point they contained both experienced and new governors; it was noticeable that in almost all of our 15 pilot study governing bodies, the elections of chairpersons in the autumn of 1988 were carried out in a manner and speed such that new governors could scarcely have known what was happening.

Although some of the chairs so elected have subsequently been replaced by others, our interviews with chairs of governors confirm that the party political governor and the old-established 'pillar of the community' governor remain central figures in our ten case-study bodies. All but one chair has substantial experience of other voluntary organizations too and most view their governor role as one in which they provide service for others and help to maintain or improve the standard of education for children. Although individual governors may initially have been motivated by their own children's presence in the education system, their desire to change a particular school or something similar, the chairs, with one exception, perceived education as a public good and saw their relationship with heads and teachers as based on advice and support rather than challenge or a battle between producers and consumers.

But can this group and others like them, who loosely at least represent the democratic and accountable collective concern model and values, survive the change in ideological climate which was signalled first by the mid- and late 1980s educational legislation? There are undoubtedly many problems for such governors, in particular the difficulties of dealing with the exigencies of school finances. Faced with a budget shortfall and possible staff redundancy, as some governing bodies in our study have been, it may be that collective concern governors face an unresolvable dilemma. Even though they may be aware that the resource problem they face is not primarily created by their school or themselves but by national public spending priorities, they no longer have the possibility of appeal to an intermediary in the form of an LEA. The latter, while it still exists, is having to divest itself of staff, and functions under the same set of imperatives as those faced by governing bodies; it cannot offer extra financial assistance in the way it once could. Central government is no longer a focus for appeal and complaint because it has devolved power to schools and governors.

There is then no longer any mechanism for effective protest against the contradictions of apparent local autonomy for schools together with the massive centrally held powers of the Department for Education. Even governors opposed to the new model and its ideological suppositions may be forced into operating it or resigning altogether. We found this especially striking at one school in the study, Lady Clare, which is a large multi-ethnic primary and had recently to make a member of staff redundant. There were a considerable number of Labour Party members on the governing body, including all but one of the LEA governors, and they consistently displayed hostility towards LMS and competition between schools. When the budget deficit first began to be apparent there was much talk of fighting any redundancy; but in the end a redundancy was made, despite governors' awareness of the impact this would have on children's learning. There was nowhere they could protest which would, in their view, have enabled any other outcome. Thus the private interests involved in running that school came to take precedence over the wider public concerns of providing the kind of education system which our children require.

Collective concern values and beliefs do persist among both established and new governors in our study. We have observed discussions about education in governing body meetings, in almost all of our ten schools over the four years of our research, which suggest real concern for and about the quality of children's learning and genuine awareness of the problems teachers face in schools. At the same time, some of those engaged in such discussions, although not always chairs of governing bodies who may be caught between wanting to support heads and needing to disagree, are not afraid to criticize what a school is doing or question a given course of action by a headteacher. But such criticism is constructive and offered in a spirit of co-operation. These governors may be parents, LEA or co-opted governors. They are distinguished by their concern for children and young people in general and by their desire to be involved. Two examples of collective concern governors were evident at Moatmeadow Secondary. One was a mother of a current pupil and the other a co-opted governor and vicar. They served on working groups, wrote reports for the governing body, came into school and one of them even went on a week of demanding outdoor pursuits with sixth-formers. Although in the context of Moatmeadow these governors might put that school first, they also displayed a much wider awareness of the needs of children and public education. Public concerns took precedence over private interests.

Consumer interest governors are different. They tend to take one of two stances. There are those who ask lots of questions, are rarely supportive of the school and head, and frequently demand to know how their school is doing in comparison to others. If they are parents of current pupils, their children's experiences are often the basis for their criticisms. Others use neighbourhood or school-gate gossip as a basis for comment. Woods (1992) sees parents who conform to this type as being empowered under the recent legislation to get more involved. But more constructive involvement does not always happen. One governor of this kind at Cotswold School complained consistently about a wide range of matters – the organization of the finances, the shared sixth-form scheme, non-challenging school visits, teacher supply problems, discipline – yet when challenged at one meeting to visit school and see for himself the new house system, he said he was far too busy, gave too much time to the task of governing already and did not see school visits as a priority. Similar views about the unimportance of school visits were expressed by other consumer interest governors in our study; this was not an isolated example.

So empowerment may only be partial and hence perhaps from the school's point of view offer criticism which is not fully informed by a knowledge of the conditions under which everything operates. The other difficulty with the notion of empowerment is that it does not extend to all social groups. Governors are not drawn equally from all social groups, as we have already seen. At Cotswold, which is basically a working-class school, the governor just mentioned stood out as being privileged in several ways: he had a degree and a senior administrative post in a higher education institution; he understood how schools worked; and he also knew a great deal about the education system in general. He was already empowered, even without being a governor, compared to most of the other parents in that school.

There is also, however, a second type of consumer interest governor, what we might term an 'iconoclastic' governor. We found them to be mostly LEA governors or, more rarely, co-opted. Their connections with a particular school were often instrumental (for example, it was in their council ward) or tangential. Some such governors wished to become governors of a school they regarded as bad with a view to improving it, but their strategies rarely focused on a target within the school. As prominent local figures such governors did not need legislation on governor involvement to empower them – they often already had access to MPs, ministers and the media. Going to the local newspaper about school exam results before talking to the school(s) concerned first is something which recurred frequently in two of our case-study secondary schools. Whatever the intentions behind such actions, they can be perceived as morale-destroying for pupils and teachers, and were seen as such by the schools concerned.

Very critical governors whom we observed in our research were only occasionally those with the most detailed knowledge of the workings of a particular school; the media and gossip were more frequent sources than school visits for this group, the polar opposite of the collective concern governors (Deem, 1991). It might well be argued that being highly critical of a school does display public interest; but in fact we found that governors who took this line rarely approached things in a manner which demonstrated this. Instead they were more concerned with an abstract ideological debate about standards, markets and competition rather than with actual children and teachers.

Consumer interest governors, whether iconoclastic or not, often believe that they are superior to teachers and know more about running schools, often as a result of their business experience, whether this is extensive or narrow. They tended in our study to be co-opted or LEA-nominated governors and less often parent governors, although, as the Cotswold example demonstrates, parent consumer interest governors do exist. Indeed it was parents to whom the rhetoric of the late 1980s legislation often seemed to refer; it was anticipated that consumer interest governors would be drawn from among parents, since LEA governors were widely considered to be representing the producers of education. But we found several consumer interest governors who were LEA nominees. These individuals represented a quite different and recent group of councillors and party members to the urban gentry from whom chairs in our study were drawn. But the circumstances in which governing bodies now operate mean that there is increased pressure on all governors to behave in ways which at best serve the interests of pupils in one school only rather than a group of schools in an area. Within the context of that school, there is also some pressure to favour the interests of high and above-average attainers rather than those who are average or below. Similarly, the pressure on governors to understand budgeting and school finance means that training needs are likely to give a low priority to issues like equal opportunities (Deem, Brehony and Hemmings, 1992).

SCHOOLS, GOVERNING BODIES AND THE MARKET

The delegation of budgets to schools, and the basing of school funding on a formula which allows money to follow pupils, encourages schools and their governors to compete with each other rather than collaborate. The further reduction in LEA jurisdiction heralded by the 1993 Education Act means that one of the major vehicles for encouraging awareness of collective interests is fast losing that capacity. Of course governing bodies may choose to co-operate with others, but this co-operation is under considerable pressure at present. There is evidence from two of our case-study bodies that the former degree of co-operation and collaboration diminished as LMS developed, though this may have been temporary.

The pressure for good Standard Assessment Task and public exam results, isolated from any data about either the social characteristics of pupils or the value added by the school, meant that some governors of both primary and secondary schools in our study during 1991 and 1992 were becoming more concerned with the measurable aspects of education than with its more intangible aspects. Whether pupils are happy, well-adjusted, work co-operatively with others, and are able to think and understand as well as regurgitate material sometimes took lower priority. Two primary governing bodies in our study put pressure on their heads, though unsuccessfully, to publish their schools' 1992 SATs results for 7-year-olds. The first league tables for secondary public exam results were published in 1992. Results which are publicly available are likely to affect demand for places in schools, although in August 1993 it was agreed that the SATs for 7- and 14-year-old pupils would not be published. However, given the widespread opposition by governors, teachers and parents to SATs in 1993, it is hard to predict the impact of those league tables which *are* published. Exploratory work by Walford (1992) suggests that while middle-class *parents* may choose schools on the basis of academic indicators, in working-class households it may be that *children* choose their school, which is unlikely to be on the basis of exam results.

The public concern versus private interest issue is most sharply seen in the treatment of issues like increasing pupil intake by governing bodies. In our study the schools with falling rolls had working-class intakes. Governors at Little Rivers, a multi-ethnic secondary school, wanted to bring more children into school. They worked in an urban area where the local education office and heads openly talked about the ways in which white parents took their children out of the area to attend schools with a majority of white pupils. This background factor to pupil recruitment in the area leads to some very difficult dilemmas. The then present and previous heads had developed multi-cultural policies for the school, the desirability of which was the basis of quite heated arguments between governors, teachers and head. At the same time, because of falling rolls the school also tried to attract new (and by implication white and/or middle-class parents) by changing the school's name, offering a glossy brochure, and setting up a sixth form. The present head also investigated, without getting full governing body support, the possibility of a new school site away from the current one, which would in his view attract a different group of parents, even though it would be hard for many existing pupils to make their way to the school on this new site. Here the importance of marketing the school meant that the collective concerns of the current pupils and the community the school served were seen as less important than acquiring a different client group which might secure the school's financial future (Deem, Brehony and New, 1993). It remained to be seen at the end of our fieldwork whether the multi-cultural policies would survive the new emphasis on marketing.

The differential allocation of money to schools on the basis of degree of popularity with pupils, and the use in formula funding of average rather than actual staffing costs, is encouraging some schools with budget shortfalls to seek extra money from private sources. In our study this had not proved possible for the schools with budget deficits because they are in relatively low-income areas. Fundraising does take place on a lavish scale in one primary school, Knighton, and one secondary school, Ashdene, both of which are located in more affluent areas but these schools did not experience budget deficits during the period of our fieldwork.

Concern about finance was often directed at private interests rather than public concerns. One example was found in the debates about the requirement to develop a policy on charging for optional activities set out by the 1988 Act. This brought forth a wave of concern in several governing bodies about how parents could be made to pay charges, and how schools could ensure that parents were still charged for outings. It produced rather less discussion about how schools could ensure that disadvantaged children did not miss out on school trips or other optional activities (Brehony and Deem, 1990).

Since the dominant political ideology in England during the early 1990s suggests that social divisions do not exist – epitomized by Prime Minister Major's vision, both pre- and post- the 1992 general election in Britain, of a classless society – it is becoming ever harder for governors to suggest that it is legitimate to raise questions about disadvantaged pupils in schools and more difficult for schools which do take such questions seriously to justify their concerns and the expenditure involved. Ironically, expenditure on brochures, logos and publicity was rarely questioned and often encouraged by the governing bodies in our study. Additionally the huge workload imposed on governors by the 1986 and 1988 legislation may reduce the pool from which governors are drawn, further diminishing support for that model of governing schools in which accountability and democracy are prominent.

CONCLUSION

The superimposing of the *consumer interest ideology* and model of governors on the *collective interest ideology* and model, together with greatly increased governor workloads under LMS, may be decreasing rather than increasing the amount of democratic involvement in the English education system. This effect may work in one of two ways. First it may constrain many potential governors from serving at all. Second it may work by putting on the agenda a range of issues which make it harder for governing bodies to promote the public good in education rather than articulate private interests, whether these are interests of individual children or individual schools. This is surely not to be welcomed in a democratic society, whatever its political orientation.

Even if the educational market argument is accepted as a valid one, there are still questions to be asked about whether enabling choice only for those with the cultural resources necessary to benefit from it, and encouraging governors to focus on one school rather than public education in general, are in the end the most helpful ways to ensure that our children are educated properly and that state educational resources are used effectively. If the consumer interest model of governing schools empowers only those already privileged in social class terms, and if the issues they raise are individualistic matters concerned only with one school and its current pupils, then the universality of state education provision is being questioned and weakened. The consumer interest model itself may also be failing to work in its own terms if it is LEA-nominated and co-opted governors rather than parent governors who are among the first to take up the cudgels of consumer interest. It is also not clear that the issues raised by, and of import to, consumer interest governors are those which will necessarily lead to more effective and efficient schools. Our case-study evidence suggests that stringent criticisms by consumer interest governors are rarely accompanied by a willingness to be involved in a concerted attempt to overcome the problems thus identified. Abstract criticisms of this kind may simply demoralize rather than revitalize schools.

The arguments I have presented here and the evidence from our case study suggest that the consumer interest ideology may indeed be in the ascendancy, and that even where its central values are rejected by some governors, the requirements and predominance of the model that flows from it are such that many governing bodies are being forced to work in a way which favours private concerns rather than public interests and accountability. I contend that, in England, despite the recent educational reforms and extensive recomposition of governing bodies, as well as the sharp increase in their duties and responsibilities, the question of how to ensure public accountability of schools through the democratic involvement of lay members of the community, while not simultaneously legitimating the articulation of private rather than public concerns, remains unsatisfactorily answered.

NOTE

The research project on which the chapter is based is funded by an Economic and Social Research Council Grant (R000 23 1799). The researchers would like to thank the governing bodies involved in the study for their help and co-operation. Thanks also to Kevin Brehony, project co-director, Sue New, who joined the project team in February 1992, and Sue Hemmings, researcher on the project from April 1990 until August 1991, without whose contributions this chapter could not have been written. The discussion of the original version of this paper at the CEDAR conference was extremely helpful in producing this revised version, and I am grateful to the participants for raising many important points which gave further food for thought. Thanks to Barry Troyna for pointing out that even collective concern governors, faced with redundancies, may come to see themselves in a different light.

REFERENCES

Ball, S. (1990a) Education, inequality and school reform: values in crisis. Inaugural lecture, King's College, London.

Ball, S. (1900b) Markets, morality and equality in education. (Hillcole Group Paper 5). London: Tufnell Press.

Ball, S., Bowe, R. with Gold, A. (1992) *Reforming Education and Changing Schools.* London: Routledge.

Brehony, K.J. (1992) 'Active citizens': the case of school governors. *International Studies in Sociology of Education* 2 (2), 199–213.

Brehony, K.J. and Deem, R. (1990) Charging for free education: an exploration of a debate in school governing bodies. *Journal of Education Policy* 5 (4), 333–45.

Brehony, K.J. and Deem, R. (1991) School governing bodies: reshaping education in their own image. Paper presented at British Educational Research Association annual conference, Nottingham Polytechnic, August.

Brehony, K.J. and Deem, R. (1992) The participating citizen – a comparative view from education. Paper presented at British Sociological Association conference, University of Kent, April.

Brigley, S. (1991) Education accountability and school governors. In Golby, M. (ed.) *Exeter Papers in School Governorship No. 3.* Tiverton, Devon: Tiverton Publications.

Dale, R. (1981) Control, accountability and William Tyndale. In Dale, R., Esland, G., Fergusson, R. and Macdonald, M. (eds) *Education and the State: Politics, Patriarchy and Practice.* London: Falmer Press.

Deem, R. (1990) The reform of school governing bodies: the power of the consumer over the producer? In Flude, M. and Hammer, M. (eds) *The Education Reform Act: Its Origins and Implications.* London: Falmer Press, pp. 153–77.

Deem, R. (1991) Bad apples with a taste for trouble. *Times Educational Supplement*, 8 February.

Deem, R. (1993) Educational reform and school governing bodies in England 1986–1992: old dogs, new tricks or new dogs, new tricks? In Preedy, M., Glatter, R. and Levacic, R. (eds) *Managing the Effective School.* London: Paul Chapman.

Deem, R. and Brehony, K.J. (1991) A labour of love. *Times Educational Supplement*, 21 June.

Deem, R. and Brehony, K. (1992) Why didn't you use a survey so you could generalise your findings? Methodological issues in a multiple-site case study of school governing bodies after the Education Reform Act. Paper presented at ESRC-funded seminar 'Methodological and Ethical Issues Associated with Research into the 1988 Education Reform Act'. Department of Education, University of Warwick, July.

Deem, R., Brehony, K.J. and Hemmings, S. (1992) Social justices, social divisions and the governing of schools. In Gill, D., Mayor, B. and Blair, M. (eds) *Racism and Education: Structures and Strategies.* London: Sage, pp. 208–25.

Deem, R., Brehony, K.J. and New, S. (1993) Education for all? Governors, schools and the miasma of the market. In Wallace, G. (ed.) *Decentralised Management in Education*. Bournemouth: Hyde Publications.

Department of Education and Science (DES)/Welsh Office (1977) *A New Partnership for Our Schools* (The Taylor Report). London: HMSO.

DES (1984) *Parental Influence at School* (Green Paper). London: HMSO.

DES (1985) *Better Schools* (White Paper). London: HMSO.

Department for Education (DfE) (1992) *Choice and Diversity in Education* (White Paper). London: HMSO.

Hammersley, M., Scarth, J. and Webb, S. (1985) Developing and testing theory: the case of research on pupil learning and examinations. In Burgess, R.G. (ed.) *Issues in Educational Research*. London: Falmer Press.

Keys, W. and Fernandes, C. (1990) *A Survey of School Governing Bodies*. Slough: NFER.

Kogan, M., Johnson, D., Packwood, T. and Whittaker, T. (1984) *School Governing Bodies*. London: Heinemann.

Meikle, J. (1992) Patten seizes schools. *The Guardian*, 29 July.

Sallis, J. (1988) *Schools, Parents and Governors*. London: Routledge.

Streatfield, D. and Jefferies, G. (1989) *Reconstitution of School Governing Bodies: Survey 2*. Slough: NFER.

Walford, G. (1992) Choice of school: lessons from Britain on inequality and democracy. Paper presented at British Sociological Association conference, University of Kent, April.

Webb, S. (1973) The education muddle and the way out. In Van der Eyken, W. (ed.) *Education, the Child and Society*. Harmondsworth: Penguin.

Westoby, A. (1989) Parental choice and voice under the 1988 Education Reform Act. In Glatter, R. (ed.) *Educational Institutions and Their Environments: Managing the Boundaries*. Milton Keynes: Open University Press.

Woods, P.A. (1992) Empowerment through choice? Initial findings of a case study investigating parental choice and school responsiveness. Paper presented at CEDAR conference, 'Accountability and Control in Educational Settings', Warwick University, April.

Chapter 6

Educational choice, control and inequity

Geoffrey Walford

Over the past decade Great Britain has experienced a variety of changes in education policy that have been introduced and justified in terms of giving parents a greater choice of school. These changes include the introduction of the assisted places scheme in 1980; the granting of greater opportunity for parents to 'express a preference' for particular state-maintained schools following the Education Acts of 1980 and 1981; the development of city technology colleges from 1986; the 1988 restructuring of the education system through grant-maintained schools, local management of schools and open enrolment; and the 1993 Act's even greater emphasis on choice and diversity. All of these policies have important implications for the democratic control of education and for educational equity.

EARLY CONCEPTS OF CHOICE

The 1944 Education Act included clauses relating to parental preferences, but they were designed to ensure that parents could indicate their wishes with regard to the religious denominational control of schools, and were not intended to give choice between individual schools (see Walford, 1990a). The allocation of children to schools of the same type was under the control of the LEA and was usually done by means of residential catchment areas for each school.

Following the Second World War the main priority was to provide sufficient schools for all children. Not only did war-damaged schools have to be repaired or replaced, there was also a need for more accommodation for the rapidly growing school-age population. In 1951 there were 2.19 million children aged 12–15 in state-funded secondary schools in England and Wales. By 1981 the figure was 3.54 million (Halsey, Heath and Ridge, 1984). The increase was due to higher birth rates, fewer early deaths, and a gradual decrease in the proportion using the private sector. In addition, the school-leaving age was raised to 16 in 1972 and an increasing number of children continued in school beyond this age. While some parents gradually began to question and appeal against the allocation of their child to a particular school, most were prepared to accept their catchment area school while there was an obvious shortage of accommodation. However, in England and Wales the number of 10-year-olds reached its peak in 1975, and there was a decline of some 30 per cent in the years until 1987. It is this dramatic demographic change that does most to explain the increased interest in parental choice of school in Britain in the late 1970s and into the 1980s.

From the mid-1970s, it became obvious that many schools had spare capacity, and the then Labour government was faced with a growing demand from parents to have the right to choose a particular school for their children. An Education Bill was produced in 1977 which was intended to allow greater choice in a context where ultimate control was still retained by the LEAs. It recognized the need for some school closures and for LEAs to be able to plan local provision to ensure high educational standards for all children.

CHOICE AFTER 1979

A general election was called in 1979 before the Labour Education Bill became law, but Mrs Thatcher's newly elected Conservative government rapidly moved to implement its own version of parental choice through the 1980 Education Act. Much of the Act was similar to the 1978 Bill proposed by Labour, simply because it aimed to solve the same problems, but the ideological emphasis was shifted towards moving schools into the market-place and generating more competition between schools. From 1982 parents were given the right to 'express a preference' for a school of their choice, and the LEA was obliged to take this preference into account. However, the Act still gave LEAs considerable powers so that they could manage falling school rolls and plan the overall provision of school places in their areas. It allowed the benefits of the community as a whole to override the benefits to individual parents by giving LEAs the right to refuse parents' preferences if this would lead to some less popular schools having unviable numbers.

Stillman and Maychell (1986; Stillman, 1986) have shown that the effect of this legislation throughout England and Wales was extremely variable. Some LEAs tried to encourage parental choice, while others endeavoured to restrict it. Those offering minimal choice justified their behaviour on the basis that catchment area schools would foster better links with the local community. They also argued that catchment areas ensured that the LEA could engage in long-term planning and hence benefit from the most efficient and effective use of resources. There were many examples of both Conservative and Labour LEAs offering very restricted choice.

The somewhat different educational system in Scotland necessitated separate legislation from that for England and Wales. The Education (Scotland) Act 1981, which was designed to introduce parallel rights for parents to 'express a preference', actually gave the local authorities less power to inhibit free choice than did the Act for England and Wales. The exemptions were more tightly drawn and the appeals procedures were interpreted by local sheriffs to be more strongly in favour of parents. The result was that the Scottish experience after 1982 can be seen as a good indication of the possible effects of the free choice of school that was not introduced in England and Wales until the passing of the 1988 Education Reform Act.

THE SCOTTISH EXPERIENCE OF CHOICE

There have been two large-scale studies of the effects of the Education (Scotland) Act 1981. The most comprehensive of these was that conducted by a group at the University of Edinburgh (Adler, Petch and Tweedie, 1989; Petch, 1986a, b; Adler and Raab, 1988) whose multi-faceted research deserves careful attention. A major part of this work was a detailed study of the number and nature of requests made by parents for a school other than their catchment area school. The group studied the three regions Lothian, Fife and Tayside during the period 1982–5 and found that, while the number of 'placing requests' (i.e. requests for a school other than the one designated) doubled over that period, it was still small. On average, by 1985, some 9 per cent of children at both primary and secondary levels were entering schools other than the local one that they would normally have attended. However, this overall average masked considerable regional variations, with some rural areas having less than 1 per cent placing requests, and some cities such as Edinburgh having more than 16 per cent. These figures immediately indicate the limited effect that increased choice can actually have in rural areas, primarily because children would have to travel long distances to attend an alternative school. Without greatly increased expenditure, significant choice of school is possible only in urban environments.

In contrast to what many critics have predicted, the research also showed that, in all the areas studied, placing requests were made from parents of all social classes. They could find no evidence to suggest that middle-class parents were making a disproportionate number of placing requests, although there was some evidence that those doing so were more likely to have stayed at school longer and to have attained higher educational qualifications. However, the nature of the requests from different social groups varied. Many requests from working-class parents were from those living in poor housing estates who wished their children to attend a school in a more middle-class or mixed social class area. In contrast, there were few middle-class parents who wished their children to attend a working-class school. The authors argue that, at the secondary level, the legislation is leading to a widening of educational inequalities and producing a two-tier system where schools are generally perceived as desirable or undesirable. But what is important here is that some 90 per cent of parents did not exercise their right of choice on behalf of their children. Well-motivated parents and children were able to opt out of local working-class schools because they saw them as undesirable, but by doing so they ensured that their judgement was likely to become a reality for those children who remained. Adler, Petch and Tweedie (1989, p. 215) argue that, while the Act has led to the integration of a few pupils from areas of multiple deprivation into alternative schools, it has probably led to increased social segregation for those remaining in the local school. Their overall findings lead them to argue that the operation of greater parental choice might benefit some children, but has acted to the detriment of children overall.

The other major Scottish study of the 1981 parental choice legislation was conducted by Macbeth, Strachan and Macaulay (1986), who concentrated on a large-scale questionnaire and interview survey with parents conducted in six areas in three regions of Scotland. Only about 2 per cent of parents actually made placing requests; most parents continued to send their child to the nearest school. There were some inconsistencies between the results derived from the two methods of investigation, but they also found that the great majority of placing requests were successful – about 93 per cent of requests being granted at the initial stage. They found that placing requests had been made by parents across the whole social range and approximately in relation to the proportion of each socio-economic category in each area, and that requests were not predominantly from a 'middle-class minority', as some critics had predicted. Placement requests had generally been towards schools with an intake of a higher socio-economic status.

They recognize, however, that many parents will already have been able to assure their choice through purchase of a house near to the desired school, but argue that the 1981 legislation had enabled another group of parents to attain their choice and had thereby made the system more egalitarian. But to recognize that many middle-class parents would already have bought a home near to their chosen school means that the finding that the proportion of each social class of parent requesting placement was roughly equal to the proportion in the population shows that the middle class had taken disproportionate advantage of the new legislation. Their findings show that some poorer parents had, indeed, taken advantage of the possibility of choice, but that more affluent families now had two separate ways of achieving their objectives, and were using both.

The research found that 86 per cent of parents knew that they had the right to make a placement request. The authors report this as a very positive finding, but it might be argued that 14 per cent not knowing is rather too large a proportion for complacency, especially as these parents are probably those with children most in need.

Both of the studies described above were based on a non-randomly selected series of case studies rather than a true national sample and are thus not generalizable. A national representative Scottish study of choice of school was conducted by a separate group at the Centre for Educational Sociology, University of Edinburgh (Echols, McPherson and Willms, 1990). Their study investigated the social class and parental education of a national cohort of young people who transferred to secondary school in 1982, the first year of the new legislation. It included analysis of those who chose the private sector as well as those who chose an alternative school in the state-maintained sector. They found that the largest single effect on the incidence of choice was not individual but structural, and arose from the local availability of options between which choices could be made. In other words, especially in the state sector, more choices were made where schools were closer together geographically. They found that it was the better-educated parents and those of higher social class who were more likely to have made a choice. For example, parents with the highest level of schooling were almost twice as likely to have made a choice of state schools than were parents with the lowest levels. They also found that the schools chosen tended to be those that had a higher social class intake and higher levels of attainment. These tended to be the older, long-established schools which had been grammar schools before the 1965 reorganization and still retained some of their former prestige. The authors believe that the legislation on parental choice has increased social segregation between schools, and that the disproportionate gains in attainment made by children with parents who are manual workers, brought about by comprehensive education, are likely to be retarded or even reversed.

A more recent and detailed analysis by the same research group (Willms and Echols, 1992) draws upon a range of questionnaire and survey data and reinforces the earlier results. They found that parents who exercised choice were likely to be more highly educated and to have more prestigious occupations than those who sent their child to the designated school. Choosers tended to select schools with higher mean socio-economic status and higher levels of attainment, but these differences in attainment were actually small once the differences in background characteristics of the pupils had been taken into account. The results suggest, once again, that the choice process is increasing inter-school segregation, which may produce greater inequalities in attainment between social class groups.

These studies show that, rather than raising standards overall, as predicted by advocates of these policy changes, greater inequalities are likely to develop. The children of well-motivated, highly educated or wealthy families are more likely to make applications and thus be accepted by the popular schools. In contrast, children from families which do not highly value education will probably not bother to make a placing request, and will find themselves in schools which have been impoverished by the loss of the more actively involved parents and pupils. The loss of these well-motivated pupils and parents means that it is likely that any pre-existing differences between schools will widen.

MORE CHOICE IN THE PRIVATE SECTOR

The assisted places scheme, also introduced in the 1980 Education Act for England and Wales and in 1981 for Scotland, was one further policy justified in terms of increasing parental choice. The scheme was officially designed to 'give able children a wider range of educational opportunities' by giving 'help with tuition fees at independent schools to parents who could not otherwise afford them' (DES, 1985). In practice, it not only helps individual parents and children, but gives substantial financial and ideological support to the private schools themselves. About 12 per cent of secondary pupils in the private sector are now supported through the assisted places scheme. Individual schools are allocated a set number of places each year and are able to fill these places using their own selection methods.

The major study of the assisted places scheme conducted by Edwards, Fitz and Whitty (1989) draws on national statistical data on the allocation and take-up of places from 1981 to 1987, and extensive case-study data drawn from interviews with pupils, parents and headteachers from the private schools involved and from state-maintained schools. Not unexpectedly with a scheme where parents initially have to be aware of the possibility of financial help and then determined enough to apply and be interviewed by the schools, there is a severe social class bias in the children selected. The authors show that, while about a third of the pupils were from single-parent families, many of them had existing links with the private sector. There was a low participation rate from manual working-class families and from families of some ethnic minorities, particularly those of Afro-Caribbean origin. Although the scheme is means tested, about one-third of children on assisted places had parents with above-average incomes. The authors suggest that a considerable proportion of assisted-place holders came from submerged middle-class backgrounds already well endowed with cultural capital. It was also very noticeable that there were considerably more boys benefiting from the scheme than girls.

It is notable that when the scheme was introduced there was no ideological linkage between the desire to increase choice and that of raising overall educational standards. Indeed, the assisted places scheme was predicated on the belief that some state schools were so bad that the only hope for academically able children was to remove them from these schools and place them in private schools. There was no suggestion that the state schools might improve as a result of this transfer.

77

CHOICE IN THE MID-1980s

As the 1980s progressed, two successive Conservative governments pushed through a series of privatizations of state-owned enterprises and services (Walford, 1990b). These moves were seen as part of a general policy of 'rolling back the frontiers of the state' and encouraging competition wherever possible. The rigours of the market were seen as the way by which higher quality and greater efficiency were to be achieved. Inevitably, education services were also the subject of various privatization measures. Cleaning and other services were contracted out to competitive tender, and it is at this point that strong links began to be made between choice and raising educational standards.

At the 1986 Conservative Party annual conference that preceded the 1987 general election, a particularly dramatic privatization policy was announced under the guise of giving greater parental choice. The Secretary of State for Education and Science announced the creation of a pilot network of 20 city technology colleges (CTCs) to cater for 11- to 18-year-olds in selected inner-city areas. These were to be private schools, run by educational trusts with close links with industry and commerce. The governing bodies of these schools were to include many representatives from industry and commerce but to exclude both parent and teacher governors. The CTCs would charge no fees, but sponsors would be expected to cover the extra costs involved in providing a highly technological curriculum and would make substantial contributions to both capital and current expenditure. They were to select children with a broad range of academic abilities from a defined catchment area. Significantly, these new schools were also supposed to act as 'beacons of excellence' for nearby LEA schools and thus raise educational standards overall.

The desire to increase technological education was a major feature of the plan, but many public political speeches at the time showed that CTCs were also designed to encourage inequality of educational provision, reintroduce selection, weaken the comprehensive system and reduce the powers of the LEAs. As the title of the promotional booklet, *City Technology Colleges: A New Choice of School* (DES, 1986), makes clear, this was all to be justified and legitimized through the ideology of increased parental choice, and the idea that greater choice would improve educational standards for all.

The results of the CTC initiative have not been as planned. There was fierce opposition to the scheme from LEAs, teachers' unions and some local action groups. More unexpectedly, many involved in industry and commerce were also against the idea and expressed the belief that technological education was better served through their involvement in many schools' rather than through concentration of their efforts and resources on a small number of CTCs. The CTCs have proved much more expensive to establish than was first thought, and sponsors have provided only about 20 per cent of the capital expenditure and little of the current expenditure. At the first CTC, at Kingshurst, Solihull, for example, sponsors provided £2.1 million towards the capital costs of establishing this new private educational trust school, but the state has given more than £8 million towards capital costs and will provide the vast majority of the ongoing current expenditure.

A preliminary study of the first CTC has been conducted by Walford and Miller (1991). While it is still too early in the life of the new college to evaluate fully its effects on the children selected and on nearby schools, some indications are illuminating. Of particular importance is the way in which children are selected for the CTC from those who apply. All of the CTCs are required to provide education for children of different abilities who are wholly or mainly drawn from the area in which the school is situated. The CTC, Kingshurst, selects children from a tightly defined catchment area which includes eight LEA secondary schools, and is thus in direct competition with these other schools for pupils. Parents are required to apply for admission to the CTC on behalf of their child. The child takes a simple non-verbal reasoning test which is used to ensure that children are selected with a range of abilities broadly representative of those who apply. They are also interviewed with a parent. In addition, parents and the child have to state that they intend the child to continue in full-time education until the age of 18. The study by Walford and Miller showed that the college took great care to ensure that it was taking children with a wide ability range, but the whole entry procedure means that selection is based on the degree of motivation of parents and children instead. Children and families who have a low level of interest in education simply do not apply.

In interviews, heads and teachers in the nearby LEA schools claimed that the CTC was selecting those very parents who have the most interest in their children's education, and those children who are most keen and enthusiastic. They argued that the CTC was selecting children who, while they might not be particularly academically able, had special skills and interests in sport, art, drama or other activities. These children were seen as invigorating the atmosphere of any school, providing models for other children, and being rewarding for teachers to teach. Heads and teachers in nearby schools saw their schools as having been impoverished by the CTC's selection of these well-motivated pupils: they saw the CTC as having only a negative effect on their schools.

The present reality is far from the optimistic future presented in 1986 and, in spite of continual government support, there are still only 15 colleges. But the symbolic significance of the CTCs is disproportionate to the number of pupils involved. Fundamentally, the CTC idea made it clear that the government wished to develop an educational system based on inequality of provision and the selection of children for those schools with the best facilities, funding and support. The CTCs may have been a faltering start, but the idea rapidly led to more radical changes.

CHOICE AND THE 1988 EDUCATION REFORM ACT

The 1988 Education Reform Act for England and Wales introduced a wide range of ideas designed to hasten market processes within education (Walford, 1990c). Through the introduction of grant-maintained schools and in the interlinked ideas of local management of schools and open enrolment, the major thrust of the Act was designed to increase competition and to encourage parents to make choices between schools. Funding to individual schools is now largely related directly to pupil numbers, and schools have their own delegated budgets. Popular schools gain extra funding as they attract more pupils, while less popular schools lose funding as their numbers decline. LEAs have lost much of their power to give extra support in areas of special need, or temporarily to adjust funding to particular schools to ensure that future needs are met. At a time of falling school rolls, this means that the choice of which schools will close is left largely to the summation of the decisions of existing parents. The needs of future parents, or the society as a whole, are forgotten.

The Act was clearly also designed to reduce the powers of LEAs in other ways. LEAs are currently allowed to retain a small proportion of their educational funding for services which are best provided centrally rather than at the school level. LEAs provide help for those with special learning difficulties, pay for local curriculum advisers, planners and administrators, develop curriculum innovations, support multi-cultural and anti-sexist work, operate field centres, media centres and a host of other activities. One of the main reasons why schools have wished to become grant maintained is that the schools receive 'their share' (in fact, a disproportionate share) of these central costs. They are then able to buy whichever of these services they wish from any supplier. The LEA thus loses power to encourage curriculum developments which it feels to be particularly relevant to the children in the region. If the grant-maintained school becomes oversubscribed, it also means that it can begin to select the children it wishes to accept. The ability of parents and children to choose a school leads to schools being able to choose the pupils they want.

Encouraged by large grants from central government, the number of schools seeking grant-maintained status is now increasing. Halpin, Fitz and Power (1993) have shown that many of the schools involved had been part of local authority schemes designed to close or reorganize schools to deal with falling school rolls. They show that many of the schools that have achieved grant-maintained status were identified by their former LEAs for closure or reorganization. In several cases this has led to whole LEA reorganization schemes having to be reworked and considerable waste of public funding as schools still continue to operate with very low pupil numbers. Almost two-thirds of their local authority respondents reported that their reorganization plans had been either abandoned or temporarily shelved after schools had decided to opt out. They argue that the individualistic decisions of single schools to opt out was inhibiting the viability of whole local schemes of provision, and resulting in negative financial and educational consequences for the other schools in the area.

REASONS FOR CHOICE AND WHO MAKES THE CHOICE

The greater choice of school that followed the 1980 Education Act for England and Wales and, in particular, the 1981 Education (Scotland) Act, has encouraged research on the criteria that parents use in making their choice. Prior to these changes, most research on choice in Great Britain had concentrated on the private sector (see Johnson, 1990; Walford, 1990b). One of the most important findings of these studies of choice in the private sector is the wide range of different factors seen as important. However, in her study of parents of boys in Headmasters' Conference schools, Fox (1985) found that the most frequently voiced criteria for choice were related to the perception that these schools could produce better academic results and develop character through discipline. However, the distance of the school from the parental home was still an important factor, even where the child boarded.

The Scottish study by Adler, Petch and Tweedie (1989) examined the reasons parents gave for choosing particular schools. Through a survey of the parents of about 600 children about to enter secondary schools and 400 about to enter primary schools, Petch (1986a, b) showed that the choice of school is most strongly influenced by pragmatic and pastoral considerations. At primary level the most important aspects were found to be the distance of the school from the home, the child's happiness, safety in travelling and sibling attendance. Very little attention was given to what the school offered in terms of educational content or teaching method. At secondary level the most important factors were the child's happiness, the child's preference and the perceived higher level of discipline at that particular school. Factors connected with academic achievement were lower down the list of priorities.

Adler, Petch and Tweedie (1989) also found that the presence of siblings, location of school and desire for the child to accompany friends were the three most important open-response reasons given for choice of secondary school. This still leaves open the reasons why the choice had been made for the sibling, but it is noticeable that academic criteria again do not feature prominently. In terms of the parents' responses to structured items, in all four of their case-study areas the most important of 32 items were that 'our child prefers the school' and 'we think our child would be happier there'.

The other Scottish study, conducted by Macbeth, Strachan and Macaulay (1986), found a rather higher percentage of parents giving reasons based on assessments of the schools themselves than has been found elsewhere. It found that parents' reported reasons were divided fairly equally between those based on assessments of the schools themselves and those related to other issues such as the ease of travelling to the school. However, Johnson (1990, p. 79) notes that there are some methodological problems associated with the way the questions were asked which raise doubts about the generalizability of this finding.

Several other relatively small-scale investigations of choice have been conducted more recently. Hunter (1991) conducted an interview survey of parents with children in 18 Inner London Education secondary schools in 1988 before the Act had come into effect. There was a deliberate oversampling of parents who send their children to single-sex schools, so the results were not representative of the Inner London Education Authority as a whole. However, she found the four most commonly cited reasons for choice were good discipline, good exam results, single-sex intake, and proximity to home. The third of these is somewhat special to London, where there is a high proportion of single-sex schools and a high ethnic minority population.

Much of the research about choice has questioned parents after the event, but the results of research conducted before the event tend to stress rather different priorities. The ILEA Secondary Transfer Project (Alston, 1985), for example, found that 65 per cent of the parents said that the fact their child wanted to go to the school was important. Proximity was mentioned by 53 per cent of the parents, while 48 per cent said 'good facilities' were important. A school's good reputation for examination results was stressed by only 38 per cent.

West and Varlaam (1991) also questioned parents before their final choice had been made. Their sample of 72 parents was drawn from six Inner London primary schools. They found the four factors most often seen as important (without prompting) were: the child wanting to go there, good discipline, emphasis on good examination results, and ease of access. More interestingly, they also found that three-quarters of the parents indicated a particular school that they did *not* wish their child to attend, mainly because of its 'bad reputation'.

West and Varlaam also asked their sample of parents why they thought their child wanted to go to a particular school. The most important reason was simply that the child wished to go to the same school as his or her friends or relations. Other reasons given were the good sports facilities, its convenient location or because it was single sex. None mentioned academic reasons.

A similar small-scale study of parents of children in Sheffield primary schools about to move to secondary was conducted by Boulton and Coldron (1989). Using a questionnaire returned by over 200 parents and interviews with 16 families, they found the most important factors influencing choice were the nearness of the school, and the future attendance at the school of the child's siblings and friends. They found that parents ranked very highly the child's feelings of security and happiness in the new school environment. As a result, there was a very strong relationship between many parents' wish for their child to be happy and the prioritizing of the preferences expressed by the child.

It would appear that the recent introduction of published 'league tables' in examination results has done little to reduce the influence on parents of children's views. In a small-scale interview study conducted in early 1993, Webster *et al.* (1993) found that 69 per cent of their sample of parents rated the views of their children as 'very important' to them in their choice of school. A further 13 per cent rated their children's views as 'important'. Interestingly, three-quarters of their respondents stated that the published examination figures for the schools were unimportant in their decision-making. Only 18 per cent stated that they had been an important part of the process, while 22 per cent registered very strong negative reactions to the official figures.

What is fascinating about the results of so many of these studies where the parents are questioned before the child enters secondary school is that parents appear to give a high priority to the wishes of their children. At the time the choice is actually made, they seem to give high status to the wishes of their 10-year-old sons and daughters. After the event, parents may rationalize their decisions in terms of the criteria they believe the researcher might want to hear, but before the event they are prepared to admit that their child's happiness in attending a particular school is an extremely important factor. Moreover, there are indications that there are systematic variations in the degree of legitimacy that parents accord to their children's views. Edwards, Fitz and Whitty (1989), for example, found that the most striking difference between parents of able children at LEA comprehensive schools and those of assisted places scheme children in private schools was the extent to which they considered their child's desire to stay with friends. Those who chose the private sector for their children were more likely to ignore their children's wishes.

Gewirtz, Ball and Bowe's (1992) study of the workings of choice and the market since 1988 has examined in detail the way in which various families respond to the market situation in which they find themselves. They identify three broad groups of parents, defined in terms of their position in relation to the market – the privileged, the frustrated and the disconnected – and show the ways in which working-class or newly immigrant families may be disadvantaged in the market. They present a picture of a complex situation where patterns of choice are generated both by choice preferences and by opportunities, and where reputation and desirability are played off against other factors. But they also show that the way in which parents play the market is strongly related to social class, and that working-class parents are much more likely than middle-class parents to see the child's views as decisive.

While children appear to play a large part in the choice-making process, until recently they have rarely been questioned themselves about their reasons for wishing to attend one school rather than another. One such small-scale study was part of the wider study of the city technology college, Kingshurst, discussed earlier (Walford, 1991). The majority of children at the school completed questionnaires and a representative sample were individually interviewed. It was found that nearly half of those interviewed believed that it had been they who had made the final choice to apply to the CTC and not their parents. A further 40 per cent stated that the decision had been a joint one with their parents. Significantly, in a specific question asking whether the fact that it was a *technology* college had been important, less than half agreed that it had. In this case the most common reason given was simply that they saw the CTC as offering them a 'good' or 'better' education, but this was often seen in terms of newer or better facilities and a better physical environment. As these children are selected with the chance that their friends from primary school might not also be selected even if they had applied, this factor had to be given low priority. In these circumstances the children choosing this very unusual school did appear to take educational aspects into consideration, but only at a very low level.

For comparison, interviews were held with 61 pupils in their first year at three nearby LEA schools which were within the CTC catchment area. Fifty-five per cent of these children stated that the choice of school had been their own decision, with a further 30 per cent saying that it had been a joint decision with their parents. Reasons given for choice were varied, with differing patterns between the three schools. In all three schools, however, the fact that friends and relations were either already attending the school or were due to do so was an important consideration. The most common response in the interviews was that the pupil simply thought it was a 'good school' or that they just 'liked it'. Negative comments about other possible schools were also common.

What is of great importance here is the high proportion of children from this largely working-class area who stated that the choice of secondary school had been made by them rather than their parents. While it must be recognized, of course, that parents may use various subtle techniques to influence their children's choice, this was not the impression gained from these interviews. Most of the children who stated that it had been their choice were adamant that they had made this decision, sometimes against the wishes of their parents.

This degree of delegation of responsibility has also been found in a small-scale study of children in two urban junior schools in northern England conducted by Thomas and Dennison (1991). In their study of 72 children, 60 per cent claimed that they made their own choice of secondary school. A further 30 per cent said it was a joint decision with their parents. Interviews with a sample of parents confirmed that most gave their children the 'biggest say' in the choice, and that their main concern was with their children's happiness. Again, decisions were made on the basis of a mixture of factors, with friendship being a major influence for children. Of those children who chose a secondary school which was not their nearest, existing patterns of friendship represented the single most important factor in accepting the longer journey.

The results from another study of slightly older children in an outer London borough indicate a smaller, but still significant, proportion of children making the choice of school themselves (West, Varlaam and Scott, 1991). Eighteen per cent of the children from 12 middle schools reported that they had made the choice of high school themselves, with a further 66 per cent reporting that it had been a joint decision with their parents or guardians. These somewhat different proportions could well be related to the social class composition of the outer London sample. This study also discusses ethnic group differences and, while the numbers involved are small, the differences are significant. Compared with white European children, a higher proportion of African/Afro-Caribbean children stated that they had made the choice themselves, while a far lower proportion of Asian pupils made this statement.

CONCLUSION

One of the main justifications that has been used for greater choice of school is that it is anticipated that popular schools will thrive while unpopular ones will close. However, this effect can only occur at a time of falling school rolls. Once less popular schools have closed in line with the falling pupil population, those remaining will be full. Without overcapacity in schools, parents will quickly find that their choices are severely curtailed, and that it is the schools who choose which children to accept rather than the parents and children choosing a school. Control will have passed to individual schools and their governing bodies. At the city technology college, Kingshurst, for example, there were over 1,000 applicants for 180 places for September 1991. Far more parents were denied their choice than granted it, and the CTC was able to select just the children it thought most suitable. That the government has begun to allow grant-maintained schools to become academically selective, and given all schools the right to select up to 10 per cent of their intake because of a 'specialism', is an indication that increased selection was an integral part of the choice ideology.

The idea that greater choice leads to higher overall standards is based on the assumption that choice of school will be made by parents, and that these parents will be well informed. It is supposedly the 'bad' schools that close and the 'good' ones that expand. However, it has been shown that parents make choices on a broad range of criteria and that academic issues appear to feature quite low on their list of priorities. There is little evidence for equating 'popular' with 'good' in terms of parental choices. However, recent evidence has shown that the child's wishes are of great importance to many parents, and that a large number of parents appear to delegate the decision of choice of school to their child. This concern with the wishes of the child may mean that she or he has a happier time at secondary school (which is not insignificant), but there is even less evidence that the choices of 10-year-old children are likely to be informed choices and primarily related to the academic effectiveness of the schools. More fundamentally, it is highly unlikely that the sum of many such choices will automatically lead to higher educational standards for all.

It does seem likely, however, that choice will lead to better-quality schooling for *some* children, because some parents and children will be more concerned and better informed about the effectiveness of various schools than others. Some parents are better able to pay for the transport of their children to school, and some are more likely to impose their decision about schooling on their children. As choices are made and pupils selected, the schools will become more differentiated. Some will be able to draw on parental financial support for new buildings and equipment or to pay for additional teachers and helpers. Other schools will not be so fortunate.

Eventually, this continuum of schools will offer different educational and social experiences to pupils, with the final decisions about recruitment made by the schools and their governing bodies. Control of education will be in the hands of a series of small, largely unelected groups. The evidence that we already have about choice suggests that this process of selection will probably be closely linked to social class and ethnicity, and will discriminate in particular against working-class children and children of Afro-Caribbean descent. There is also likely to be greater segregation of social and ethnic groups and less mutual understanding. The pre-existing social and economic order of wealth and privilege is likely to be confirmed. In summary, the main purpose of the recent moves towards greater choice is not to build a more democratic and fair educational system but to rebuild a more differentiated system which will more closely aid social reproduction. The ideology of choice acts partially to mask this process and, while it may allow a few individuals to benefit, the majority have much to lose.

NOTE

This chapter draws in part upon my article 'Educational choice and equity in Great Britain', *Educational Policy*, Spring 1992, and the ideas are also developed in my book *Choice and Equity in Education* (Cassell, 1994). Some of the interviews of parents reported in this chapter were conducted by Henry Miller and Sharon Gewirtz, to whom I am grateful.

REFERENCES

Adler, M., Petch, A. and Tweedie, J. (1989) *Parental Choice and Educational Policy.* Edinburgh: Edinburgh University Press.

Adler, M. and Raab, C.D. (1988) Exit, choice and loyalty: the impact of parental choice on admissions to secondary schools in Edinburgh and Dundee. *Journal of Education Policy* 3 (2), 155–79.

Alston, C. (1985) *Secondary Transfer Project. Bulletin 3: The Views of Parents before Transfer.* London: ILEA.

Ball, S.J., Bowe, R. and Gewirtz, S. (1993) Circuits of schooling: a sociological exploration of parental choice of school in social class contexts. To be published.

Boulton, P. and Coldron, J. (1989) *The Pattern and Process of Parental Choice* (Project Report). Sheffield: Sheffield City Polytechnic.

Department of Education and Science (DES) (1985) *Assisted Places at Independent Schools.* London: HMSO.

DES (1986) *City Technology Colleges: A New Choice of School.* London: HMSO.

Echols, F., McPherson, A. and Willms, J.D. (1990) Parental choice in Scotland. *Journal of Education Policy* 5 (3), 207–22.

Edwards, T., Fitz, J. and Whitty, G. (1989) *The State and Private Education: An Evaluation of the Assisted Places Scheme.* London: Falmer Press.

Fox, I. (1985) *Private Schools and Public Issues.* London: Macmillan.

Gewirtz, S., Ball, S. and Bowe, R. (1992) Parents, privilege and the education market place. Paper presented at the British Educational Research Association Annual Conference, 26–29 August.

Halpin, D., Fitz, J. and Power, S. (1993) *The Early Impact and Long Term Implications of the Grant-Maintained Schools Policy.* Stoke-on-Trent: Trentham.

Halsey, A.H. (1980) Schools. In Halsey, A.H. (ed.) *British Social Trends since 1900.* London: Macmillan.

Halsey, A., Heath, A. and Ridge, J. (1984) The political arithmetic of public schools. In Walford, G. (ed.) *British Public Schools: Policy and Practice.* Lewes: Falmer Press.

Hunter, J.B. (1991) Which school? A study of parents' choice of secondary school. *Educational Research* 33 (1), 31–41.

Johnson, D. (1990) *Parental Choice in Education.* London: Unwin Hyman.

Macbeth, A., Strachan, D. and Macaulay, C. (1986) *Parental Choice of School in Scotland* (Parental Choice Project). Glasgow: Department of Education, University of Glasgow.

Petch, A. (1986a) Parental choice at entry to primary school. *Research Papers in Education* 1 (1), 26–47.

Petch, A. (1986b) Parents' reasons for choosing secondary schools. In Stillman, A. (ed.) *The Balancing Act of 1980: Parents, Politics and Education.* Windsor: NFER–Nelson.

Stillman, A. (ed.) (1986) *The Balancing Act of 1980: Parents, Politics and Education.* Windsor: NFER–Nelson.

Stillman, A. and Maychell, K. (1986) *Choosing Schools: Parents, LEAs and the 1980 Education Act.* Windsor: NFER–Nelson.

Thomas, A. and Dennison, B. (1991) Parental or pupil choice – who really decides in urban schools? *Educational Management and Administration* 19 (4), 243–9.

Walford, G. (1990a) Developing choice in British education. *Compare* 20 (1), 67–81.

Walford, G. (1990b) *Privatization and Privilege in Education.* London: Routledge.

Walford, G. (1990c) The 1988 Education Reform Act for England and Wales: paths to privatization. *Educational Policy* 4 (2), 127–44.

Walford, G. (1991) Choice of school at the first city technology college. *Educational Studies* 17 (1), 65–75.

Walford, G. and Miller, H. (1991) *City Technology College.* Buckingham: Open University Press.

Webster, A., Owen, G. and Crome, D. (1993) *School Marketing: Making It Easy for Parents to Select Your School.* Bristol: Avec Designs.

West, A. and Varlaam, A. (1991) Choosing a secondary school: parents of junior school children. *Educational Research* 33 (1), 22–30.

West, A., Varlaam, A. and Scott, G. (1991) Choice of high school: pupils' perceptions. *Educational Research* 33 (3), 207–15.

Willms, J.D. and Echols, F. (1992) Alert and inert clients: the Scottish experience of parental choice of schools. *Economics of Education Review* 11 (4), 339–50.

Chapter 7

Constituting good practice: HMI and its influence on policy and pedagogy

John Lee and John Fitz

Her Majesty's Inspectorate (HMI) is, and more pertinently has been, one of the most influential agencies within the English education system. All other educational institutions are subject to its inspectorial gaze, and their activities have been more or less directly influenced by it. How the Inspectorate exercised the powers that it had been given constitutionally is an interesting question for researchers. Teachers and, more recently, teacher educators have been aware that their activities were evaluated against centrally generated models of good practice. This is one way by which the Inspectorate traditionally exercised its authority. Those models had not been consensually agreed and in the past had remained something of a mystery. But Inspectorate documents first published in the mid-1970s have indicated an Inspectorate view of what 'good practice' is. More important, as we argue in this chapter, the Inspectorate's recent activities can be interpreted as a concerted attempt to implement as widely as possible its model of good practice.

The primary aim of this chapter is to identify, document and analyse HMI's notion of 'good practice'. Our investigations have developed into two other complementary areas. First, in seeking to understand the elements of good practice we were drawn into the history of the process by which contemporary ideas of it were constructed and applied. Second, researching the policy documents of HMI raises a methodological issue: how does one research powerful, 'élite' institutions such as the Inspectorate?

Our work on HMI's model of 'good practice' has focused on documentary sources, including documents written by the Inspectorate, commentaries on these and other secondary sources which have described and analysed the nature and function of HMI. Special attention has been paid to three categories of documents. First, the 'baseline documents', produced in 1978–9, provide an insight into HMI's more public responses to the Great Debate initiated by Callaghan's Ruskin speech in 1976. The *Primary Survey*, published in 1978, and the *Secondary Survey* (DES, 1979) reported on and identified weaknesses in curriculum practices in schools.

The second category comprises school inspection reports. Under instruction from Sir Keith Joseph, Inspectorate reports on educational institutions were made public documents from 1983 onwards. We surveyed more than 60 of the inspection reports published in 1983–4. We have read, however, more recent inspection reports in the course of our inquiry. A systematic analysis of the reports published over the last decade is something we hope to undertake in the near future.

The various documents relating to teacher education is the third category. Within these we have focused on the circulars which have specified the components of teacher education courses, with particular reference to the criteria these courses have to meet to be accredited. The 1984 and 1989 Council for the Accreditation of Teacher Education (CATE) Circulars (DES, 1984, 1989) are important in so far as they represent the considerable influence that the Inspectorate's model of good practice has had on initial teacher training institutions, and they also demonstrate its consistency since 1978.

The documents referred to above and other Inspectorate documents in the public domain are statements about public policy and have to be interpreted in that light (Campbell, 1989). One of the arguments we advance in this chapter concerns the role of the Inspectorate as policy-maker, evidenced by its output since 1978. This provided us with the second complementary area of enquiry, namely how does one conduct research on a powerful educational institution much of whose work is not open to public scrutiny.

This question is important because it relates to our earlier concern about how the Inspectorate arrived at a view about good practice. Here we supplemented documentary analysis with studies of policy-making within the DES (e.g. Salter and Tapper, 1981; Ball, 1990) and with interviews with retired inspectors. These persons agreed to be interviewed, although in line with recent policy research they have not been personally identified. The interviews enabled us to check the account of good practice we had discerned in the documents and changes in the role of HMI with an insider's perception and interpretation of policy issues. Clearly, a more fully developed investigation of the Inspectorate would need to draw on other sources, both within HMI and the DES, and from other external but contemporary influential policy-making agencies, such as teacher unions.

There are other related problems for the researcher in respect of school inspection reports that have been placed in the public domain. The problem for the researcher is that the Inspectorate never explicitly stated any criteria by which good practice can be judged. HMI documents are written in a curiously 'distanced' prose. Although they appear to have been created with Gowers's advice in mind, they are so devoid of rhetorical devices as to make their meaning opaque. There seems to be an attempt never to make a direct statement about practice. The only statements that provide hard information are those that say how HMI collected evidence at an operational level. We have not at this point attempted to replicate Abbot's study, which used a form of content analysis to reconstruct the criteria that HMI employed in their inspection visits (Abbot, 1990). That study indicates a way in which private agendas can be rendered more public and provides a basis for a more extensive investigation of school reports.

In view of these acknowledged constraints, the arguments we present below are to be regarded as provisional, and await confirmation after a more extensive programme of research. How this might be pursued is indicated by the structure of this chapter. We address first the changing role of the Inspectorate, in the period following the Ruskin speech, up to the publication of the CATE criteria and the National Curriculum. We then discuss the policy-making role of HMI and the significance of its publications. The study further focuses on the implications of the 'baseline' documents and the Inspectorate's first curriculum proposals, and then considers the CATE criteria. It concludes with a discussion of the Inspectorate's model of pedagogical practice and the implications of the creation of the Office for Standards in Education (OFSTED) as a non-ministerial department of state.

CHANGING ROLE OF HMI

While the principal purpose of HMI was to advise Ministers, on the basis of first-hand inspections, about the state of educational provision, since the 1944 Education Act its work may be crudely characterized as falling into three phases. It is not suggested that these phases are mutually exclusive, but even so they provide ways of categorizing the behaviour of the Inspectorate and of considering its role with respect to making policy.

In the first phase from the 1944 Act until the ending of full school inspection, inspection reports were confidential and the Inspectorate as a whole had a low public profile. Though lack of documents makes it difficult to gain a clear picture of HMI operations, we can draw on Leonard Clark's rather romantic memoir of the period, which offers us a snapshot of HMI operating in this phase: 'It was my habit, as it was with most of us, to watch the teachers at work, hear the children read, set them arithmetic and composition tests, and then give our findings to the teachers' (Clark, 1976, p. 41).

Although this account refers to the period just before the Second World War, Clark was clearly following the same sorts of procedures in the immediate post-war period. Commenting on his transfer to London in 1954, he makes clear that it was inspection rather than advice that was of utmost importance: 'The London County Council had its own large and powerful Inspectorate; its elementary schools were rarely visited by HMI until after the war.' Clark also tells us that 'The writing of reports has never been ... easy', presumably because the criticism and praise of a school needed to be couched in such a way that 'development' was encouraged. The only full report readily available from the period of confidentiality is that on Summerhill School published in full in Neill's book (Neill, 1968). The language of the report suggests a 'gentlemanly, scholarly' individual at home at the high table of some ancient college.

The other major role of the Inspectorate, according to Clark, was the giving of lectures to groups of teachers. It was this role that enabled individual members of the Inspectorate to take 'charismatic' leadership roles. Clark lists a small group of inspectors involved in these courses, and among that small group comments particularly on Robin Tanner and Christian Schiller. Tanner 'was a brilliant teacher' who had a profound influence on Clark himself. Clark provides us with a little vignette of what was probably the first HMI course devoted to 'progressive' primary education. Led by Schiller, 'a visionary, [and] a pioneer in the philosophy of modern primary education', the course focused on drama, music and poetry. Momentous as this course might now seem, these inspectors acted as individuals rather than as members of a policy-making body. Schiller's influence on primary education came about by his personal selection of people to work with, not through the publication of official documents. (After leaving the Inspectorate, Schiller taught at the London Institute of Education and here operated in a similar charismatic fashion. He published little, leaving his 'disciples' to collect and publish his lectures. Tanner's influence on the teaching of art and its importance in the curriculum of all schools should not be underestimated.) Clark's memoir makes no mention of HMI as policy-makers. The focus of his work was inspection, giving lectures, and in his case sitting as an HMI assessor on the National Book League. He paints a picture of inspectors rarely meeting as a body and working in small and relatively isolated groups. Not at all concerned with policy or even politics, they were an independent body ensuring that schools fulfilled their role. In contrast to his London County Council colleagues:

> At no time did I envy the lot of the Chief Inspectorate for the London County Council. He was often caught between the devil and the deep blue sea, and had to satisfy several masters. There were occasions when their expert advice, and that of their colleagues, was not always accepted by the Education Committee, nor, in some cases, by the more militant teachers in the schools. The Chief Inspector always seemed to be having crises and problems to deal with, and had to proceed cautiously before definite action was taken.
>
> (Clark, 1976, p. 141)

According to Clark, he and Matthew Arnold would 'in the end be looking for the same things, if not perhaps the same values'.

The distinctive feature of the second phase is the abandonment of whole-school inspection, and a general move towards the inspector as adviser and professional friend. The Inspectorate appears to have accepted with enthusiasm the recommendation of the Select Committee on Education and Science that full-scale formal inspections should be discontinued. During this period the Inspectorate sought to influence practice in schools not by critical inspection reports but by proposing 'good' practice. In addition, individual members of the Inspectorate defined 'new' areas of concern. The Inspectorate sought out practitioners who, in their opinion, were creating good practice, and by the use of short courses put those individuals in front of a wider professional audience. Inspectors such as Harold Gardiner and Edith Biggs were representative of the most proactive inspectors. They sought to influence the teaching of English and mathematics respectively; arguably both were proponents of, and protectors of, 'progressive' methods in these subjects. Even before the abandonment of full school inspection HMI Biggs was responsible for the preparation of Schools Council Curriculum Bulletin 1, *Mathematics in Primary Schools* (1965). Significant features of this seminal document in primary mathematics education are its lists of materials found in 'good' classrooms, assignments used on in-service courses, suggestions for classroom experiments, notes for use in in-service courses, and a chapter called 'Straight from the classroom'. Biggs may serve as an example of the close involvement of HMI in the work of the Schools Council; in the case of some individuals work on council curriculum projects appears to have led to recruitment to the Inspectorate.

The Inspectorate began to develop a curriculum area that came to be called multi-cultural education. Inspectors created courses on which teachers could share classroom experience and plan curriculum change. An early course held at Whitelands College focused on the education of West Indian pupils and brought teachers into contact with a group of colleagues who had visited Jamaica under HMI leadership. It provided some knowledge of Jamaican culture, and examples of current 'good' practice. A later course held at the College of St Mathias brought together teachers of secondary-age pupils and introduced them to teachers getting West Indian pupils to write in dialect, teachers using dance and drama, and newly established LEA projects aimed at curriculum change in the education of West Indian pupils.

This is a period of educational optimism during which the Inspectorate operated to create educational change at the grass roots rather than operating in the grander cabinets of policy-making. Many found their 'natural home' in a variety of Schools Council projects, which they put before teachers in the courses that HMI organized. The HMI short course booklets from the end of the 1960s until the end of the 1970s reveal an enormous range of courses all aimed at encouraging and developing good practice. Eric Bolton, former Senior Chief Inspector, acknowledges that during this phase the Inspectorate continued to provide 'objective' information and presumably advice to both the Minister and the Ministry (Bolton, 1991). In the same article he comments on the 'shock to the nation' of the primary and secondary surveys published in 1978 and 1979, and seems to signal an inspectoral view that the advisory strategy had been ineffective in policy change. In Bolton's view, this is the beginning of a new phase.

This third phase is characterized by a much more public role for the HMI, and, we argue, for the first time they are seen to take an explicit role in policy-making and in the politics of education. Sir Keith Joseph's insistence that schools should be fully inspected and that the reports be published pushed the Inspectorate into the public arena. The interview with Eric Bolton (1991) suggests that after his initial reticence to enter the public arena there was almost a relish in the 'new' role of policy-making. If we accept Bolton's account, the Inspectorate had a major responsibility for creating the conditions for the development and widespread acceptance of a 'national curriculum' by drawing attention to the differences in provision in secondary schools, and by laying out its structure in the 'Curriculum Matters' series. In the case of primary schools the Inspectorate expressed concerns about lack of breadth in the curriculum and the management and leadership of schools.

The question of when inspectors became policy-makers rather than advisers is difficult to answer. Clark's comments on the travails of the LCC Chief Inspector indicate a distaste for the rough world of politics and policy-making. Equally difficult to answer is why after over a hundred years the Inspectorate should so radically alter its position. Our interview data suggest that in the mid-1970s the Staff Inspectorate predicted that politicians would become increasingly interested in curriculum matters and associated questions of standards in schools. Perry, for example, makes clear that in her view the debate initiated by the Ruskin speech has at its centre 'the quality of what actually went on in schools' (quoted in Ball, 1990, pp. 140–2). In doing this, HMI was bound to become a policy-maker since the kinds of question that ministers would ask 'were questions that the HMI could answer' (ibid., p. 140). Perry also makes clear that the evidence upon which the Ruskin speech drew came from the Inspectorate: in her words 'something was badly wrong with the education system' and 'this had been coming through certainly before '76. I would date it from '73, '74' (ibid., p. 141).

If we accept Perry's view, then the Callaghan speech created the climate in which the two critical surveys could be published and, more importantly, used as a launching pad from which HMI could establish a public policy-making role. Rather than the surveys being a response to an agenda set by politicians, bureaucrats and pressure groups, they are the first real evidence of HMI as independent policy-makers rather than advisers presenting options. Crucially, the 'bad news' they contained had already been used to inform and persuade policy positions, and thus they appear in a 'friendly' climate. Attacks on the position expressed and the later curriculum documents were dismissed as coming either from teachers seeking to protect their privilege or from out-of-touch educationalists with no appreciation of the needs of the economy or the training needs of young people. We would concur with the Centre for Contemporary Cultural Studies (CCCS) analysis that the 'Yellow Book' was written by DES in 1975–6 on Callaghan's instructions to unpick teacher domination of the curriculum (CCCS, 1981).

The rationale for the change, expressed somewhat idiosyncratically by Perry, was dependent on the Inspectorate's informed view that 'something is rotten in the state of Denmark' (in Ball, 1990, p. 141). Although we have no access to school reports before 1983 we can examine the two survey documents to establish whether they present evidence of crisis. Allowing for the peculiarity of HMI prose, it is difficult to see how Perry's view can be substantiated. In the 60 or so reports that we have reviewed there is no evidence to back Perry's view. Rather the reverse: on the whole, inspectors report orderly classrooms, careful teaching, and proper attention to basic skills of literacy and numeracy. Inspectors' concerns in these reports, as in the two surveys and the annual reports, is for a broader curriculum, the matching of tasks to pupils' abilities, and progression and development. With the exception of inner-city schools, the Inspectorate seems to be relatively happy with levels of achievement, although it draws attention to the variability of curriculum provision.

INSPECTORATE ACTIVITIES AND SOURCES OF INFLUENCE

The scope of the Inspectorate's work and the legal basis of it were most recently stated in 1983 (DES, 1991c). A ministerial policy statement put before Parliament in that year identified the following functions:

(a) assess standards and trends and advise the Secretary of State on the national performance of the education system;

(b) identify and disseminate good practice and promising developments and identify weaknesses requiring attention;

(c) provide advice and assistance, via day to day contacts, contributions to training and its publications, to those with responsibilities for and in the system.

(DES, 1991c, p. 1)

The constitutional position of the Inspectorate, however, was no guarantee of either its legitimacy or its effectiveness. In the face of mounting criticism of HMI, predominantly from the New Right (see Burchill, 1991), the Inspectorate was at some pains to make known the basis of its contribution to quality monitoring in Education.

The basic case made by the Inspectorate for its efficacy as both policy advisers and policy-maker was the 'authenticity' of its evidence: 'The standing and status of the Inspectorate's advice, for what it's worth to me, is the extent to which it's based on inspection' (Bolton, 1991, p. 4) What the Inspectorate was most proud of was its knowledge of what was going on in schools and colleges, knowledge that came from inspectors' own observations. The pamphlet *HMI in the 1990s* states explicity how inspection was carried out:

> HMI's judgements are based on *observation*, that is on first-hand evidence of the learning and teaching, the examination of pupils' and students' work and records, and discussion with pupils and students and with teachers. HM Inspectors do not make judgements on hearsay, although they include such evidence in some cases where it confirms the judgements made from first-hand observations. Nor are Inspectors' observations and judgements of what is going on decided by predetermined criteria. Inspectors, over a long period of inspection, decide what they think of what they have seen, work out criteria and, where appropriate, apply them.
>
> (DES, 1990b, pp. 7, 8)

This collective defence of the value and validity of HMI judgements is given further emphasis in former Senior Inspector Salter's response to Burchill's criticism of the Inspectorate's work. He argues that the strength of HMI's judgements was founded on long experience of observation and evaluation and knowledge of national standards, that the judgements were based on evidence, and were collective (Salter, 1991). We have also heard this view stated in a private meeting with an inspector. In that forum, however, the priority given to the Inspectorate's direct observation of institutional practice was made more profound by an admission that little notice was taken of published or ongoing research in areas where the Inspectorate might have an interest.

It was this mode of operation, direct observation and collective judgement, that gave the inspectors the confidence to attempt to change practice at the grass roots and to operate on the national scene. Drawing on these observations, HMI has proposed models of good practice, in the past by applauding individual teachers, more recently in published critical reports. The inspectors' confidence in being able to recognize, define and disseminate good pratice was reflected in their statement about remedial action:

> Where HM Inspectors are able to raise issues arising from their inspections with *those who need to know*, action is often taken well in advance of the publication of the inspection report to put right shortcomings and to *support and extend good practice*.
>
> (DES, 1990a, p. 14; our emphasis)

Not merely does the Inspectorate have the confidence to know what good practice is, it is also clear about who needs to know. In the earlier phase of HMI practice, Clark (1976) was clear that those who needed to know about poor practice in schools were managers, governors and, most importantly, LEAs. The phrase 'those who need to know' has different overtones for the contemporary Inspectorate: it suggests a policy-making rather than an advisory role.

Here is its second line of defence. By virtue of its constitutional position, 'those who need to know' respond to its judgements and by this means the inspections have a real effect on institutions and those responsible for them. Salter notes, for example, that 'Many schools could testify that HMI inspections have led to better teaching and learning, more balanced curricula, more effective management, improved use of resources – even change of head' (Salter, 1991, p. 270). It is likely that these claims are true and that many institutions have become more effective teaching and learning environments. This emphasis on the inspectorial role, however, misses the broader influence that HMI has had, and has sought to exert, on the system.

In his Ruskin College speech in 1976, the then Prime Minister, James Callaghan, posed a number of questions to and about the education system, including, 'What is the role of the Inspectorate in respect of national standards and their maintenance?' (CCCS, 1981). One visible response to that challenge was a proactive Inspectorate, evidenced by the output of reports and other publications concerned with the nature and quality of education. The flow of documents from 1977 onwards can be interpreted as evidence of the Inspectorate's attempts to determine the form and direction of educational change, particularly in the areas of curriculum, institutional management and school effectiveness. Campbell for example, argues that, taken together, the documents indicate that: 'HM Inspectors have taken a directly interventionist role in policy formulation, despite their constitutional position and regardless of the cautiously laundered language in which they write' (Campbell, 1989, p. 165). Although the spate of publications post-1977 is sufficient to indicate a change in the policy field there remains some uncertainty as to the weight to be given to these documents as policy instruments which have influenced the form of educational provision.

In his consideration of the status of HMI documents, Campbell urges caution in the way we relate public documents to policy issues (Campbell, 1989, p. 163). He argues that the processes, including the 'horse trading', that precede HMI publications are not open to examination and so the documents themselves may hide uneven degrees of support for the values or policies they promulgate. He continues: 'what meanings can be legitimately attached to public documents and what impact they have, all raise the need to be extremely cautious and tentative in the way we treat policy issues' (ibid.).

Nevertheless, we would argue that in the documents there is a family of concerns which in themselves identify the direction in which HMI sought to steer the activities of education institutions. In other words, inspectors, in and through their inspection and monitoring of the quality of education, have moved one step further. Through OFSTED, they still continue to visit educational establishments and report what they find. However, through its documents HMI has also identified, approved and promulgated a view about what constitutes good and desirable content and practice in education.

These desired characteristics, we argue, formed the core of the Inspectorate's policy concerning the composition of the curriculum, pedagogy and effective management of schools and other institutions. We will outline our argument through a consideration and analysis of curriculum documents, summative reports of phase-related provision, annual reports on the education system as a whole and school reports.

THE 'BASELINE SURVEYS'

Reviewing the period under discussion, the Inspectorate focused attention on a selective number of curriculum and pedagogical issues. These emerged early, in 1978, and have since then remained stable areas of concern, comment and evaluation. In the absence of published reports of school inspections, and in light of the new policy role that HMI was forging for itself, the *1978 Primary Survey* is probably the first public policy statement recording an Inspectorate view of good practice (DES, 1978).

In the case of the *Primary Survey* the desperate picture that Perry paints is not easily substantiated. The behaviour of children is noted to be responsible and co-operative, except in a few classes. There are warnings about the problems of size arising from falling roles but no clear backing for large establishments. In considering the curriculum HMI notes that a high priority is given to the teaching of reading, writing and mathematics. The Inspectorate's concern does not seem to be only low achievement but also the much more difficult problem of 'matching' tasks so that the intellectual needs of the more able are met and systematic development occurs for the average.

The most strident recommendations relate to the need for curriculum breadth:

> The general progress of children and their competence in the basic skills appear to have benefited where they were involved in a programme of work that included art and craft, history and geography, music and physical education, and science, as well as language, mathematics and religious and moral education, although not necessarily as separate items on a timetable.

> (DES, 1978, p. 107)

In particular, they raise the issue of matching as needing attention since 'it is broadly the case that the more able children within a class were the least likely to be doing work that was sufficiently challenging'. In considering the question of specialist subject teaching they are broadly neutral, going for the middle ground in stating that all primary teachers need broad curriculum knowledge but that, where needed, schools might follow the practice of music teaching and offer some specialist teaching, particularly in science.

The only properly critical comments refer to children in inner-city schools, and these are hardly acerbic. The survey notes that teachers are more likely to underestimate the capability of inner-city children, that more resources and teachers are probably needed, and that further study is required 'of how improvements may be brought about'. In the recommendation relating to teacher education there is an indication of what will later appear in the CATE criteria, which as we argue are the most obvious evidence of HMI not simply as policy-makers but as successful policy-makers. It is clear that the HMI view is that there is no room for complacency, but it does not seen to be presenting a picture of unmitigated disaster.

The survey of secondary education, while more openly critical, also hardly presents a picture of disaster. It makes clear that inspectors have the same worries over curriculum breadth and coverage as were raised in the Ruskin speech. It is perhaps not unreasonable to suggest that HMI internal notes of school inspection were used in the writing of the Yellow Book, and that the writers of the speech had access to them. This has been confirmed by an HMI informant.

We analysed a sample of reports of inspection of secondary schools conducted between October 1982 and March 1984, 24 in all. All these reports were written as a result of visits relating to 'a national monitoring of secondary education'. We paid particular attention to comments relating to curriculum organization, the use of differing teaching styles, differentiation and match, and pupils' behaviour and attitudes. Surprisingly, even allowing for the laundered language, there is little direct criticism of lack of curriculum breath and balance. Of the 24 only 11 have such direct statements. It is the general organization of the curriculum rather than schools' ability to offer a range of subjects to pupils that the inspectors criticize. They express concern for the creation of effective faculties and for the lack of cross-curricular work. The reports record schools in which the pupils behave well and in which classroom relationships are harmonious; schools that are striving to provide a good education for those in their charge. Concern is expressed, although it is muted, for differentiation, lack of planning for the most and least able, and the use of new technologies.

It is the concluding chapter of the *Primary Survey*, the first of the baseline documents where we find themes which have now become familiar, and the most coherent statements about the constitutive elements of 'good practice'. These include the following:

> pupil progress is related to a quiet working atmosphere and work of appropriate level of difficulty (i.e. 'match') (8.6, 8.33);

> location of school influences levels of performance (8.11);

> the less able are generally catered for better that the more able (8.21, 8.33);

> teachers should employ a range of teaching strategies, including whole-class teaching (8.22, 8.61);

> subject specialist teachers are of value in promoting learning of all children and the recognition that 'teachers' need for a thorough knowledge of the subject becomes more marked as the children get older' (8.12, p. 113, 8.25, 8.35, 8.42, 8.44);

> there was uneven delivery of curriculum areas beyond the 'basics', notably in science, crafts, history and geography (lack of breadth, lack of progression in these areas (8.26, 8.28));

> there is a need for continuity across phases (8.31);

> teachers had low expectations of inner-city children (8.37);

> staff should be deployed with special regard to class size, age range, subject specialization and non-contact time (8.46, 8.51, 8.52);

continuing professional development for teachers is important (8.61).

(Figures in parentheses refer to paragraph numbers in the *Primary Survey*.)

The *Primary Survey* can be interpreted as a very early delineation of precisely what was 'rotten in the state of Denmark', in respect of primary school practice at least, although some of the areas of concern have resonances in the secondary schools survey, *Aspects of Secondary Education in England* (DES, 1979). The categories of concern have since been indentified and consolidated in later writings as curriculum breadth, differentiation, 'match', subject specialization, teaching with regard to 'fitness for purpose' (group/whole-class teaching), and teachers' expectations and staff development (e.g. Richards, 1986). How these are developed into a prescriptive model of good practice we shall discuss in more detail below.

In summary, the 1978 survey and the later documents reported that although work in maths and English is satisfactory, 'there is a wide variation in what is taught and what is learnt'. The problem here is that the Inspectorate focuses on absences. In order to discover what is absent it is necessary to turn to the 1980 DES publication *A View of the Curriculum* (DES, 1980), and to the series Curriculum Matters, particularly *The Curriculum 5–16* (Curriculum Matters 2: CM2) (HMI, 1985).

CURRICULUM MATTERS

It is clear that the Inspectorate was concerned with the wide variation in curriculum provision in secondary schools revealed in the secondary survey. It must also be noted that these concerns became public after the Ruskin College speech and in the opening years of Thatcher's premiership. At this point the Inspectorate states, 'The curriculum, whether for a school as a whole or for an individual pupil, has to be presented as more than a series of subjects and lessons in the timetable.' Programmes need to be measured against necessary knowledge, skills, understanding and experience in relation to pupils' capabilities.

In *The Curriculum 5–16* the Inspectorate is clearly setting out an argument about the curriculum which demonstrates its independence from the DES, and is based on collective experience and wisdom. A lack of progression and development through the years of compulsory schooling is noted, and as a result 'teaching reverts to an undemanding level for pupils'. The Inspectorate states that there must be 'unity of purpose throughout the 5 to 16 age span'. 'The curriculum should aim to be broad by bringing all pupils into contact with an agreed range of areas of learning and experience.' These areas are set out under the following headings:

aesthetic and creative
human and social
linguistic and literary
mathematical
moral
physical
scientific
spiritual
technological

This list, the Inspectorate argues, provides breadth and balance, qualities lacking in many of the schools they visited. Although the Inspectorate's most powerful argument for a common curriculum is couched in terms of areas of learning and experience, the subsequent pamphlets in the series describe the curriculum in conventional subject terms. It is interesting to note that *English from 5 to 16* (HMI, 1984) was published as Curriculum Matters 1 while *The Curriculum 5–16* (HMI, 1985) was published as No. 2. If the Inspectorate from 1985 to 1987 was publicly arguing the case for the National Curriculum, and effectively determining its content, in retrospect it seems either to have begun one argument and abandoned it, or deliberately to have presented alternatives leaving political policy-makers to decide.

In the general argument about curriculum set out in *A View of the Curriculum* (DES, 1990) and *The Curriculum 5–16* (HMI, 1985), the question of pedagogy is of equal significance to curriculum content and organization. In its observation of teaching, the Inspectorate has been consistently critical of teachers' lack of consideration of differentiation. In *A View of the Curriculum*, for example, we find the following:

> If it is to be effective, the school curriculum must allow for differences. It must contribute to children's present well being, whatever the age and stage of growth and development they have reached, and their ability to take advantage of the opportunities available to them.

(DES, 1980, p. 2)

The Curriculum 5–16 explicitly makes recommendations about grouping as a response to the problem of differentiation. Schools need that flexibility in organization if 'groupings are to match the learning which it is planned should take place' (HMI, 1983, p. 12). The term 'differentiation' is used as a subheading and is defined as 'the identification of the learning needs of individual pupils by sensitive observation on the part of the teacher'. This forms an operational definition of the concept of 'match', a metaphor employed by the Inspectorate in all its school reports. Even at this stage of creating a climate under which a common curriculum could come to fruition, the Inspectorate was equally concerned with pedagogy.

CONSTITUTING GOOD PRACTICE

Let us now set out the principles that underpinned the Inspectorate's view of the curriculum and its delivery:

- It should be broadly conceived via the nine areas of experience, and it should be common to all students, thus overcoming the problem of variability.
- The curriculum can only be effectively delivered by teachers with a profound knowledge of their subject area, and the phase-related needs of learners. In the case of primary schools, that expertise might exist within, and be deployed across, the staff as a whole (e.g. subject co-ordinators).
- Emphasis is placed on effective teaching and learning and this is

predicated upon teachers having a firm grasp of sound principles of classroom management: creating an orderly environment, employing teaching style(s) guided by 'fitness for purpose', high expectations, and the competence to meet differentiation.

- There is regard for progression as it relates to longitudinal assessment, record-keeping and management both of curriculum and personal development.
- Subject specialization (in primary schools) is needed as a means of providing challenges to all learners.
- Firm and consistent policies on staff development are necessary as these relate to upskilling professional practice.

Central to the principles of good practice outlined above is teaching quality, *and* the quality of the teaching force. And here the Inspectorate had identified and was concerned about variations, probably unacceptable in its view, in the effectiveness of both the teaching and the composition of the profession. While a 'common curriculum' might smooth out variations in what was taught, how were variations in how things were taught, and the variety of competencies among teachers, to be addressed? HMI's approaches to these questions were signalled in Curriculum Matters 2 and later consolidated in the CATE criteria of 1984.

The policy arguments embodied in documents such as Curriculum Matters 2 arise not only from HMI classroom observations but also from policy discussions within the senior team. Although Curriculum Matters was presented as a series of publications intended to be non-prescriptive, provide a public language with which to discuss and analyse curricular issues and to stimulate debate, we are by no means certain that this was the way things were viewed by all of the Inspectorate. Commentary by HMI Colin Richards on the implications of Curriculum Matters 2 provides some interesting insights on how that series has been interpreted, and applied. One component of the curriculum framework proposed 'comprises a set of broad criteria which can be applied when appraising the whole school curriculum or just one of its parts' (Richards, 1986, p. 6). The criteria Richards refers to are breadth, balance, relevance, differentiation, progression and continuity. To emphasize the extent and importance of their intended application, we quote Richards's interpretation of their significance:

> Such general criteria and the challenging questions they entail need to be applied not only to the curricular policies and *practices* of individual schools *but also to curricular policy statements emanating from whatever source.*

> (ibid.; our emphasis)

First, these criteria can be used to measure teaching quality within individual classrooms; second, they can be employed to model good pedagogical practice within schools; and third, they can be and have been employed in the evaluation of educational institutions in England and overseas. Reports on aspects of primary schooling in France and teaching and learning in New York are examples of the latter (see DES, 1991b).

There is a more general point to be made about these criteria. They are indicative, post-1977, of the Inspectorate's preparedness to take the commanding heights in the field of curriculum innovation, planning and change. It is *their* instruments which will be employed to evaluate curriculum policy from 'whatever source'.

Modelling good practice among existing teachers is one strategy. The second, and we believe equally important, area of HMI intervention was teacher education. Here was a key site for the introduction, consolidation and dissemination of effective teaching practices, and the site to institutionalize and develop pedagogy believed to be appropriate to raising levels of achievement.

POLICY TO PRACTICE: THE CATE CRITERIA

The concern expressed by HMI for the quality of education in schools found its strongest expression not in the details of the National Curriculum but in the criteria for the accreditation of initial teacher training courses (the CATE criteria) (DES, 1984, known as Circular 3/84; DES, 1989, Circular 24/89). HMI is best seen as one of a variety of actors who brought about the National Curriculum, significant but not dominant. In the writing of the curriculum itself arguably HMI 'lost' control to the subject committees, the result being the complex and detailed curriculum now in place about which HMI has expressed some doubts concerning deliverability, particularly at primary level. The question of the CATE criteria is very different. These reflect entirely the descriptions and criticisms HMI has made since the mid-1970s. HMI has always been of the opinion that it is the type of teacher which is the key to improved standards. In our discussion below we show how closely the criteria and HMI statements match.

Section 4 focuses attention on subject studies and their application. Criteria 4.1 and 4.2 require that intending teachers should learn a subject, or at most two subjects, at their own level. The need for subject knowledge is made clear in Curriculum Matters 2 (HMI, 1985), and has been reinforced in the recent Alexander, Rose and Woodhead report (DES, 1992). It is worth noting that HMI Rose has been presenting a strong argument for subject knowledge and subject teaching for a number of years. Criterion 4.6 specifies that all primary intending teachers must be concerned with the teaching of their subject specialism, and must have some 'structured school experience' related to it. Under 4.7 the students are required to be able to plan subject teaching for their age range, make assessments of pupils, and be prepared to advise colleagues who lack subject knowledge. The whole question of ensuring that schools are able to meet the requirements of a broad and balanced curriculum is established in both the primary and secondary surveys, in the various Curriculum Matters documents, and was raised in the Yellow Book.

The criteria set out in section 5 relate to both the breadth of the curriculum and to what can be described as the 'core'. A cause of concern flagged in the *Primary Survey* and echoed in published school reports is the lack of breadth in many primary schools. Criterion 5.3 explicitly addresses this issue. While it is true that the criteria in 24/89 make explicit reference to the National Curriculum's foundation subjects it is noteworthy that 3/84 addressed exactly the same concerns. Criterion 5.2 focuses attention on English, mathematics and science by specifying the time students must spend on studies in these subjects. Circular 3/84 did not include science in this accountancy exercise. HMI observations of school practice, we argue, led it to include science.

As we have shown, HMI focused attention on differentiation, not simply with respect to pupils with special educational needs, but also with respect to those deemed to be more able. The *Primary Survey* noted a lack of attention to the more able, and to the fact that work tended not to 'stretch' such pupils. The criteria clustered under 6.3 refer explicitly to the need for students to learn how to 'identify gifted pupils and pupils with special educational needs or with learning difficulties; and to understand the ways in which the potential of such pupils can be developed'. In addition, clearly echoing HMI concerns that achievement in inner-city schools is unsatisfactory, students are to be prepared to teach pupils of the whole range of social and ethnic backgrounds and to promote equal opportunities. Criterion 6.6 deals with the question of information technology, an attempt to ensure that all new entrants to the profession are well versed in the use of new technologies. A constant theme of HMI writing has been the need for professional updating. In 6.8 it is stated that courses should have 'explicit objectives to secure that students recognise the need to maintain their professional competence through regular updating and inservice training'.

The criteria that initial teacher training (ITT) courses are expected to meet are the clearest expression of HMI's influence as policy-makers. We would argue that its success in establishing them was quite remarkable. This focus on ITT can be seen as a continuation of HMI attempts to control the profession and to promote its own view of quality. It can be argued that the attempts to create professional change through advice and short courses were relatively unsuccessful, but if the content of ITT was specified and controlled, then the system could be moved in the desired direction. In short, we argue it is a version of 'give me the man until the age of seven . . .'

INSPECTION IN THE 1990s: HMI AND PEDAGOGY

From September 1993 the inspection of schools has been conducted by a radically different organization. The relatively small, cohesive team of HMI has ceased to exist; in its place there will be teams of inspectors who will bid for inspection contracts. The purpose of this change is to create an 'inspection market' in line with other market-orientated policies in education. At this point it is not clear how the new arrangements will work. Critics from the right, particularly those associated with the Centre for Policy Studies, are unhappy that schools will not be able to choose their inspection team from, to use the words of John Burchill, Chief Inspector for the London Borough of Wandsworth, 'the Yellow Pages'. The House of Lords' amendment to the 1992 Act giving OFSTED the responsibility for determining who should be awarded tenders is likely to be a contentious issue. Critics from the New Right are already able to point to the fact that the training and leadership of the new inspection teams has fallen to ex-HMI inspectors; and over two-thirds of the contracts for inspections to be conducted in 1993–4 have been awarded to local authority teams. At a Centre for Policy Studies conference held on 5 July 1993, Sheila Lawlor pointed to OFSTED as the continuation of HMI by other means, and noted that there was a real danger that the view of teaching and learning proposed by HMI would continue to be imposed on schools. It is to the question of pedagogy that we now briefly turn.

HMI's concern for meeting the needs of pupils at different ages and stages of development suggests a Piagetian psychological model. All of HMI's reports from the recent past make use of the metaphor of 'match' in discussion of the organization of learning tasks in classrooms. At first sight it would appear that the sort of pedagogy which relies on Piaget (use of first-hand experience, relating tasks to the child's stage of development, and the need to invoke children's previous understanding) is the model HMI wished to promote. However, its use of the term 'match' is inconsistent: it is used to discuss both the meeting of needs of individuals and the need for teachers to make curriculum match. The Inspectorate does not specify pedagogy by drawing on psychological theory except in so far as it meets their concerns when 'inspecting'. Nor does it draw on a developed sociology. Although HMI reports record concern for levels of achievement, especially in inner-city schools, they do not make pedagogical statements directly related to social class. The area in which HMI makes strongest recommendations is that of 'multi-ethnic education'. Drawing on inspectors' observations of work in multi-ethnic schools, it makes clear what teachers should know, and how the curriculum should be altered to meet the ethnic and cultural imperatives seen in schools. This has its strongest expression in CATE criteria grouped as 6.3: 'Students should learn to guard against preconceptions based on race, gender, religion or other attributes of pupils and understand the need to promote equal opportunities.'

The government hopes that OFSTED's new inspection system will have a profound effect on schools. The motto adopted reflects this: 'Improvement through inspection'. For the first time, the process of inspection is clearly laid out and the aims of inspection made explicit. The two documents *Framework for Inspection* and the *Handbook for Inspection* (OFSTED, 1993a, b) are both detailed and prescriptive. In a recent article, Anthea Millett, OFSTED's Director of Inspection, discusses the new procedures. The primary aim of inspection is not to provide indicators of individual schools' 'success', but to effect change: 'I see inspection as uniquely placed to bring about change where it matters – in the classroom' (Millett, 1993, p. 12). At this point it seems that OFSTED's mission is pedagogical. Significantly, in the same article Millett states:

> Inspection can help in two *other* ways: by creating the best-ever knowledge base about the educational service, which will offer society a full account of how schools and pupils are doing throughout the country; and by providing assurance to taxpayers and politicians that public money is being spent and managed efficiently by schools.
>
> (ibid., p. 12; our emphasis)

Unlike HMI, OFSTED looks outward to the system, and is expected to offer the kind of critique that will create changes in pedagogy, presumably in the ways preferred by the Secretary of State. How pedagogical recommendations or prescriptions will be expressed through the inspection process and report is not yet clear. David Singleton notes: 'It's now much clearer what the audience for the report is. Previously we had to do a difficult balancing act. We were writing for the Secretary of State, for the public and for the profession. Under the current framework it's clear that we're writing for a lay audience.' Underlying this is the notion of parents as consumers who will choose the 'best schools' and/or force pedagogical changes on those given an unfavourable report.

HMI based its view of the curriculum directly on inspectors' own experience of classrooms. What pedagogical 'theory' it had was classroom led. The idea of 'match', we would argue, is a common-sense notion based on HMI observations. It seems that no particular model of teaching can or should be recommended; it should merely be good of its kind. While this kind of pragmatism is attractive (it would suggest that HMI was not wedded to dogma), it has had the profound drawback of locking HMI into the dichotomous debate over progressivism. Until comparatively recently, inspectors were concerned with how teachers taught rather than what they taught. In making judgements of quality they sought to discover whether teachers fulfilled their intentions and whether lessons were planned for progression and development; they were also concerned with questions of order and discipline. The new inspection teams, at least at present, will inevitably be making the same sorts of pragmatic judgement about quality, but without the security or cosiness of the close-knit HMI network.

It has been argued in this chapter that as HMI sought to become a policy-maker it is possible to detect a changing view of pedagogy and what counts as quality. The 1992 Act has radically altered the relationship between inspectors and politicians. There will no longer be a relatively small cohesive body charged with the duty of providing advice to the Secretary of State. It is difficult to see how the annual report from Her Majesty's Chief Inspector (DES, 1991a) can have the same impact as the recent annual reports from the previous Chief Inspector. On the other hand, such reports were a recent innovation, and, as we have argued, HMI struggled to become an explicit policy-maker. It may well be that because of the way that OFSTED focuses on the system rather than on policy-makers and politicians, it will have a more rapid and profound effect on pedgogy. At present these things are unknown, but what we do know is that there will continue to be a fierce ideological battle for the 'soul of education'. The foregrounding of inspection of how schools provide for the 'spiritual, moral, cultural and social development' of pupils may provide an opportunity to ensure that teachers and schools inculcate the sorts of moral and social ideas spoken of as 'Victorian values'. Since John Patten has been Secretary of State for Education it appears that the New Right has been in the ascendancy. If at least some of them have their way, ex-HMI inspectors and local authority inspectors will be excluded from inspection, leaving schools to the vagaries of inexperienced and possibly antagonistic individuals.

REFERENCES

Abbot, D.M. (1990) What do HMI look for? *Education 3–13*, 18 (1), 47.

Ball, S.J. (1990) *Politics and Policy Making in Education: Explorations in Policy Sociology*. London: Routledge.

Bolton, E. (1991) A view from the room at the top. *Times Educational Supplement*, 21 June.

Burchill, J. (1991) *Inspecting Schools: Breaking the Monopoly*. London: Centre for Policy Studies.

Campbell, R.J. (1989) HMI and aspects of public policy for primary school curriculum. In Hargreaves, A. and Reynolds, D. (eds) *Education Policy: Controversies and Critiques*. Lewes: Falmer Press.

Centre for Contemporary Cultural Studies (CCCS) *Unpopular Education*. London: Hutchinson.

Clark, L. (1976) *The Inspector Remembers*. London: Dennis Dobson.

Department of Education and Science (DES) (1978) *Primary Education in England: A Survey by HMI*. London: DES.

DES (1979) *Aspects of Secondary Education in England: A Survey by HMI*. London: HMSO.

DES (1980) *A View of the Curriculum*. London: HMSO.

DES (1984) *Initial Teacher Training: Approval of Courses* (Circular 3/84). London: HMSO.

DES (1989) *Initial Teacher Training: Approval of Courses* (Circular 24/89). London: HMSO.

DES (1990a) *Standards in Education, Annual Report of HM Senior Chief Inspector*. London: HMSO.

DES (1990b) *HMSO in the 1990s: The Work of HM Inspectors*. London: DES.

DES (1991a) *Standards in Education, Annual Report of HM Senior Chief Inspector*. London: HMSO.

DES (1991b) *Aspects of Primary Education in France*. London: HMSO.

DES (1991c) *HMI: Its Work and Publications 1991*. London: HMSO.

DES (1992) *Curriculum Organisation and Classroom Practice in Primary Schools*. London: HMSO.

Her Majesty's Inspectorate (HMI) (1984) *English from 5 tc 16* (Curriculum Matters 1). London: HMSO.

HMI (1985) *The Curriculum 5–16* (Curriculum Matters 2). London: HMSO.

Millett, A. (1993) How inspectors can actually help. *Times Educational Supplement*, 25 June.

Neill, A.S. (1968) *Summerhill*. London: Gollancz.

Office for Standards in Education (OFSTED) (1993a) *Framework for the Inspection of Schools*. London: HMSO.

OFSTED (1993b) *Handbook for the Inspection of Schools*. London: HMSO.

Richards, C. (1986) The curriculum from 5–16. *Education 3–13*, 14 (1), 3.

Salter, B. and Tapper, T. (1981) *Education Politics and the State*. London: Grant McIntyre.

Salter, M. (1991) A matter of judgement. *Education*, 4 October, 270.

Schools Council (1965) *Curriculum Bulletins Number 1: Mathematics in Primary Schools*. London: HMSO.

Chapter 8

Professionalism, judgement and the inspection of schools

Jon Nixon and Jean Rudduck

Over the past decade professional judgement – as it relates to education and schooling – has become increasingly politicized and problematic: politicized because of the structures of public accountability that now surround it; problematic because of the unresolved tensions between these structures and the ways in which professionals have traditionally exercised their judgement. This chapter offers an analysis of these unresolved tensions as they relate to the changing role of a particular professional group and is based on evidence gathered by the authors in the course of an ESRC-funded research project.

Our starting point is the situation of local education authority (LEA) advisers/inspectors in a time of transition.[1] That situation has tended to be characterized in terms of a general shift from advice to inspection and a more specific shift from implicit to explicit criteria for judgement. However, the evidence we have gathered from interviewing over 70 LEA advisers/inspectors across six LEAs leads us to conclude that preoccupation with the surface features of the implicit–explicit criteria issue can lead to a caricaturing of the nature of professional judgement. There is, we argue, a strong tacit component to professional judgement which cannot be circumscribed by the simple expedient of making explicit the criteria by which it is supposed to operate. School inspection – whether conducted by the LEA or others – should, we conclude, be based on a much clearer understanding of the nature of professional judgement and of the authority by which it is exercised.

BY WHAT AUTHORITY?

The local inspection of schools – when and where it existed – traditionally derived its authority from the partnership between schools, LEAs and central government. Always vulnerable, that partnership is now under severe strain. Changes in legislation regarding school government together with the delegation of school budgets have occasioned a significant shift in the locus of authority. The possibility of schools opting out of LEA control and assuming grant-maintained status – and the financial inducements offered by central government for them to do so – has confirmed this shift and placed LEAs in an increasingly difficult position.

The effect of these changes has been to dislocate various occupational groups from their own traditional practices and, in some cases, their professional values. As Philippa Cordingley and Maurice Kogan have suggested, 'over time, power distributions change, and it should not be unexpected that a period of strong local and professional rule will be followed by centralisation and de-professionalisation' (1993, p. 101). Equally, however, it should not be unexpected that this process of deprofessionalization will have a significant impact on the morale and outlook of the groups concerned, especially when it is accompanied by 'an all-but-pathological hatred of LEAs and educationists' (Kogan, 1993). Teachers, headteachers, teacher educators and LEA personnel have all suffered the demoralizing side-effects of the increasingly centralized control of an education service whose professional expertise is treated with open disdain by government Ministers.

For LEA advisers/inspectors, this situation presents a quite specific dilemma. Forced to adopt an increasingly inspectorial role, they are being systematically divested of the traditional expertise-based authority by which they might have expected to fulfil that role. They are, therefore, heavily reliant on the goodwill and trust of schools and on their own willingness and capacity to negotiate a credible and workable identity for themselves within the new accountability culture. By making explicit to schools their own criteria of inspection they were, during the period we carried out our research, trying to maintain the spirit of partnership between schools and LEAs, while at the same time ensuring that their own recently acquired inspectorial responsibilities were adequately fulfilled.[2]

The Education (Schools) Act 1992 has undoubtedly complicated this already difficult task in certain crucial respects. Lacking any explicit statement on the purpose of school inspection, the Act implies that inspection can offer adequate consumer advice to parents through the obligatory reporting procedures, while at the same time improving the quality of teaching and learning by its requirement of a written statement of the action to be taken by the school in the light of the inspection ('the action plan'). The assumption is that, through the new legislative framework, inspection will be able to provide for both 'the head and the school as customers' and 'the parents and governors as customers' (Coopers & Lybrand Deloitte, 1992b, p. 13). This is a questionable assumption that severely tests traditional notions of partnership and support upon which advisers/inspectors have routinely relied.

Nevertheless, the 1992 Act does offer some consolation to LEA advisers/inspectors, in that LEAs will be free to provide an inspection service for schools (whether maintained by the LEA or not) within their area; on condition, that is, that the full costs of inspection are recovered through charges and that no advisers/inspectors act as inspectors for a school with which they have a connection that may cast doubt on their impartiality. While the second of these conditions may well be used to drive a wedge between advice and support on the one hand and inspection on the other, LEA-based teams are certainly eligible to tender for school inspections and are in many cases successfully doing so. The involvement of LEAs – and the continuing influence of LEA advisers/inspectors on the inspection process – is far from over.

THE STUDY

The period during which our research was planned and conducted (October 1990– December 1991) was one of considerable change and uncertainty. LEAs were in the process of responding to the 1988 Education Reform Act and the 1989 Audit

Commission Report (*Assuring Quality in Education*) and were also trying to foresee the full implications of the Education (Schools) Bill in its passage through Parliament.[3] This chapter is to some extent, therefore, an essay in local history: an analysis of the work of a particular professional group in six very different localities at a time of transition.

The research aimed at understanding how that change was impacting upon local inspection. It also sought:

- to elicit the often tacit criteria for judgement that LEA advisers/inspectors have employed when working with schools;
- to examine the ways in which criteria function within the local inspection process; and
- to consider whether frameworks of criteria afford a coherent and consistent approach to the inspection of schools.

We adopted qualitative research methods, focusing on the work of adviser/inspector teams in six different LEAs. While in-depth interviewing was our major research instrument, we also made use of documentary data. The interviews were semi-structured and covered a range of issues. Within the interviews we worked from the concrete examples and recollections offered by the interviewees. In addition, we explored how respondents perceived the new situation, their relationships with schools, and the ways in which communal frameworks for judgement were being developed within the current working group of advisers/inspectors.

Events moved rapidly after the completion of the fieldwork: the Education (Schools) Bill was enacted with significant amendments; a general election took place and a new government formed under the premiership of John Major; and a White Paper was announced though not, at the time of writing, published (see DfE, 1992). This made the task of analysis a challenging one and meant that, in drawing conclusions, we had to rely heavily on conjecture and inference.

THE CHANGING ROLE OF THE LEA ADVISER/INSPECTOR

The situation we moved into proved to be complex. Its complexity grows out of the ambiguities and ambivalence of transition. The transition can be simply described as the move from advising to inspecting, but the process has generated considerable personal stress and uncertainty.

The traditional strengths and value affiliations of advisers/inspectors were vividly recalled by one of our interviewees:

Colleagues here did not take up jobs as advisers to monitor what was going on in schools. That wasn't one of their expectations. They came in to be specialist advisers – to give support and advice and to get heavily involved in in-service education and training.

This kind of characterization was common across the LEAs we studied. Advisers/inspectors have invariably worked their way through the school and/or further education systems and enjoyed successful and fulfilling careers on the way. Those who have taught within primary schools have often held one or more headships.

Those who have come up through secondary schools and further education are more likely to have been heads of department/faculty or house/year heads. They are, therefore, by background and inclination very much *senior insiders*.

For many existing advisers/inspectors the transition from teaching was occasioned by their involvement in local curriculum development or assessment initiatives which would be likely to have carried with them some responsibility for the delivery and organization of in-service education and training. Their decision to enter the advisory service, in other words, was influenced by their perception of themselves as supportive agents of change. It was their enthusiasm for, and evident skills in, working alongside teachers to improve the practice of schooling that, for many, made advisory work appear an attractive and appropriate option.

Transition also had to be understood in terms of the relative emphasis that is placed on the specialist and generalist roles of advisers/inspectors. Broad trends are difficult to plot, since different teams have traditionally allocated roles and responsibilities in very different ways. Nevertheless, Stillman and Grant detected 'over the past few years ... a move towards increasing the generalist role' (1989, p. 195), and Nebesnuick reported that the majority of the 50 LEA schemes he had surveyed were responding to the 1988 Education Reform Act 'with a move from subject-specific advice to a broader-based monitoring and inspection service' (1990, p. 8).

These trends are certainly in line with the experiences of those whom we interviewed, as the following autobiographical sketches (extracted from the interview evidence) reveal:

A primary adviser/inspector:

I had an interesting training because it included both junior and secondary. My first post – the post I applied for and got – should have been teaching expressive arts in a secondary school in a new town. But they'd misjudged everything. They asked me if I'd go into a junior school because they'd got the numbers wrong, which I agreed to do for one year only but at the end of the year decided that I didn't actually want to go back into secondary. It was a very challenging and difficult situation, but I enjoyed it immensely and found myself wanting to stay with the children and watch them develop. From then on I worked on a number of junior and primary schools in the same LEA and got one or two promotions fairly early – I suppose because they saw me as a reasonably innovative teacher who liked working in team situations, which was very unusual at that time. I was even able to round my experience off by working in the early years and in nursery education. Then, at 27, I switched LEAs in order to become deputy head of an open-plan school, which is probably why I got the position because I'd had open-plan experience on my travels. The following year the head of the school moved on. I didn't apply for the headship first time round and they didn't appoint. But I did apply when the post was re-advertised. So, at 28, I got my first headship – which was pretty good because it was a large school. That was very exciting and I stayed there for eight years because there were so many changes and I felt so involved. I did a lot of in-service work across the LEA as well. I was very, very happy. Ultimately I moved on to an even larger school in a totally different area. Having been there for nine years – longer than I'd anticipated because the job was so challenging in terms of changing staff attitudes – I began to feel it was about time I went for an adviser's post. I'd been encouraged for years by the authority, but I'd not felt in a position to go for it. Anyway, I started applying and had a couple of interviews, as one does, and came here. Well, I very nearly didn't, really. It was my staff who encouraged me to come down, and it felt right. So here I am. I've been here for nearly two years now.

A secondary adviser/inspector:

I began teaching in 1962 and taught for seven years in two grammar schools. Then I became a college lecturer for three years between 1967 and 1970, before going back into school teaching. About that time I became a project officer for the Schools Council History 13–16 Project for two years. In a way I suppose that was the most exciting thing I've been associated with and certainly, if I'm talking about history, that would be the high point. After that I went into the advisory service of the LEA where I was working and acted as history and social studies adviser. That was from 1974 to 1978. Then from 1978 I came here and have remained here ever since, though my job has changed three or four times. When I first came I really did think it was a beast of a job. I was senior adviser for a particular area but was also required, in curriculum terms, to be lead adviser across the authority for history, geography and matters spiritual. Looking back it was a very heavy job. Gradually, though, I began to shed the curriculum responsibilities. First of all RE went. Then later geography went. And then, finally, I was divested of history. Then, in the brave new world of the late '80s, the attached adviser role and the notion of area teams were ushered in. So I became a full-time senior adviser attached to one of the new teams and helping to develop the attached adviser role. There was a lot of heart-searching about it, and those advisers, like myself, who had come in with experience and expertise and great enthusiasm for a particular curriculum area found it extremely difficult to lose all that. What one really had to offer was suddenly removed and we all became generalists. Latterly that's what I've been required to concentrate on – plus, from the summer of '89, I took over developments relating to the Elton Report on school discipline. I've really enjoyed that, because it's something like the old days when you had an innovation to develop. Now, everyone is so busy changing that there's no time left for innovation.

The pattern, however, is neither uniform nor static. LEAs have found it necessary to go on rethinking, and sometimes redefining, tasks and duties in response to the changing balance of power between themselves and school governing bodies. For example, as the National Curriculum impacts upon schools, some LEAs have thought it prudent to restrengthen the subject-specific advice which they feel raises their credibility with schools. This, for the advisers/inspectors concerned, may amount to a second significant shift of emphasis in a comparatively short space of time – away from a generalist role that they are still only developing and back to a more traditional curriculum specialist role.

It was evident from our interviews that advisers/inspectors were experiencing considerable disorientation as they sought ways of utilizing past talents and sustaining past commitments within the new culture. From their perspective the 'danger of a split between those who judge and those who help to repair' (Hargreaves, 1990, p. 235) is very real. Increased by recent legislation, that danger now represents a considerable threat to the professional self-identity of LEA advisers/inspectors.[4] Indeed, as Michael Apple warned, 'a general principle emerges here: in one's labour, lack of use leads to loss' (1986, p. 176)

COPING WITH TRANSITION

The transition has tended to be characterized in terms of a move from implicit to explicit criteria for judgement. Each of the LEAs we visited had already developed or was in the process of developing lists of agreed criteria for use by advisers/inspectors. However, the interview data have led us to conclude that preoccupation with the surface features of the implicit–explicit criteria issue can lead to a caricaturing of the nature of professional judgement. We also thought it important to understand the social and political significance of this preoccupation with identifying explicit criteria for judgement.

The lists of criteria developed by LEAs are, in the main, substantial and comprehensive, and far too extensive to quote in entirety. However, the following brief extracts (taken from the much longer composite lists of two different LEAs) give some indication of the terms within which they are couched:

Extract 1: Curriculum planning and organization (LEA 1)

- The curriculum is planned as a coherent whole which ensures progression.
- The curriculum is broad, balanced and relevant.
- All pupils have access to the National Curriculum for a reasonable time.
- There is a close match between pupil need and teaching.
- Pupils are given time and encouragement to complete tasks.
- Pupils are encouraged to work in a variety of ways.
- There is an orderly atmosphere which is work centred.
- Classroom procedures and routines are consistent and made explicit to pupils.
- Effective use is made of high-quality and relevant display.
- Detailed and comprehensive schemes of work are available for all courses.
- Courses set up in National Curriculum subject areas enable the Programmes of Study in the appropriate Key Stage to be delivered and all relevant attainment targets to be met.
- The school is enabling the achievement of pupils of the appropriate level of attainment in all areas of the National Curriculum.

Extract 2: Pupil experiences (LEA 2)

- What evidence is there that the content of the curriculum is relevant to the age and ability of each child?
- What evidence is there that there are suitably differentiated aims and objectives within and between classes?
- To what extent are differentiated tasks available which lead to positive achievements for all?
- How are the most able children challenged and extended?
- How are activities linked to real purposes and how are children helped to see and understand these links?
- What variety of teaching and learning strategies are in use and are they, broadly speaking, appropriate to the content being addressed?
- How are children encouraged to share with their teachers responsibility for their own learning?
- To what extent are children's achievements measured in terms which are criterion referenced?
- How are children of all abilities encouraged to recognize and celebrate their success?
- What evidence is there that the best use is being made of the available human and material resources within the school/classrooms?
- To what extent does the cross-curricular work recognize skills common to different curriculum areas and provide reinforcement whilst avoiding unplanned duplication?

In reviewing these lists some pertinent questions can be raised by using the kind of analysis put forward by Richard Rorty (1989). Criteria, claims Rorty, 'are never more than the platitudes which contextually define the terms of a final vocabulary in use'. He goes on: things 'can be made to look good or bad simply by being redescribed' (1989, p. 75). Criteria, in other words, tell us what to look for (breadth, order, relevance, discrimination, etc.), but don't help us to question what we find. They operate on the assumption that there is a 'we' out there that is in the know and for whom the key terms constitute an unquestionable 'final vocabulary'. That is why it is important to ask whether the lists of criteria that new inspectors spend time in constructing are, at some level, a diversion from the profoundly complicated task of understanding the nature of professional judgement and applying it in a whole-school context.

The production of public lists of criteria is undoubtedly serving both social and political ends. For instance, they play a part in helping individual advisers realize their new role as team members with a predominantly inspectorial purpose. One of the ways in which advisers/inspectors are responding to their changing role is to rely heavily on a team approach to inspection whereby individuals are able to share perceptions and insights within an agreed framework of explicit criteria. Regular team meetings fulfil an important function in this respect – at any one time an individual adviser/inspector is likely to be a member of several different teams each with a distinct pattern of regional and/or curriculum responsibilities. 'We appreciate', as one interviewee commented with a touch of irony, 'that inspection is a team activity.'

At the same time lists of agreed criteria work as a bridge between the advisers/inspectors and teachers in schools. 'We are', as one interviewee put it, 'only making judgements based on criteria that schools have agreed are appropriate.' The seeming openness and straightforwardness of these agreed criteria serve to soften the hard and divisive edge of teacher suspicion. They also help the school to feel some sense of 'ownership' and the adviser/inspector to feel less uncomfortable about 'judging' people who were her or his former colleagues. 'Inspection', as John Pearce (1992) puts it, 'thus rests on a degree of consensus between inspectors and schools, either generic or, nowadays more likely, constructed for the occasion' – and, importantly, constructed around explicit criteria.

Considerable efforts have been made by advisers/inspectors to foster a sense of commitment by schools to these lists of criteria. In one LEA we were told that 'the criteria were drawn up by working groups which included school and college representatives', and this was the procedure adopted in at least one other LEA. Even in those LEAs where the criteria were initially drafted by the advisers/inspectors themselves, they were 'discussed with schools and then modified taking their views into account' and, in one case, developed and extended by the schools themselves: 'We have encouraged schools – and some of them are beginning to do it – to use our criteria, which are quite broad and general, to develop their own progress indicators.'

We see the issue of implicit–explicit criteria as interesting and important in relation to the task of judgement, but currently distorted both by the personal complexity of the situation and by the social and political dimensions of the new relationships. There is, we feel, a need to go behind – or beyond – the implicit–explicit criteria issue and to look into the nature of professional judgement itself, particularly as it relates to the school as a whole.

THE WORKINGS OF PROFESSIONAL JUDGEMENT

The advisers/inspectors whom we interviewed all had a clear idea of what makes a good classroom and a good lesson. Moreover, their views coincided across LEAs, curriculum areas and primary- and secondary-phase responsibilities. One of the clearest messages to emerge from this study is that pupil learning remains the main focus of LEA inspection.

This may seem unremarkable. It is worth bearing in mind, however, that schools could be – and sometimes are – judged by criteria that suggest a focus very different from that defined by our interviewees. The Chartered Institute of Public Finance and Accountancy (1988), for example, has suggested a more explicitly managerial focus, in which 'management of the quality of learning and of the curriculum' is only one of six sets of criteria; while Coopers & Lybrand (1988), in an appendix to their report to the DES on the local management of schools, similarly outlined a much broader range of 'input considerations' and 'process and outcome indicators'.

None of the advisers/inspectors we interviewed sought to exclude the broader managerial and financial considerations. These were, however, generally of secondary importance. The real cutting edge of LEA inspection, as perceived by the advisers/inspectors themselves, is the overriding emphasis it places on the quality of learning in particular classrooms and subjects and on how this is reflected in the achievement and progress of individual pupils and in their level of engagement with their work.

In practice, school inspection invariably focuses upon the individual lesson and the individual classroom. What emerges is not so much a perspective on the whole school as an aggregation of more or less independent observations. To that extent the emphasis on the team approach may actually mask the failure to achieve a fully integrated perspective.

This is not to say that shared judgements and a sense of what one interviewee termed 'collective house responsibility' are unimportant. They are, but for reasons different from the ones often suggested. They do not in themselves lead to a surer inspectorial grasp of the whole-school effect. For that to be achieved local adviser/ inspector services may need to relinquish some of their current preoccupation with particular classrooms or subjects in order to look more systematically at overall patterns of achievement and at trends.

Despite this clarity of focus on learning, there remains a strong element of connoisseurship in the approach adopted by advisers/inspectors. 'I don't think', as one interviewee put it, 'that we can develop criteria which are so watertight, so well-defined and so sharp that they remove professional judgements'. The explanations offered by our interviewees as to how they form judgements about specific schools sit uneasily, therefore, beside the emphasis on explicit criteria. In offering such explanations interviewees rarely began by setting out the criteria against which the judgement had been made. Indeed, in their view, professional judgement would seem to operate by very different kinds of principles:

> You may well finish up at the end of a visit somewhere slightly different from where you thought you were going. That's the nature of journeys which are worth taking. It's not a question of getting on the 22 bus and knowing what the terminus is. It's a question of saying, 'I think we want to go in that direction. I wonder what we will find.' Maybe what you find is not quite in that direction. It's over there a bit and it's not quite what you expected.

Here, epistemologically, we come very close to what Michael Polanyi and Harry Prosch termed 'questing' or 'strategic' intuition, which (they argue) provides the means whereby 'we are … able to know (in some anticipatory, intuitive sense) enough of what we do not know as yet in an explicit sense (because we have not yet discovered it) to enable us to locate a good problem and begin to take groping but effective steps towards its solution' (1975, p. 178). Politically, we are perhaps closer to Ernest House's notion of evaluation as persuasion, whereby evaluation (or in this case inspection) 'persuades rather than convinces, argues rather than demonstrates, is credible rather than certain, is variably accepted rather than compelling' (1980, p. 73). The adviser/inspector cannot know exactly where the bus will end up, because the terminus is located – beyond enquiry – within the field of action.

The important point to emphasize is that this kind of 'not knowing' is an aspect of all human understanding: one can only reject it by refusing to get on the bus (which is not an option). Anthony Giddens has discussed it as a key element in his theory of structuration in terms of 'what actors know (believe) about social conditions, including especially the conditions of their own action, but cannot express discursively' (1984, p. 375). This 'practical consciousness', as he terms it, is of fundamental importance and, where it is excluded, 'a very wide area of knowledgeability is simply occluded from view' (ibid., p. xxx). Indeed, he argues, 'what agents know about what they do, and why they do it – their knowledgeability as agents – is largely carried in practical consciousness' (ibid., p. xxiii).

Not surprisingly this tacit element is particularly strong when judgement becomes problematic. Advisers/inspectors know what makes a good school and can recognize it. They also know a poor school when they see one. It is the very many schools falling between these extremes that present the problems:

> The middle ground to me is where it becomes very difficult. It's easy to spot very good lessons and to know what's good about them. And it's easy to know what's bad. It's all the shades of grey in between that prove difficult.

In rationalizing the way in which they form judgements in such situations, advisers/inspectors stress the strong element of progressive focusing implicit in the process of school inspection. They tend, for example, to shift from ascertaining what 'bits' of desirable practice are in place (and which, by implication, are missing) to exploring the quality of those 'bits' and the extent to which they add up to something coherent and worth while. The significant shift here is from criteria that operate as principles of compliance to those which operate as standards of performance.

But there are other shifts of focus which at first sight are less easy to rationalize. One interviewee, for example, described how, if she had a sense of 'poor quality' in 'what's delivered to the children', she would begin to ask questions about the overall 'management of the school'. Concerns about teaching and learning in the classroom might thus occasion a lateral shift of focus to different aspects of school practice – shifts, that is, that presuppose a strong sense by advisers/inspectors of the complex and indeterminate relation between different aspects of school practice. In that sense judgement as exercised by advisers/inspectors is to a large extent guided and focused by their own insider knowledge and belief about schools and by their own professional values.

It is difficult to see how some such element would not be part of any serious inspection carried out by senior insiders with their traditional strengths and loyalties. However, if advisers/inspectors are to retain this element – and at the same time retain their credibility with schools – they will need to articulate it with much greater clarity and coherence than at present. The skilful use by advisers/inspectors of tacit criteria can all too easily appear to be a failure to make those criteria explicit – rather than the sensitive exercise of a particular kind of professional judgement. Within a context where their credibility is at stake, this can put advisers/inspectors at considerable risk.

RECONCEPTUALIZING SCHOOL INSPECTION

What is required is a radical reconceptualization of the role of local inspection with a view to highlighting the nature and central importance of professional judgement. This raises important and, as yet, unresolved issues to do with credibility and authority – issues which are largely beyond the control of LEA advisers/inspectors themselves and which require, for their resolution, a broader and more fully co-ordinated response.

The need for reconceptualization raises two further issues which are closer to the immediate concerns and responsibilities of those who manage the local inspection of schools. The first of these issues relates to the notions of partnership and consensus that are so firmly embedded within the practice of LEA advisers/inspectors. Formerly those notions existed, in a relatively uncomplicated fashion, against the backdrop of LEA control. That backdrop is now threadbare – and the current emphasis on agreed lists of criteria can seem little more than a patching exercise. It will be necessary, in constructing an alternative basis for partnership between schools and any local inspection service, to look beyond lists of agreed criteria to the principles underlying professional judgement.

It will also be necessary to acknowledge the highly problematic nature of constructing a consensus around actual judgements, since these are necessarily singular and open to question. To that extent professional judgement – as Lyotard (1988, p. 38) puts it – is in the predicament of having to carry 'with it the promise of universalisation', but only 'as a constitutive feature of its singularity'. Whatever consensus is achieved across the complex institutional boundaries of school inspection will need to recognize the central importance of professional judgement, while at the same time acknowledging the unpredictability and diversity of the actual judgements that are made. No framework can eradicate that unpredictability and diversity without also spiriting away the very process of judgement itself.

This means that the kind of consensus that coalesces around school inspection ought, in certain respects, to approximate more closely to that which has traditionally been associated with the research community. It ought, in other words, to involve agreement about the procedures and processes for generating and refining judgements, without in any way ensuring agreement on which, if any, judgements should be given final assent. If all judgements are conjectural in the sense of being open to refutation (Popper, 1963), then school inspection should perhaps be less concerned with pronouncing upon educational quality and more concerned with informing professional debate and discussion by questioning current assumptions about quality. So conceived, the end of inspection – to borrow some words of David Hiley (1988, p. 145) – would be 'not to achieve the truth ... but to keep the conversation going by constantly calling current agreement into question and sending the conversation off in new directions'.

The second issue relates to the need for a whole-school perspective. Despite the 'team' context, individual LEA advisers/inspectors are in practice continuing to focus on individual lessons, individual pupils and individual classrooms, while in theory offering more general – and more generalizable – insights into the institution as a whole. To that extent the situation may not be very different from that noted by David Winkley, who remarked that 'inspectorial reports tend to have the air of administrative accumulations of enormous amounts of information, like thousands of single-frame photographs' (1985, p. 124). Moreover, the heavy emphasis now placed on classroom observation can serve to compound this problem. It will be necessary, therefore, for advisers/inspectors to gain a much stronger sense of the whole-school effect – and this will almost certainly involve the development of more sophisticated data-gathering techniques and of different patterns of recruitment from a wider range of research and evaluation backgrounds.

115

At another level it will also involve some clarification of what exactly constitutes the 'whole school'. This current emphasis includes – and sometimes confuses – a number of strands which, although related, need to be distinguished for the purposes of analysis. The 'whole school' has, of course, something to do with notions of curriculum coherence, of organizational planning and of management structure, but this notional complementarity needs to be made explicit and its relation to pedagogical practice spelt out. Advisers/inspectors could – and ought to – have a major role to play in this process of clarification.

There are, in particular, some important questions relating to curriculum coherence that advisers/inspectors could help schools to address. All too often coherence is simply assumed to be a function of the breadth and balance of a specific curriculum. Arguably, however, coherence must also be defined in terms of the experience of the learner: what David Hargreaves has called 'coherence-in-the-experience-of-the-pupil' (1987, p. 10). This is not to deny in any way the importance of those other two elements in the curriculum equation (breadth and balance), which are more likely to be defined in terms of the sets of skills and bodies of knowledge associated with particular fields of study; but to affirm, rather, that a broad and balanced curriculum must appear such to those for whom it is designed. Only in this light can the curriculum – and, indeed, the school effect – be viewed as in any way 'whole' (see Nixon, 1992, pp. 51–8).

LEA inspection services, with their detailed knowledge of the history and current practice of specific schools, are well placed to develop a model of inspection grounded in professional judgement and a commitment to school improvement. At its best, LEA inspection is sensitive in its grasp of local factors, rigorous in its gathering and sifting of evidence and punctilious in its reporting procedures. If, however, it is to take full advantage of the possibilities inherent in the new legislative framework, it will need to rethink its current role and practices in terms of some of the more specific points raised in this chapter. These include the following:

- In order to ensure that school inspection is gaining a firm grip on the whole-school effect, it will be necessary to recruit inspectors from a wider range of professional backgrounds including those with a background in educational research and evaluation.
- Similarly, it will be necessary to ensure that the analytic and research skills of existing advisers/inspectors are extended and their understanding of the role of research in the inspection process deepened.
- The partnership between schools and school inspection services will need to be redefined in terms of a much more sophisticated understanding of how – and within what kinds of epistemological constraints – professional judgement operates.

What has been important about LEA inspection at its best is the relation it has assumed between complex judgements of value and equally complex decisions regarding the practice and policy of schooling. School inspection should not be seen as some kind of consumer advice service – or even the educational equivalent of a serious book review which may or may not persuade us to purchase. It should aspire primarily to inform the decisions and practices of those who are responsible for the day-to-day management of schools and for the quality of teaching and learning that takes place within them. Whatever systems and procedures are eventually put in place – and these may vary across regions – the emphasis on inspection as a means of helping schools to help themselves will, we believe, remain of paramount importance.

CONCLUSION: RECLAIMING PROFESSIONALISM

In a recent review of the future role of LEAs, Coopers & Lybrand Deloitte (1992a) have outlined a number of criteria 'to be applied in determining the future shape of the management, organisation and administrative framework for the education service'. The first of these criteria they define as a 'plurality of interest . . . reflected in the allocation of powers and responsibilities to different levels in the system' (1992a, p. 14). The LEA, they argue, is both a significant element within this plurality and a means of protecting – and responding to – the multiplicity of interests that comprise it. This stress on plurality chimes in well with what Kathryn Riley (1992) of the Institute of Local Government Studies sees as a possible future role of the LEA. 'One particular model for the future,' she argues, 'albeit an optimistic one, is the interactive LEA.' This new role would be one 'that locates the LEA centrally in the local education arena but that also recognises the centrality of the other key movers: central government; TECs (Training and Enterprise Councils); schools, institutions and governors; the local community'. The 'interactive LEA' is thus 'the linchpin between the centre and the locality', which 'articulates clearly values of quality and equality' and is 'concerned with the management of influence as well as the management of action' (Riley, 1992, p. 21).

A similar view emerges from the Local Government Management Board's recent national survey of internal organizational change in local government in England and Wales. According to the preliminary findings of this survey, chief education officers (CEOs) increasingly 'characterise their authority in terms of a partner to, and enabler of, school-based activity . . . with almost all LEAs now characterising themselves in this way, compared with only four out of ten, according to CEOs' recollections of 1988' (LGMB, 1993, p. 1). Any such shift in the characterization of authority will necessarily bring with it changes in the role of the professional. For the professional groups concerned those changes already involve a greater emphasis on managing the boundaries between provider and client, together with a clear acknowledgement 'that professionalism no longer has the same protection from user critique and control' (Cordingley and Kogan, 1993, p. 105). All the indications are that this shift towards an 'enabler' role is a significant factor within the development of a new professionalism.

It should be borne in mind, therefore, that the 'new professionalism' is located in a market-place that is both school driven *and* centrally controlled: devolved budgets but a single set of purse-strings. While there may be advantages to this system, there are certainly drawbacks. For, as Stewart Ranson points out, the competition created by the market constitutes 'a zero-sum game in which if there are to be winners there are sadly always going to be losers' (1993, p. 2).[5] There is also the constant risk that, in having to respond to the various push and pull factors to which such a system inevitably gives rise, LEAs could fail to meet their prime obligation to public service through the altruistic use of specialized knowledge and expertise. It is only this knowledge and expertise – and the principled use professionals make of it – that prevents school inspection from becoming a tool of centralized management.

LEAs have, we believe, a continuing and significant role to play in the future of school inspection because of the premium they have in the past placed on the professional judgement of those who are *senior insiders* to the school system. We also believe that those who have been professionally involved as LEA advisers/inspectors share certain understandings which need carrying forward, if only because of the serious challenge they present to current policy and practice as it relates to school inspection.[6] This chapter has attempted to explore some of those understandings, which on the basis of our interview evidence may be summarized as follows:

- School inspection is concerned primarily with the exercise of professional judgement, not with the measurement of school performance against predetermined norms and standards.
- Professional judgement may operate with reference to explicit criteria, but these cannot in themselves define – or circumscribe – a process which necessarily includes a strong tacit or inferential element.
- That element is what currently gives to local inspection its diagnostic edge and helps define its functions in terms of school improvement as well as public accountability.

NOTES

This chapter is based on a published paper (*Research Papers in Education* 8 (2), 1993, 135–48). We would like to thank the editors and publisher of *Research Papers in Education* for permission to reprint substantial sections of the earlier paper. We would also like to thank the two anonymous *rapporteurs* whose comments on our end-of-award report for the ESRC were challenging and helpful.

1. Throughout this chapter we have used the rather cumbersome term 'adviser/inspector' because of the variety of usage across LEAs – a minority continue to use 'adviser', but the majority have adopted the designation 'inspector'. In all settings the functions of the advisers/inspectors have moved closer to inspection.

2. In so doing they were also staying one move ahead in a game that, since the formation of the Office for Standards in Education, has become increasingly dominated by explicit – and centrally defined – criteria (see HMCIS, 1992).

3. For recent retrospects of the work of LEA advisers/inspectors, see Riley (1992) and Wilcox (1992). The latter reminds us that as early as 1985 Sir Keith Joseph issued a 'draft statement', which never moved beyond the draft stage but raised a number of issues that have since been addressed by the 1992 Education (Schools) Act. It would seem that the political agenda relating to school inspection was drawn up some time ago.

4. The threat, however, has been around for some time. Reporting on a study of the observational work of LEA advisers/inspectors carried out between 1977 and 1979, Rob Walker remarked: 'Advisers/inspectors see their position as under threat. The research topic is therefore a sensitive one, for the particular subjects of the study and for the professional group as a whole' (1981, p. 13).

5. Attempts to explain this state of affairs *solely* in terms of the workings of a central

locus of power should, however, be treated with some scepticism. As Dowding *et al.* usefully point out:

> Social relations involving power, like bargaining games between actors, cannot be argued *a priori* to have either zero-sum or positive-sum outcomes across the board. Instead they are variable-sum, depending on many detailed situational effects, in particular the distribution of power and 'advantage' (or luck), and the structure of the decision situation. Some results produced by the exercise of outcome and social power will be positive-sum, some zero-sum, and others negative-sum.
>
> (1993, pp. 15–16)

6. The national framework for school inspection (HMCIS, 1992) was issued after we had conducted our interviews and requires its own analysis. It would seem, however, to do very little in the way of resolving the tensions and contradictions highlighted in the present chapter.

REFERENCES

Apple, M.W. (1986) Are teachers losing control of their skills and curriculum? *Journal of Curriculum Studies* 18 (2), 177–84.

Audit Commission (1989) *Assuring Quality in Education: The Role of LEA Inspectors and Advisers.* London: HMSO.

Chartered Institute of Public Finance and Accountancy (1988) *Performance Indicators in Schools: A Contribution to the Debate.* London: Chartered Institute of Public Finance and Accountancy.

Coopers & Lybrand (1988) *Local Management of Schools.* London: HMSO.

Coopers & Lybrand Deloitte (1992a) *The Future Role of Local Education Authorities* (Review of Local Government, Paper No. 13). London: Association of County Councils (February).

Coopers & Lybrand Deloitte (1992b) *The Future Role of Inspectors and Advisers: A Practical Guide.* Haywards Heath: National Association of Inspectors and Educational Advisers (May).

Cordingley, P. and Kogan, M. (1993) *In Support of Education: The Functioning of Local Government.* London: Jessica Kingsley.

Department for Education (1992) *Choice and Diversity: A New Framework for Schools* (White Paper: Cm 2021). London: HMSO.

Dowding, K., Dunleavy, P., King, D. and Margetts, H. (1993) Rational choice and community power structures: a new research agenda. Paper presented at the annual meeting of the American Political Science Association, Washington Hilton, 2–5 September.

Giddens, A. (1984) *The Constitution of Society: Outline of the Theory of Structuration.* Oxford: Polity Press.

Hargreaves, D. (1987) The quest for school curriculum: directions and destinations. *School Science Review* 69 (246), 7–16.

Hargreaves, D. (1990) Accountability and school improvement in the work of LEA inspectors: the rhetoric and beyond. *Journal of Education Policy* 5 (3), 230–9.

Her Majesty's Chief Inspector of Schools (HMCIS) (1992) *Handbook for the Inspection of Schools.* London: OFSTED.

Hiley, D. (1988) *Philosophy in Question: Essays on a Pyrrhonian Theme*. Chicago: University of Chicago Press.

House, E.R. (1980) *Evaluating with Validity*. London: Sage Publications.

Joseph, K. (1985) *Education Advisory Services Should Be Reviewed* (Draft statement). London: DES (10 September).

Kogan, M. (1993) Cut out the blather. *Times Educational Supplement*, 16 July.

Local Government Management Board (LGMB) (1993) *Survey of Internal Organisational Change in Local Government: Interim Report 4*. Luton: Local Government Management Board.

Lyotard, J-F. (1988) *Peregrinations: Law, Form, Event*. New York: Columbia University Press.

Nebesnuick, D. (1990) *Monitoring and Evaluation and the 1988 Education Reform Act*. Windsor: NFER–Nelson.

Nixon, J. (1992) *Evaluating the Whole Curriculum*. Milton Keynes: Open University Press.

Pearce, J. (1992) On closer inspection. *Education* 179 (1), 13.

Polanyi, M. and Prosch, M. (1975) *Meaning*. Chicago: University of Chicago Press.

Popper, K. (1963) *Conjectures and Refutations*. London: Routledge & Kegan Paul.

Ranson, S. (1993) *Local Democracy for the Learning Society* (National Commission on Education Briefing No. 18). London: National Commission on Education.

Riley, K. (1992) The changing framework and purposes of education authorities. *Research Papers in Education* 7 (1), 3–25.

Rorty, R. (1989) *Contingency, Irony and Solidarity*. Cambridge: Cambridge University Press.

Stillman, A. and Grant, M. (1989) *The LEA Adviser: A Changing Role*. Windsor: NFER–Nelson.

Walker, R. (1981) *The Observational Work of LEA Inspectors and Advisers*. University of East Anglia: Centre for Applied Research in Education.

Wilcox, B. (1992) *Time-Constrained Evaluation*. London: Routledge.

Winkley, D. (1985) *Diplomats and Detectives: LEA Advisers at Work*. London: Robert Royce.

Chapter 9

Language and educational control: the construction of the LINC controversy

Alison Sealey

> Every time the question of the language surfaces, in one way or another, it means that a series of other problems are coming to the fore: the formation and enlargement of the governing class, the need to establish more intimate and secure relationships between the governing groups and the national-popular mass, in other words to reorganise the cultural hegemony.
>
> (Gramsci, 1985, pp. 183–4)

This chapter explores some aspects of the relationship between the control of educational policy and language: language as an area of the school curriculum and language as the medium through which decisions about government education policy are communicated to the public. The chapter takes as a case study the press coverage of a specific conflict between the government – in the shape of the then Department of Education and Science – and a national education project. The project, Language in the National Curriculum (LINC), was financed by the DES through an education support grant, and was commissioned by the DES to produce materials for the in-service training of teachers throughout the country. In the summer of 1991, the decision by education Ministers not to publish the materials produced by the project was widely reported in the press. This chapter begins by summarizing the events which led up to the press reporting of the decision to ban the materials. The second part explores some of the reasons why the specific aspect of the teaching of English, which was the concern of the LINC project, should be the subject of such intense controversy, and in the final section an analysis is presented of a number of the newspaper articles which dealt with that controversy.

THE HISTORY OF THE LINC PROJECT

The impetus for the establishment of the LINC project might be traced back over a considerable period, as is indicated by the discussion of conflicts surrounding English teaching in the second section of this chapter. The project's immediate provenance, however, may perhaps be located in the publication of two reports by Her Majesty's Inspectors (DES, 1984, 1986),[1] after which Kenneth Baker (then Secretary of State for Education) announced, in January 1987: 'I have been struck by a particular gap. Pupils need to know about the workings of the English language if they are to use it effectively' (DES press release, 16 January 1987). This curious metaphor heralded the launch of the Committee of Inquiry into the Teaching of English Language, under the chairmanship of Sir John Kingman. This appointment (of a mathematician rather than an English specialist), together with other aspects of the composition of the committee, aroused hostility at the time among many members of the English teaching profession, and did nothing to lessen their anxieties that the subject was being manipulated by government for particular ideological reasons.[2] The committee's terms of reference included the recommendation of a model of the English language . . . which would

    i   serve as the basis of how teachers are trained to understand how the
        English language works;
   ii   inform professional discussion of all aspects of English teaching.
(DES, 1988, Appendix 1, p. 73)

Many of the recommendations made in the subsequent report (known as the Kingman Report: DES, 1988) concerned the training of teachers in the area of English language, both prior to and during their teaching careers, and Baker's provision of an educational support grant to finance the in-service training of teachers constituted a response to the recommendation: 'that English generally and knowledge about language in particular be included in the list of national priority areas under the Local Authority Training Grants Scheme with effect from the earliest possible date' (DES, 1988, p. 70).

    This in-service 'Kingman Project' was structured as follows. Ron Carter, Director of the Centre for English Studies at the University of Nottingham, was appointed as national director; there were 25 regional co-ordinator posts (typically filled by people with experience as English advisers or as lecturers in English in education), and each participating LEA (which included all but one in England and Wales) appointed a primary advisory teacher. By the time the project got under way in September 1989, the English Working Group, under the chairmanship of Professor Brian Cox, had produced the report which was to form the basis of the original National Curriculum for English (the Cox Report: DES, 1989). In one chapter, 'Knowledge about language', the Report referred to the post-Kingman training programme:

> As is argued at length in the Kingman Report, substantial programmes of teacher training are required if teachers are themselves to know enough to enable them to design with confidence programmes of study about language. Such training is now under way.
(DES, 1989, para. 6.3)

Those working on the project therefore abandoned the 'Kingman' label, and, acknowledging a responsibility to support the implementation of English in the National Curriculum, adopted the name LINC – Language in the National Curriculum. The terms of reference of the project *did not include research* – into the teaching of 'knowledge about language' (or 'grammar', or 'English'), or into what children know about language, or how their knowledge about language develops or is facilitated. The rationale for and implications of this omission of a research element are discussed below. The emphasis of the project was on the training of practising teachers: 'The remit of the project is to mediate to teachers the wide view of the language curriculum taken by the Kingman and Cox (1989) Reports and enshrined within all National Curriculum requirements for English' (Ron Carter, press statement, 24 June 1991).

The grant, then, funded the production, trialling and revision of a package of training materials for teachers; the salaries of project personnel in LEAs and regional consortia throughout the country; and the actual programme of training of school-based teachers, including attendance at centre-based courses with supply cover, travel and the like, as well as follow-up work in participants' own schools, regional conferences and local publications for the dissemination of teacher-developed strategies and so on.

In June 1991 Tim Eggar, Minister of State for Education, announced that the training materials, widely available in draft form, were not to be published after all, and this ban on formal publication has never been lifted. In an article in *The Times Educational Supplement*, Eggar explained this decision thus: 'Why? The reason is simple. The LINC units were not designed nor are they suitable for classroom use as *teaching* materials' (Eggar, 1991; original emphasis). Eggar's 'simple' reasoning, however, is not convincing: the brief was to produce materials for teachers which HMSO would publish and the DES would distribute *as* materials for teachers; their unsuitability for classroom teaching is not at issue. Another justification for the ban which is put forward in this article is that the materials are 'way above the head of the lay reader with an interest in how his children will in future be taught about language'. This argument too is misleading, given that the audience for the materials was never intended to be 'the lay reader'. It is not the aim of the current chapter to describe or evaluate the materials themselves, nor indeed to explore in any depth the precise reason for the ministerial ban, which has been the subject of various commentaries. Goddard (1991), for example, suggests that Ministers were 'uneasy' about the materials, which looked to them 'a big dodgy'. To understand what this might mean, and why the controversy about LINC was reported as it was in large sections of the press, it is necessary to be aware of the political significance attaching to 'English' as a subject in the school curriculum.

ENGLISH LANGUAGE AND POLITICAL IDEOLOGIES

Various commentators have observed that English maintains a particular importance in debates about education and policy: 'since the beginnings of mass public education in England and Wales, the teaching of English has been a focus of keen political interest and political control' (Ball, Kenny and Gardiner, 1990, p. 47). The LINC controversy throws into relief issues that arise from various characteristics of English as a school subject – English as language, English as literacy, English as literature – and conflicting theoretical perspectives on literature and 'culture'. Fundamental contradictions have been identified in the enterprise of teaching English which help to account for the conflicts that arise. On the one hand, attempts may be made to deploy English, and literature in particular, in the struggle to 'save our souls and heal the state' (Gordon, speaking at the beginning of this century, quoted in Ball, Kenny and Gardiner, 1990, p. 49): 'From the earliest days of state education writers and authorities on English teaching began to blur the distinction between literacy as a technical skill and as a moral technology.'

A key role for literature and culture as 'civilizing' influences, articulated by, for instance, Arnold, or Newbolt, is observable in contemporary government policy. English becomes a repository of moral values and an agent of social cohesion. While Newbolt explicitly elevates English to a key role in the state education system, Baker articulates a specific role for the subject in the broader project of introducing a national curriculum (claimed to be a means of 'raising standards', of which more below):

> for English children no form of knowledge can take precedence of a knowledge of English, no form of literature can take precedence of English literature: and ... the two are so inextricably connected as to form the only basis possible for a national education.
>
> (Newbolt, 1921, p. 14)

> I see the national curriculum as a way of increasing our social coherence. ... The cohesive role of the national curriculum will provide our society with a greater sense of identity.
>
> (Baker, in *The Guardian*, 16 September 1987, quoted in Johnson, 1991)

> I am working towards *national agreement* on the aims and objectives of English teaching in schools in order to improve standards. ... We need to equip teachers with a proper model of the language to help improve their teaching.
>
> (DES press notice, 16 January 1987; emphasis added)

A role for language and literature in the maintenance of the social order is not confined to the school curriculum. For example, Terry Eagleton – a literary theorist – highlights the wider role of literature, culture, or the humanities in general in government's 'legitimating ideology':

> From time to time, not least in the throes of political crisis, you need to remind yourself collectively of the values by which you're supposed to be living; and the role of the humanities is then to be wheeled in from offstage to provide an answer to this question.
>
> (Eagleton, 1991, p. 5)

In these manifestations, English teaching may be constructed as a vehicle for promoting national cohesion and unity, enforcing literacy as a 'moral technology', and promulgating through literature ideologies and theories which legitimize the social order. However, perceived from other positions, the discipline of 'English' has, far from consolidating and perpetuating a homogeneous system of values, been an important site of expressions of diversity: 'English is not a "subject" in the conventional sense of that term.... It spreads across the curriculum and defies encapsulation.... The whole makes up a bewildering set of networkings in a constant state of flux' (Mittins, 1988, p. 51).

Moreover, those who teach English have a reputation for valuing diversity and creativity, and perhaps for being 'among the most resistant to the very idea of evaluation and accountability' (Allen, 1991, p. 3). As biddable agents of 'moral technology', then, English teachers have been notoriously unreliable. In his review of 'English and English society at a time of change', Medway observes: 'not only does English not align itself with establishment values; it displays a tendency to anti-authoritarianism' (Medway, 1990, p. 33). Hence the tension inherent in a subject through which attempts are made to legitimize particular ideologies with reference to literature. Contradiction in the subject of English itself is expressed by Green thus: 'English teaching is to be regarded as an instance of cultural politics, with a dynamic interplay of progressive and reactionary elements' (Green, 1990, p. 156).

The LINC project was intended to focus specifically on language, with less direct reference to literature (although, of course, recent developments in linguistics influenced the design of the materials, so that whole texts rather than decontextualized or unconvincingly contrived 'bits' of language provided the material for linguistic and pedagogic analysis). An important characteristic of 'English' as language, which distinguishes it from other school subjects, is its dual role as the means of instruction as well as a subject in its own right. Although the idea is not new, the establishment of English as a 'core' subject in the National Curriculum underlines the point:

> In the school curriculum English is unique: the child begins to acquire language before school, without it no other processes of thought and study can take place, and it continues to be central throughout life.
>
> (DES, 1989, para. 1.13)

Snow considers the tensions and contradictions that arise in the study in schools of English *language*:

> We have to be subject to the rules of grammar, in order to be the author of a meaningful sentence. In language we experience the world through the ideologies which English, since Arnold and Newbolt, has promoted. Language is the medium in which we acquire identities through the educational practices of examination and morally managed growth. . . . All this certainly involves a curbing of idealised notions of individual freedom, but, at the same moment, entry into language is also the possibility of making meaning, of becoming the subject of one's own utterances and actions, of understanding and transforming the world.
>
> (Snow, 1991, p. 22)

In their identification of this tension in learning language, between constraints and opportunities, such remarks go some way towards accounting for the controversy about LINC. Knowledge as regulation is incompatible with knowledge as 'critical awareness'. Thus, when an education project on 'knowledge about language' which was intended to contribute to the former was perceived instead to be more identified with the latter, ministerial concern was predictable:

> There is useful material in the LINC units for in-service training: the material specifically related to grammar. . . . But there is a lot more which is a distraction from the main task of teaching children to write, spell and punctuate correctly. A number of fashionable secondary agendas have pushed into the foreground.
>
> (Eggar, 1991)

Another place where English language and education policy converage is the issue of 'standards' – most obviously, of course, in the phrase 'Standard English'. 'Standards' is a word rich in connotations: as well as the sense it carries of agreed measures or norms, there is its association with 'high standards', and with the 'standard bearers' around whom members of a group rally – especially in times of conflict. It has been an important and continuing feature of the discourse in which English teaching is discussed that connections are made between linguistic 'standards' and moral 'standards'. Those whose conception of the nature of language emphasizes its susceptibility to 'rules', and who attribute high priority to the privileged *form* of English, the 'standard', may make quite explicit connections with moral virtue and social responsibility. Such a tendency is to be found not only in the Newbolt Report of the 1920s but also in contemporary observations about English teaching:

> The Elementary School might exert a more permanently humanising influence on its products if it were not for the mistake of some teachers in treating English as . . . a mere subject . . . they have to fight against the powerful influence of evil habits of speech contracted in home and street. The teachers' struggle is thus not with ignorance but with a perverted power . . . the lesson in English is not merely one occasion for the inculcation of knowledge, it is an initiation into the corporate life of man.
>
> (Newbolt, 1921, pp. 57–60)

> The overthrow of grammar coincided with the acceptance of the equivalent of creative writing in social behaviour. As nice points of grammar were mockingly dismissed as pedantic and irrelevant, so was punctiliousness in such matters as honesty, responsibility, property, gratitude, apology and so on.
>
> (Rae, 1982)

Another reason for the fierceness of the defence of 'Standard English', whenever a threat is perceived, is a belief in the power of the 'standard' form of the language to facilitate harmony and consensus, and even to unite the nation.[3] As suggested above, this idea has a long history:

> Two causes, both accidental and conventional rather than national, at present distinguish and divide one class from another in England. The first of these is a marked difference in their modes of speech. If the teaching of the language were properly provided for, the difference between educated and uneducated speech, which at present causes so much prejudice and difficulty of intercourse on both sides, would gradually disappear.
>
> (Newbolt, 1921, pp. 21–2)

Later in the same passage, as this theme is developed, the teaching of English is drawn together not only with social unity but also with patriotism:

> The English people might learn as a whole to regard their own language, first with respect, and then with a genuine feeling of pride and affection. ... Such a feeling for our own native language would be a bond of union between classes, and would beget the right kind of national pride.
>
> (ibid.)

It is interesting that the semantic field from which Newbolt drew in 1921 was of abstract qualities associated with noble emotions, while in 1988 we are offered a metaphor associated with the world of finance:

> Standard English: the language itself exists like a great social bank on which we all draw and to which we all contribute.
>
> (DES, 1988, p.14)

Once again, diversity and complexity are at odds with the concept of the standard as a tool of conformity and cohesion. A conception of language which sees it as heterogeneous rather than monolithic, critical rather than accepting, is antithetical to the project of laying down rules and prescribing standards. Halliday suggests that the academic discipline of linguistics constitutes a challenge to popular, common-sense perceptions:

> there is a real sense in which linguistics is threatening; it's uncomfortable, and it's subversive. It's uncomfortable because it strips us of the fortifications that protect and surround some of our deepest prejudices. As long as we keep linguistics at bay we can go on believing what we want to believe about language, both our own and everybody else's. ... More than any other human phenomenon, language reflects and reveals the inequalities that are enshrined in the social process. When we study language systematically ... we see into the power structure that lies behind our everyday social relationships, the hierarchical statuses that are accorded to different groups within society.
>
> (Halliday, 1979, p. 14)

Goddard (1991) describes how the banned LINC materials, in taking cognizance of 'the fact that power relations are an inherent feature of language', draw on 'a whole body of theory, developed within philosophy, literary studies, discourse analysis and linguistics, which commands widespread acceptance'. Simultaneously, the LINC project is construed, in the press reports examined below, as an example of the abstruse, irrelevant *educational* theory which it is currently fashionable to attack.[4]

The excerpts from the newspaper reports about the LINC affair which follow position their readers to subscribe to the common-sense belief that teaching is a practical activity, and an enterprise which is distorted by the influence of 'theory'. Similarly, the texts assume a readership which is familiar with the popular 'prejudices' about matters such as regional dialects and Standard English, readers who will 'go on believing what [they] want to believe about language' (Halliday, 1979, p. 14).

THE PRESS REPORTING OF THE LINC CONTROVERSY

The final part of this chapter considers how the news of Ministers' decision to prevent publication of the materials was described in the press, and explores some of the discursive devices by which the controversy is constructed and conveyed to the reader. Referring to the LINC materials themselves, in his article 'Why LINC matters', Goddard emphasizes that they

> do not seek to promote the crude, simplistic approach to textual analysis which has been characterised as 'unmasking ideology' ... [which] conjures up absurd visions of an omniscient elite cunningly manipulating pliant masses who yet could rise up and overthrow their masters if only they could be taught to read critically. One does not have to be Michel Foucault to suspect that the operations of power within discourse are likely to be rather less straightforward than this.
>
> (Goddard, 1991, p. 38)

It is not my intention in analysing these newspaper texts to oversimplify the processes by which ideologies are constructed and perpetuated. As a limited case study, the analysis is merely intended to illustrate some aspects of the discursive construction of a controversy in this particular area of educational policy.

The choice of texts for analysis is necessarily selective. While some articles in the professional press (such as *The Times Educational Supplement* and the journal *Education*), as well as a full-page spread in *The Independent*, attempted to explore in some detail a range of the issues raised by the Ministers' decision, and to represent more than one point of view, many other pieces took a partisan stance in their reporting. In the news items, feature articles and editorial comment appearing in certain newspapers, the story was consistently constructed so as to present LINC as a wasteful research project which, staffed by left-wing ideologues from the educational establishment, had produced a set of incomprehensible findings, so alien to common-sense notions of the teaching of correct English that Ministers had no choice but to ban the 'report'.

How was this achieved? First, on the issue of language itself, LINC is castigated for failing to promote the unifying, monolithic, 'correct' standard. Implicit in this criticism is the concept that there is a unity in the system of values to which everyone aspires – membership is universally sought of a club whose language is the best, the desirable norm, 'the Queen's English':

> Properly spoken and written language is the lifeline which any conscientious schooling system can offer to every child, from whatever background. It is the only possible path to real social equality. ... To teach people how to speak and write their language properly and well is to give them a ticket to freedom. Being 'tolerant' of their 'differences' is another way of writing them off.
>
> (Daley, 1991)

Paradoxically, some critics of the LINC project have turned the notion of a quest for a spurious unity against the 'progressives', with Walden, for example, in the *Daily Telegraph*, decrying 'our dangerously uniform system of comprehensive education'.

On the other hand, where the LINC approach recognizes the importance of variation in language use, this too is held against it. For example, two assumptions articulated in the LINC project materials are that:

> Language is penetrated with social and cultural values and also carries meanings related to each user's identity.

> Language reveals and conceals much about human relationships. There are intimate connections, for example, between language and social power, language and culture and language and gender.
>
> (Carter, 1990, p. 5)

Beliefs such as these are represented by LINC's critics as a philosophy which: 'reshape[s] English on multi-cultural, anti-racist and anti-sexist lines ... [into] a form of social engineering whose basic purpose is to instil in the minds of impressionable youngsters the self-evident virtues of socialist *levelling down*' (Honeyford, 1991, p. 6; emphasis added).

The paradigm implicit in the discourse is a hierarchy in which Standard English, the Queen's English, the literary canon and traditional values shine from the summit. All people, equally, 'from whatever background' (Daley, 1991), should have the freedom to move – upwards – and join this united haven of excellence. Of course a fundamental contradiction in this model is that the notion of open access expressed by its advocates itself subverts the hierarchy which peaks at the point of excellence. If everyone left behind their 'impoverished, ungrammatical, virtually impenetrable uses of language' (Daley, 1991) and converged on the pinnacle, the whole structure would presumably topple. Nevertheless, the crime of which 'the educational establishment' stands accused is the denial of access to the havens of the élite. In this scenario, the subversive educationalists are fully aware of the agreed hierarchies of language forms and cultures, but, because of 'guilt-ridden middle-class sentimentality' (ibid.), they indulge in 'criminal abnegation of educational responsibility' by 'offering a child no exit from his "social and cultural context"' and thus 'burying his mental feet in concrete' (ibid.).

An alternative charge against people belonging to 'the educational establishment' is their disregard of the agreed hierarchy. Now, rather than wilfully denying children access to what is great and good, the demons of the left seek to interfere with the rightful status of different forms of language and 'to put ethnic and regional variations on a par with the Queen's English' (Massey, 1991b, p. 5).

Another part of the agenda, as suggested above, is the demonization of the educational 'expert'. Newspaper reports about the LINC controversy have capitalized on the opportunity presented for stating the case against the 'educational establishment':

> The point is that a fraudulent system of thought ... has taken control of the entire institution: many schools, most local education authorities, the

Inspectorate, the teacher training colleges and the educational institutes.

(Walden, 1991)

the report reflects the ineradicable prejudice of large swathes of the education profession.

(*Daily Telegraph*, 28 June 1991)

What are the characteristics of the perpetrators of this 'fraud'? The first difficulty for those who want to construct these demons is to demonstrate the extent of their influence while at the same time emphasizing their marginality. This problem is solved by explaining that 'the unteachable élite' (Walden, 1991) have, while the right-minded majority ('the healthy lay mind') weren't looking, crept up stealthily on the entire education system and taken it over. For example:

Mr Eggar said the way in which the Government's straightforward idea to improve grammar teaching had been 'captured' by the trendies, turning it into an 'abstract argument between educational theorists', was a salutary lesson.

(Massey, 1991b)

The 'fraudulent system of thought': 'has the power to frustrate all reform. It appoints its own successors. It disseminates its own doctrines in a deformed, hermetic language incomprehensible to the healthy lay mind. It suppresses opposition' (Walden, 1991).

At the same time, those identified with it are no more than a 'clique', an 'élite' (Walden, 1991), a 'lunatic fringe', an 'ideological pressure group' (Honeyford, 1991). Nowhere in these texts is there an acknowledgement that the power to make appointments to curriculum working groups, or projects such as LINC, and to construct the brief to which they will work, is actually in the hands of government.

The second characteristic which the demons must be seen to possess is a surfeit of knowledge, expertise or theory. Members of the educational establishment cannot be forgiven for having some knowledge of the area in which they have spent years studying and gaining experience. The bitter resentment experienced by those who have had to turn to 'experts' for advice is palpable in the texts that denigrate them. Both Jones and Johnson provide explanations:

Those whom the right thought that, through their great victories of the 1980s, they had evicted from the premises where educational policy is made, promptly reappeared through the back door, to have an important influence on the . . . programmes of study.

(Jones, 1990, p. 3)

The minister may show off about his competence in poetry or history, but when it comes to teaching English, mathematics, or science his genius has limits. Given professional hostility to [Education Reform] Act and [National] curriculum, and the paucity of educational ideas on the Right, the government depends on the very groups it attacks.

(Johnson, 1991, p. 74)[5]

Thus, any specialist terminology used by, for example, the authors of LINC materials, is routinely referred to as 'jargon' – even 'sub-scientific jargon' (*Daily Telegraph*, 28 June 1991) – while the word 'theory' is often accompanied in these texts by adjectives such as 'impenetrable'.

Part of the process by which 'theory' itself is demonized is the portrayal of disembodied 'system[s] of thought' (Walden, 1991), rather than people, as responsible for the sorry state of affairs described. The LINC materials have, in several reports 'found their way into classrooms' – a use of the linguistic device of personification which serves to suggest insidious underhandedness. Similarly, 'fashionable secondary agendas have pushed into the foreground' (Eggar, 1991).

Although people themselves are sometimes the agents of action, it is as the originators of ideas that they are often attacked. This component of the discourse plays on the stereotype of the eccentric professor who lacks all common sense. Alongside him (*sic*) is the less studious victim swept along with a theory which has no valid foundation but which has fashionable appeal. Thus we read of 'sundry experts', 'assorted radical experts', 'assorted ideologue-practitioners' and 'the trendies' (Honeyford, 1991), 'the systematised shenanigans of educational cranks' (Walden, 1991), 'so-called experts' (Massey, 1991a) and 'trendy academics' (Graham, 1991). Hapless victims include 'the minds of impressionable youngsters' (Honeyford, 1991), pupils who 'would be harmed' if exposed to the materials (MacGregor, 1991), and also students at:

> teacher training institutions, where [LINC's] voodoo theories about the nature of language will appeal to the impressionable mind of the young woman with low A-levels in 'soft' subjects who . . . is the typical student in these establishments.
>
> (Walden, 1991)

The innocent dupes are important in the cast: their situation justifies the protective paternalism of those who know better, the politicians and the authors of the feature articles – 'the report we had to ban, by Tim Eggar' (Massey, 1991b); 'I am reliably informed', 'worrying documents . . . have come into my possession', 'it is vital for the Government to understand' (Honeyford, 1991). Furthermore, the attribution of wicked motives to the entire teaching force would presumably not hold sufficient popular appeal.

Several reports, having built up the associations of 'theories' and 'expertise' with 'trendy', 'wacky' (Hymas, 1991) academics, conclude that the solution is to 'deconstruct . . . the institutes of education' (*Daily Telegraph*, 28 June 1991). The fact that Professor Ron Carter is a linguist directing a university department not of education but of English studies is not permitted to stand in the way of this line of argument. In Walden's piece, 'the educational institutes and the teacher training colleges' are identified as 'the source of the problem', and they are likened to 'institutes of Marxism-Leninism in Eastern Europe'. He suggests that 'whether "education" is a genuine academic discipline which deserves to be funded like any other is a serious question', and comes to the conclusion that the government should set about 'the dissolution of the academic monasteries': 'If a university wishes to keep such a department, it must find the money itself, as believers in alchemy or homoeopathy are obliged to do' (Walden, 1991).

The marginalization of academic, researched, theoretically grounded approaches to education is, as has been observed, part of a broader political agenda, which might perhaps account for the persistent description of the LINC materials – in-service training materials – in terms such as an 'investigation', a 'study', 'findings' (Massey, 1991a, b); a 'reading report', the 'biggest-ever study of language teaching' (Mac-Gregor, 1991) and a 'vast report' (*Sunday Express*, 16 June 1991).

Another target which critics have managed to include in their attacks, along with academics and fashionable theories – 'all the old balderdash' (Graham, 1991) – is 'bureaucracy': 'My simple mind boggles at the thought of such bureaucratic insanity' (Telfer, 1991): 'Mad, bad bureaucracy – Has there ever been such an example of mad, bad, bureaucratic waste as the one just provided for the nation by the Department of Education and Science?' (*Sunday Express*, 16 June 1991). Presumably the implication is that centrally funded initiatives waste money, in contrast to systems of locally managed budgets. Madness and badness, as illustrated above, are two of the characteristics attributed to LINC – its personnel, its theories, its materials. There are some interesting juxtapositions of themes which help to convey the message: Honeyford's piece ties in the LINC story with an attack on 'the trendy, multi-cultural lobby' and also on Terry Eagleton, 'self-confessed and unrepentant Marxist' (Honeyford, 1991). Another report includes in the same column as its LINC story a paragraph about 'Marxists ... leading an attack on religious education in schools' (MacGregor, 1991), while in another the adjacent story happens to be headed 'Homosexual foster fathers for boy, 15' (Clare, 1991).

To help construct associations with the madness of 'Them', the discourse of the newspaper articles is sprinkled with terms such as 'barmy', 'lunatic' (Honeyford, 1991), and 'insanity' (Telfer, 1991). By contrast, terms which help to construct the 'Us' emphasize simplicity and health: 'the healthy lay mind' (Walden, 1991); 'my simple mind boggles' (Telfer, 1991). Badness is present in the two senses of 'low quality' and 'evil'. It is an important aspect of the vilification of 'theory' that the LINC materials should at once be 'too sophisticated by far' (Eggar, 1991), 'elaborate' (MacGregor, 1991) and 'complicated' (Hymas, 1991) and yet also 'incredibly banal ... [with a] lack of hard edge' (Massey, 1991b). Other terms used to stress the inferiority of the materials include 'waffle' (Massey, 1991b), 'trendy tripe' (*Sunday Express*, 16 June 1991), 'turgidities', 'inanities', 'desolate language' (Walden, 1991), and 'desolating banality of thought and phrase' (*Daily Telegraph*, 28 June 1991). While these devices imply mere incompetence, others remind the reader that there is a sinister side to the activities of the demons: 'fraudulent', 'harmful' (Walden, 1991), 'an ideological pressure group bent on destroying the concept of correctness in language and literature', 'insidious' (Honeyford, 1991), 'a criminal abnegation of educational responsibility' (Daley, 1991).

The most explicit demonization is in Walden's piece, which refers to 'voodoo theories about the nature of language' and, in questioning whether ' "education" is a genuine academic discipline', likens it to 'homoeopathy' and 'alchemy'. The construction in this text of the education establishment as a cultish following, shrouded in mystery, is supported by the contrast with the 'lay' majority, and by the recommendation of 'the dissolution of the educational monasteries'.

With the 'goodies' and 'baddies' clearly identified for the readership, the next stage is obviously confrontation, and there is a sense of urgency: the educational establishment is said to be 'tightening its grip' (Walden, 1991); it is moving on a 'continued march' (Honeyford, 1991) – what are the 'traditionalists' (Hymas, 1991), the government, 'we' (Graham, 1991) to do? Several of the texts provide no-nonsense answers. Swift, decisive, combative action has already been taken in the way Ministers have dealt with the LINC materials: 'scrapped' (MacGregor, 1991), 'vetoed' (Massey, 1991a), 'rejected' (Graham, 1991), 'had to ban' (Massey, 1991b). All that remains is the final phase, the logical conclusion: 'halt the ... march' (Honeyford, 1991), mount 'a frontal attack on [the "ed-biz"]'s citadels' and 'expel the unteachable élite' (Walden, 1991). Walden concludes by reassuring the 'impatient' 'public': 'Mr Kenneth Clarke [then Secretary of State for Education] is the man to do it. If Mr Major is serious about education, he will lend his support.'

CONCLUSION

One of the central theses on which the LINC materials rest is that language and the uses to which people put it are complex things to understand. So too are the processes – sociological, psychological, political, economic and linguistic – which are researched by those who wish to analyse and understand better what goes on as teachers teach and children learn in schools. Complexity, however, does not have populist appeal, and is harder to condense into newspaper headlines. The LINC controversy is only one example of the compression of complex educational issues into binary opposite slogans: real books versus phonics; abstract theory versus practical training; trendy experiments versus the traditional basics. The types of discourse employed in the texts discussed here are themselves illustrations of a basic assumption, quoted earlier, which is explored in the LINC materials, that: 'Language reveals and conceals much about human relationships. There are intimate connections, for example, between language and social power.'

Eggar (1991) cites this statement as an example of the 'fashionable secondary agendas [which] have pushed into the foreground', yet so threatening are such concepts to government that all traces of them have been effectively eradicated from the proposals for the redrafted English National Curriculum which appeared in April 1993. The remit to which the proposals were written promotes an instrumental notion of 'grammar' in its requirement to: 'recast the requirements for knowledge about language in reading and writing in order to define the essential knowledge and understanding of grammar needed at Key Stages 1 and 2' (DfE, 1993, p. 1). The proposals thus implicitly dismiss knowledge about the relationship between language and social relations as irrelevant to children's education.

In this chapter I have argued that language plays a central role in the enterprise of controlling the curriculum, and that the case study illustrates two senses in which this is so: what children are to learn about language and the language used to communicate education policy to the public are important sites of struggle in educational politics.

NOTES

1. It was in the context of the establishment of the apparatus for the wide-ranging reforms in education which were to be embodied in the Education Reform Act 1988 that HMI began production of a 'series of discussion documents ... intended as a contribution to the process of developing general agreement about curricular aims

objectives, of which the first focussed on English' (DES, 1986, p. 40). These publications introduced the term 'knowledge about language', and, while it was recognized that this might be contentious, the extent of criticism of this aspect of the Report in the responses to it was far greater than the Report's authors had anticipated:

> Nothing divided the respondents more than the issue of knowledge about language.... The growth of a stronger accord might be assisted by an enquiry to focus attention on the matter, with the ultimate object of drawing up recommendations as to what might be taught to intending teachers, to those in post and to pupils in schools.
>
> (DES, 1986, p. 40)

2. Harold Rosen described it as:

> a committee which left people agape with incredulity. The collective credentials of the members revealed shocking and obvious omissions. Had you asked those who played an active part in the field of English teaching they would have come up with a list of those who were *not* asked. The list of members constitutes a calculated insult to the English teaching fraternity.
>
> (Rosen, 1988, p. 2)

3. Such enterprises are not confined to the teaching of English in this country. See, for example, Morgan (1990) on the deployment of English studies as 'an arm of imperialism', with particular reference to the Canadian curriculum.
4. This trend is illustrated by the developments in teacher education. A belief that teaching is a practical activity which is learned by experience and distorted by academic study has long been articulated by writers associated with the New Right who are influential in the formation of government policy. See, for example, O'Hear (1991) and Lawlor (1990). Consistent with this view was Kenneth Clarke's announcement, early in 1992, of new arrangements for the training of teachers which would give more weight to practical experience and reduce the time available for the academic study of educational issues.
5. The handling of this issue since the LINC controversy would suggest that Ministers sought even more assiduously to avoid dependence on those whose views they mistrusted when they began the revision of the English National Curriculum. Appointments to the National Curriculum Council (NCC) and the School Examinations and Assessment Council (SEAC) included Joan Clanchy and John Marenbon, from both of whom sympathy with the government's reforms might have been expected. Both resigned early in 1993, voicing publicly criticism of the way business had been conducted. Clanchy objected to 'only being given Centre for Policy Studies pamphlets to read by way of homework', and to 'the obsession with Standard English' in the revised Programmes of Study (*Times Educational Supplement*, 5 March 1993 and *The Guardian*, 20 April 1993). Marenbon was quoted as saying that the government's plans for the National Curriculum were 'awful' and would be bad for English in universities as well as in schools (*Times Higher Educational Supplement*, 14 May 1993).

REFERENCES

Allen, D. (1991) Evaluating the English department. In Dougill, P. (ed.) *Developing English*. Milton Keynes: Open University Press.

Ball, S., Kenny, A. and Gardiner, D. (1990) Literacy, politics and the teaching of English. In Goodson, I. and Medway, P. (eds) *Bringing English to Order*. Lewes: Falmer Press.

Carter, R. (ed.) (1990) *Knowledge about Language and the Curriculum: the LINC Reader*. Sevenoaks: Hodder & Stoughton.

Clare, J. (1991) Writing is on the wall for literature. *Daily Telegraph*, 28 June.

Daley, J. (1991) Every child's freedom ticket. *Times Educational Supplement*, 28 June.

Department of Education and Science (DES) (1986) *English from 5 to 16*. London: HMSO.

DES (1988) *Report of the Committee of Inquiry into the Teaching of English Language* (The Kingman Report). London: HMSO.

DES (1989) *English for Ages 5 to 16* (The Cox Report). London: HMSO.

Department for Education (DfE) (1993) *English for Ages 5 to 16 (1993)*. London: HMSO.

Eagleton, T. (1991) The enemy within. *English in Education* 25 (3), Autumn, 3–9.

Eggar, T. (1991) Correct use of English is essential. *Times Educational Supplement*, 28 June.

Goddard, R. (1991) Why LINC matters. *English in Education* 25 (3), Autumn, 32–9.

Graham, C. (1991) Will we ever learn? *Evening Chronicle*, 18 June.

Gramsci, A. (1985) *Selections from Cultural Writings*, quoted in Crowley, T. (1989) *The Politics of Discourse: The Standard Language Question in British Cultural Debates*. London: Macmillan.

Green, B. (1990) A dividing practice: 'literature', English teaching and cultural politics. In Goodson I. and Medway, P. (eds) *Bringing English to Order*. Lewes: Falmer Press.

Halliday, M. (1979) Linguistics in teacher education. In Carter, R. (ed.) (1982) *Linguistics and the Teacher*. London: Routledge & Kegan Paul.

Honeyford, R. (1991) Why are our schools still run by cranks? *Daily Mail*, 26 June.

Hymas, C. (1991) Ministers veto 'wacky' grammar teaching guide. *Sunday Times*, 23 June.

Johnson, R. (1991) A new road to serfdom? A critical history of the 1988 Act. In Department of Cultural Studies (ed.) *Education Limited: Schooling, Training and the New Right in England since 1979*. London: Unwin Hyman.

Jones, K. (1990) The National Curriculum: working for hegemony. Paper presented at British Education Research Association Conference, University of East Anglia, Norwich, September.

Lawlor, S. (1990) *Teachers Mistaught*. London: Centre for Policy Studies.

MacGregor, I. (1991) 'Trendy' reading report scrapped. *Daily Express*, 15 June.

Massey, R. (1991a) Schools report becomes a study in farce. *Daily Mail*, 26 June.

Massey, R. (1991b) Bad grammar and the report we had to ban, by Tim Eggar. *Daily Mail*, 26 June.

Medway, P. (1990) Into the sixties: English and English society at a time of change. In Goodson, I. and Medway P. (eds) *Bringing English to Order*. Lewes: Falmer Press.

135

Mittins, B. (1988) *English: Not the Naming of Parts*. Sheffield: NATE.

Morgan, R. (1990) The 'Englishness' of English teaching. In Goodson, I. and Medway, P. (eds) *Bringing English to Order*. Lewes: Falmer Press.

Newbolt, H. (1921) *The Teaching of English in England*. London: HMSO.

O'Hear, A. (1991) Getting the teachers we deserve. *The Guardian*, 19 March.

Rae, J. (1982) The decline and fall of English grammar, *The Observer*, 7 February; quoted in Cameron, D. and Bourne, J. (1988) No common ground: Kingman, grammar and the nation. *Language and Education* 2 (3), 147–60.

Rosen, H. (1988) Struck by a particular gap. In Jones, M. and West, A. (eds) *Learning Me Your Language: Perspectives on the Teaching of English*. Cheltenham: Stanley Thorne.

Snow, J. (1991) On the subject of English. *English in Education* 25 (3), 18–27.

Telfer, B. (1991) '£21m "wasted" on English lessons' report. *Newcastle Evening Post*, 17 June.

Walden, G. (1991) Why the government must expel the unteachable élite. *Daily Telegraph*, 3 July.

Chapter 10

Accountable to whom? Researchers and researched in education

Robert G. Burgess

Accountability is now firmly on the research agenda in education. But we might ask: What is it? What form does it take? What are its implications? While it is relatively easy to pose these questions in relation to the world of schools, classrooms and curricula, it is rare for us to pose such questions in relation to those of us who are engaged in social and educational research. Indeed, as researchers we rarely scrutinize the activities of higher education in general and higher education teachers and researchers in particular (Burgess, 1986). However, it could be argued that we have begun in recent years to reflect on the methodology used in social and educational research (Burgess, 1984; Walford, 1987, 1991). But have we asked in what ways we are accountable, what form accountability takes, and what its implications are for research in education? It is these questions that form the focus of this chapter.

A DEFINITION OF ACCOUNTABILITY?

In searching for definitions of accountability, and the form accountability can take, there is still no better source than the review conducted by Kogan in the mid-1980s in which he looked at educational accountability in terms of models and frames for analysis (Kogan, 1986). In his review, Kogan examines different definitions of educational accountability and summarizes the situation by discussing accountability that 'assumes institutional authority to call an individual or a group to account for their actions' (Kogan, 1986, p. 26). He continues: 'it is to be contrasted with responsibility which is the moral sense of duty to perform appropriately' (ibid.). While this definition is useful, it does not take us far enough, given the parameters of Kogan's discussion. Accordingly, I favour the approach adopted by Becher and his colleagues (Becher *et al.*, 1979; Becher, Eraut and Knight, 1981). In particular, they point to the importance of a more diffuse usage of the term accountability, in contrast to Kogan, who defines accountability in terms of rendering accounts to those in authority. Indeed, Becher and Eraut (1977) have indicated that, while it is important to avoid confusion with general responsibilities towards individuals, it does not go far enough. They follow the notion that an individual is:

> accountable to all those who have placed one in a position of trust, and that accountability should be expressed in terms intended to secure the

continued renewal of that trust. In practice, the broader definition may well be the more appropriate, because moves to strengthen formal accountability gain support from those who have simply ceased to trust.

(Becher and Eraut, 1977, p. 11)

While such a definition points to the key characteristics of accountability and by implication issues of control, it does not subdivide the different facets of accountability. Indeed, Becher *et al.* (1979) distinguished three aspects of accountability: answerability to one's clients (moral accountability); responsibility to oneself and one's colleagues (professional accountability); and accountability in the strict sense to one's employers or political masters (contractual accountability).

It is the purpose of this chapter to consider these different facets of accountability and the extent to which they give rise to a series of questions about the conduct of social and educational research. We will touch on moral and political issues in social and educational research and the way they impinge on the research process and our reflection on it.

MORAL ACCOUNTABILITY

Traditionally, moral accountability has involved responsibility to clients. In the case of researchers, this might suggest accountability to those who are researched. I think we need to raise questions concerning to whom we are accountable. It may seem to be a simple matter to suggest that accountability is of immediate concern to the individual or group with whom the researcher is working. For example, in the study of a comprehensive school, are we accountable to the individual teacher with whom we are conducting an interview, or to the broader group of teachers that the individual represents, or to all those who work within comprehensive schools? Indeed, we could go further and explore accountability in relation to a range of different groups involved in comprehensive schooling.

Access may have been gained to a comprehensive school through an individual headteacher, or through the governors of a school, or through a local education authority. In these circumstances, the accountability which is placed upon us in conducting a one-to-one interview with a probationary teacher may lead us to believe that we are accountable to an individual teacher. But are we accountable to a broader group? To headteachers, governors and others? In this sense, moral accountability places before us questions concerning the extent to which we are accountable to a range of audiences: sponsors, gatekeepers and those who are researched. It also raises questions about whether we are accountable to an individual or, on a collective basis, to a group and whether there are significant audiences to whom we are accountable in the course of conducting our research. In this context, what starts out as a simple question concerning the responsibilities of the researcher to the researched takes us into a network of relationships, which then raises questions about the audience or audiences to whom we may be accountable.

This example has pointed to the multiple audiences involved in any piece of educational research concerning schools. Indeed, it points to the importance of considering sponsors and sponsorship in social and educational research as well as the relationship between researcher and researched, for it is within this complex web that issues of accountability arise. To explore this further I will examine three projects that I have been involved with in recent years. First, a project on nursery education in Salford LEA where interviews were conducted with heads of nursery schools, nursery centres and some primary schools (Burgess, Hughes and Moxon, 1989). Here, it would be easy to talk about the accountability we had to the headteachers who were interviewed in our study. However, the study was concerned with educational provision for the under-5s in Salford and had been commissioned by the LEA. Furthermore, the research had been specified by the local authority to the extent that we were required to interview all heads of nursery schools and nursery centres in Salford, together with the headteachers of 12 primary schools where nursery classes were located. While headteachers were anonymous within the report (where pseudonyms were used), they were not so anonymous to the LEA, given that officers and advisers had been involved in the principles of selection associated with the study. While we might argue that our team had exercised methodological expertise in discussing the principles of selection and the way in which these principles would be deployed in selecting primary schools within the study, it was, nevertheless, officers and advisers who were involved in the selection of particular schools and by implication the headteachers who were to be interviewed. In such circumstances we might ask: should we have warned those who were to be interviewed of the extent to which they were identifiable? Or was identifiability a low risk in this study?

There were further issues to explore in relation to our study as the researchers and the researched were accountable to a wider community of pupils, parents, governors, councillors, members of the local authority education committee and so on, who were involved in policy and practice associated with nursery education. Here, ethical questions arise about whether the ends justify the means, and whether one should outline to individuals the different networks within which the research is located. Within the Salford nursery project it was evident that some headteachers were concerned about whether their comments would be reported back verbatim to the local education authority, while others moved closer to tape recorders as if to make sure that the information would be communicated directly to the officers and advisers within the LEA offices. Yet there is a further problem. While we, as researchers, may have an idea as to how the material is to be written up and disseminated, this may not accord with the views of those with whom we work. Accordingly, we have an obligation to explain the conditions under which a study will be conducted, not only in terms of data collection, but also in terms of data analysis, dissemination and writing – another important dimension of the accountability of the researcher to the researched, for the researcher is ultimately responsible for the selection of theoretical frameworks and concepts that will assist in understanding and exploring the situations observed.

A further project where these issues have come to the fore has been a curriculum evaluation conducted on behalf of Hampshire LEA (Burgess *et al.*, 1989). This project, entitled 'Energy Education in the Curriculum', was commissioned by the LEA as a means of evaluating the extent to which curriculum materials were being used effectively within various primary schools in the New Forest. It was the task of our team to visit each primary school involved in this piece of curriculum development to conduct interviews with heads, class teachers and pupils. On the basis of our evaluation, it was intended that the curriculum materials would be modified for wider dissemination in Hampshire schools and, in turn, schools throughout the UK. While this was the initial objective it carried with it a major assumption: that the Warwick team would find work of such value that further money could be invested in disseminating the curriculum materials more widely within Hampshire and the UK. But therein lay our problem. Our evaluation was to encompass not only the take-up and impact of the materials on the schools, pupils and teachers, but also curriculum content (Burgess, 1991).

To begin the study, we conducted an analysis of the curriculum materials. Here, difficulties immediately arose. The materials contained examples of racism and sexism and also scientific inaccuracy – all issues which we drew to the attention of the course team in our final report. Furthermore, the implementation of the materials was far from straightforward, so we suggested ways in which the curriculum materials could be revised before the project was to be disseminated more broadly within Hampshire and elsewhere. At one level this task had been established for us by the curriculum development team, but it was not a task on which an 'answer' was required. Indeed, our report (Burgess, Hughes and Moxon, 1989) was destined to be seen not only by the course team and the officers associated with it, but also by officers with other responsibilities in the authority who were involved in policy recommendations about funding for the future development of the materials. Indeed, I have been told by the officer who was responsible for the project that our evaluation cost the team financially, since the local authority would not provide further funds for this curriculum project without certain identified deficiencies being rectified. At one level, we could argue that our project was such that we were accountable not only to the members of the curriculum development team but also to the members of the local authority, and in turn to pupils and teachers who might utilize these curriculum materials in Hampshire and elsewhere. In these circumstances, we might ask: to whom were we ultimately accountable? Were there significant others in this project and significant audiences who would determine the way in which we would report our study? There is no simple answer. Even if separate reports are generated for different audiences, it still means that the investigator has to consider the way in which data are made accessible to a wide range of groups and the extent to which data may be utilized for social and political purposes other than those for which the study was originally commissioned. The researcher may be accountable to a wide range of audiences, but there are also questions of control. Here, control refers not only to the interaction of the researcher and the researched, but also to the relationship between the researcher and the audience. Data dissemination therefore raises key issues of accountability and control.

At this point it may be easy to suggest that these kinds of problem do not arise on projects which are funded by a research council, government department or charitable trust. Yet if we look at the way in which these bodies have defined their remit, we find that there is a requirement to fulfil certain conditions to an academic or policy-focused community. Charitable trusts, such as Joseph Rowntree, require the individual researcher to contribute to the policy arena, while the Economic and Social Research Council (ESRC) would say that its fundamental reason for funding social research is to advance the knowledge base of the social sciences through theoretical and methodological development rather than through direct contributions to policy formulation and the policy-making process (though researchers are now required to communicate with the user community). In this sense, researchers are accountable to those who are funding the research and need to take into account the way research questions are framed, projects designed and data collected, as well as the way in which data analysis and report writing occurs. It is too simple to suggest that researchers have complete freedom in these circumstances compared with research and evaluation projects that are conducted on behalf of a particular local education authority. In relation to this, we need to begin to explore the extent to which researchers hold particular responsibilities to themselves and to the research community.

PROFESSIONAL ACCOUNTABILITY

When professional accountability has been discussed in relation to social and educational research, it has usually been in relation to ethical codes, and statements of ethical principles. It is essential that all members of professional associations take the issues contained in such codes and statements into account when conducting their projects. Professional accountability usually comes down to questions of responsibilities of researchers to themselves and to the wider professional organization (British Sociological Association, 1992). But what does this mean in practice?

Often an area that is hidden from view in the social sciences is the way in which research projects are designed and subsequently funded. Here, there are questions about the ways in which research designs are specified and contracts written. If an investigator undercosts a project, or suggests short cuts that are not in accord with professional competence, then questions arise about the way in which an investigation can be pursued. When designing projects, formulating questions, outlining timetables and costing initiatives, it becomes appropriate to think not only of oneself, but also of the broader research community to which we belong and the extent to which that community might confront considerable difficulties in the light of the way a project is designed. But it is not merely questions of research design, problem formulation and contractual relations that occur at the beginning of the project. There are also the conditions which are placed upon the researcher. Here it is important to consider the extent to which an individual will comply with any restrictions that might be placed upon his or her ability to do research and to place the evidence in the public domain. Once again, it is not merely the individual and his or her responsibilities that are at issue, but also a much broader community of researchers. Furthermore, there is the question of the right that the researcher has to disseminate and publish findings. Some research contracts (especially with government departments) specify carefully the extent to which data can be disseminated. Often it is stated that the data do not belong to the researcher. However, one might question the extent to which data are owned by an investigator in any investigation – but what implications does this have?

If we take Stenhouse's notion that 'research is systematic enquiry that is subsequently made public' (Stenhouse, 1975), then we need to consider the responsibilities we have to the profession in respect of publication. Are there no circumstances in which projects should be established despite the fact that restrictions are placed on publication? Or is it more important to engage in a project and subsequently to argue for the release of data and the right to publish? I tend to favour the latter course of action as it gives opportunities for young social scientists and educational researchers to gain research experience. I also favour a situation whereby one might engage in a project that delivers data which are useful to the sponsor, while simultaneously delivering data that have the potential to advance our understanding of the conduct of social and educational research – a subject on which the sponsor may well grant permission for publication. A recent example comes to mind. I have been engaged with two colleagues in conducting a study on behalf of the National Council for Educational Technology (Burgess, Phtiaka and Pole, 1991). The project has concerned the use of information technology in the teaching of English. We were required to deliver a confidential report for internal use by members of NCET staff. Is this 'research', and to whom are we accountable?

First, we need to look at the conditions that were negotiated. It was important not only to collect data on the impact of information technology on the teaching of English, but to consider the way in which the study would be conducted. It was agreed that we would conduct a survey by means of telephone interviews, a field on which there is relatively little work reported in journals and methodology textbooks. It is our intention to write up our experiences of telephone interviews so that we understand the problems and possibilities associated with that methodology, which in my view justifies engaging in this project. On the one hand the project delivers data to the sponsor, and on the other delivers fundamental evidence for the social science community on telephone interviewing while ensuring the career development and experience of the researchers employed on the project.

But this may be a relatively simple example, as statements of ethical principles and codes of moral guidance often focus on the simple and clear-cut. In reality, social and educational research is associated with considerable complexity when one considers the responsibilities of the researcher to the researched, and to a number of other bodies. When the question is asked: 'Where do the researchers' responsibilities lie?', we automatically need to examine the overlap of research and social life. Here I take as my example an ESRC-funded research project entitled 'Becoming a Postgraduate Social Science Student'. This two-year project, funded by the ESRC, was located in nine higher education institutions where we have studied the way in which first-year postgraduate students are socialized into the academic community through departments of business studies, economics and sociology. As this study was funded by the ESRC no conditions were attached to it in terms of the way in which the report was to be written (apart from the normal requirement that a report be supplied to the research council three months after the end of the project; Burgess, Hockey and Pole, 1992). But in this project we are engaged in an investigation where there are a number of overlapping memberships and loyalties. If I take my own example, I am a member of a sociology department, and a member of the professional association for sociologists (the British Sociological Association), I am involved in establishing graduate education on a university-wide basis at the University of Warwick, and at the time of the study I was a member of the ESRC Training Board.

The project, which involved studying a number of familiar settings, including settings of which I am a member, raised such questions as: to whom am I accountable? and in what circumstances? Consideration has had to be given to such issues as accountability to myself and to a variety of other groups and organizations. This topic was raised very early on in the conduct of the research in one of our research team meetings where we discussed whether, given that I was an ESRC Training Board member, the other two investigators should identify the sites within which they were working, or for that matter the people with whom they worked. After some discussion, we decided this was a simple-minded notion, given that I had already agreed through the research design to be responsible for the selection of the research sites, for some of the interviews with registrars, deans of faculties and heads of department and also with the handling of data analysis and some writing. In these circumstances, identification of research sites and some of the personnel was inevitable among team members.

Here the purposes of the project are important. We were not conducting a piece of market research for sociology departments or universities. We were not engaged in an evaluation of sociology teaching and supervision at graduate level on behalf of the British Sociological Association or any other public body, nor were we looking at the extent to which ESRC policy had been implemented. Our research did not just relate to students funded by the ESRC but to all students, regardless of origin and regardless of funding body, for our project was centrally concerned with a sociological topic – the socialization of postgraduate students – and an educational topic – the training versus education debate in the arena of postgraduate study. Our project was concerned with fundamental issues in sociology and education as well as policy issues. So while we might deliver data of use to the sociology and education research communities, to the profession and to the ESRC, we were not 'hired hands' who were checking up on colleagues in other institutions on behalf of the Research Council. We had carefully specified our research questions and in doing so had looked at ways in which we could contribute towards the study of higher education in general, and the analysis of postgraduate education in particular, as well as to sociological studies of occupational socialization – a basic research issue that has been explored in relation to a range of communities, and to which our research will add. Yet there are still questions of accountability that impinge upon fieldwork situations.

When I conducted interviews in a range of higher education institutions, I thought it was important to begin by outlining the context of the study and the roles I take in a range of overlapping communities associated with the project. I then pointed out that I was responsible for establishing graduate education across the whole of the University of Warwick. I also told those I interviewed that I was a member of the ESRC Training Board. However, in each of these instances, I emphasized that I was there as a researcher, not as a member of the University of Warwick who was attempting to find out how other institutions work in order to utilize that information, nor to check the extent to which the institution was or was not implementing ESRC policy on graduate education in the social sciences. This was a significant element to emphasize so that the limits of the research were clear. It was also important to establish a relationship with those with whom I worked, and this in turn highlighted the professional responsibilities of the researcher to the researched in this context. But in this project the sponsor was not cast in the role of employer – another situation which holds implications for accountability.

CONTRACTUAL ACCOUNTABILITY

Within the literature, contractual accountability usually refers to accountability to employers and to political masters, but in the relationship which a researcher enters into, who is the employed? Is the employer the sponsor or the institution to which the research belongs? Here the independence of the researcher becomes paramount. If the researcher were to be directly employed by a sponsor it might limit what could be disseminated in any research report. Furthermore, it might limit any critical comments the researcher might wish to make about the subject of study. If one takes organizations such as a Research Council, the Leverhulme Trust, and the National Council for Education Technology (NCET), I think it is essential that these grants are held by the institution rather than the individual. This results in some 'distance' between the sponsor and the researcher and allows a degree of independence to be maintained. The researcher must remember that the independence of the organization is often valued by those who commission the research. In the case of our telephone interview project for the National Council for Educational Technology, we were commissioned by two members of NCET who had been responsible for the implementation of the use of information technology in the teaching of English. In this sense, we were engaged in an evaluation of their work. In addition to NCET, they were also our sponsors, yet they made it clear they did not want a simple 'rubber-stamping' job, as they in turn were to be held to account within their organization. They wanted the independence of the university researcher who would examine, evaluate, criticize and disseminate data concerning their world and their work. Researchers engaged in any enquiry of this kind need to consider to whom they are responsible, and in what circumstances.

Secondly, they must establish the extent to which they are responsible; that is, for what they are responsible. This leads us to consider the implications of accountability for researchers and the expectations that different parties bring to any piece of social and educational research. Here it is essential for the researcher to consider the expectations that those who sponsor research have of the investigation, and to make those expectations clear when the research is commissioned. The researcher must explain to others the decisions that have been taken and the actions and activities that matter most in relation to a piece of research. Once the ground rules are established in any investigation, the level of accountability placed by the sponsor on the researcher, by the researcher on the researched, and indeed by the researched upon the researcher, becomes much more clear. However, these negotiated relationships (between researcher and sponsor) are not equal; for example, the researcher may understand the implications of publication better than the sponsor. Meanwhile, the sponsor may provide funds which will allow the researcher to continue to develop a career.

CONCLUSION

Within this chapter I have attempted to outline some issues concerning the accountability of researchers in conducting social and educational research. I am not suggesting that we need yet another code of ethics or statement of ethical principles around which the researcher should operate (e.g. British Sociological Association, 1992; British Educational Research Association, 1992). Instead, I would suggest that we need to consider another dimension to research, namely self-evaluation and self-criticism in relation to our investigations. A checklist of issues is required when considering the establishment of any project:

1. What research questions are to be posed, and in what circumstances?

2. What data are to be collected? What data are to be made public and to whom? In what circumstances?
3. What data are to be analysed and written up?
4. What form will dissemination take?
5. To whom will dissemination occur, and in what circumstances?

Fundamental to these issues is the relationship between researcher and researched, researcher and sponsor, and sponsor, researcher and researched. It is a complex web of interaction in which any researcher is engaged. Alongside this is the question of the accounts that the researcher offers, and the public's right to know. We need to ask ourselves: to whom are we accountable in each of our projects? The answer is far from simple. There are multiple audiences to whom we are related and with whom we need to work in order to sustain the knowledge base of education and the social sciences, while simultaneously influencing the world of policy and practice. A clear research agenda for us all.

REFERENCES

Becher, T. and Eraut, M.R. (1977) *Accountability in the Middle Years of Schooling*. Swindon: SSRC.

Becher, T., Eraut, M. and Knight, J. (1981) *Policies for Educational Accountability*. London: Heinemann.

Becher, T., Eraut, M., Booth, J., Canning, T. and Knight, J. (1979) *Accountability in the Middle Years of Schooling* (Final Report) Swindon: SSRC.

British Educational Research Association (1992) *Ethical Guidelines for Educational Research*. Birmingham: BERA.

British Sociological Association (1992) *Statement of Ethical Principles*. London: BSA.

Burgess, R.G. (ed.) (1984) *The Research Process in Educational Settings: Ten Case Studies*. Lewes: Falmer Press.

Burgess, R.G. (1986) *Sociology, Education and Schools*. London: Batsford.

Burgess, R.G. (1991) Paying the piper and calling the tune. Paper presented at the American Educational Research Association Conference, Chicago, April.

Burgess, R.G., Candappa, M., Galloway, S. and Sanday, A. (1989) *Energy Education and the Curriculum*. Coventry: CEDAR, University of Warwick.

Burgess, R.G., Hockey, J. and Pole, C.J. (1992) *Becoming a Postgraduate Student* (Final Report). Swindon: ESRC.

Burgess, R.G., Hughes, C. and Moxon, S. (1989) *Educating the Under Fives in Salford*. Coventry: CEDAR, University of Warwick.

Burgess, R.G., Phtiaka, H. and Pole, C.J. (1991) *An Evaluation of NCET's Impact on the Use of IT in the Teaching of English*. Report to the National Council for Educational Technology, Coventry.

Kogan, M. (1986) *Educational Accountability: An Analytic Overview*. London: Heinemann.

Stenhouse, L. (1975) *An Introduction to Curriculum Research and Development*. London: Heinemann.

Walford, G. (ed.) (1987) *Doing Sociology of Education*. Lewes: Falmer Press.

Walford, G. (ed.) (1991) *Doing Educational Research*. London: Routledge.

Chapter 11

Accountability and values

Mark Halstead

THE CONCEPT OF ACCOUNTABILITY

Philosophical interest in the concept of accountability is very much alive, not only in relation to education, but in many areas of public service, including the police and medical services. At the heart of any discussion of accountability lie questions about *who* is accountable *to whom, for what, in what manner* and *in what circumstances?* These questions open up what for philosophers are the central issues in educational accountability. For example, where, precisely, is the authority to hold educators to account located? What is the relationship between accountability, the autonomy of teachers and the control of education? Are there degrees of accountability? Should students themselves be held accountable for what they learn or fail to learn (cf. Wagner, 1989, ch. 6)? Do accountability procedures impinge on teachers' rights, or on their professional expertise? What values are presupposed in the desire to make teachers more accountable? How can educators take account of the conflicting wishes and demands of the various parties with a legitimate interest in education in a pluralist society? Is it possible that education has become too accountable, answerable to too wide a spectrum of interest?

Before any of these questions can be seriously discussed, however, it is necessary that we should reflect on the nature of accountability itself and the full range of its implications. The concept of accountability is far from unproblematic. Indeed, it is one of considerable complexity, and much of the confusion in debates about accountability arises from the fact that people often mean different things by the term and therefore talk at cross purposes. Attempts in the 1970s and early 1980s to distinguish between moral and legal accountability, or between professional and contractual accountability, or between 'being called to account' and 'taking account of', did not always bring clarity to the debate. There is still a need to disentangle the various usages of the term and to set them out in such a way that their relationship and overlapping meanings become clear. In the present chapter I intend to examine the basic elements and conditions of accountability, to discuss six forms which it might take in the educational context and to examine the values which lie behind the notion.

Dictionaries (for example the *Concise Oxford*) usually define 'accountability' either in terms of an agent's obligation to 'give an account' of his actions or as 'responsibility'. Neither definition is adequate without qualification. To define accountability in terms of *delivering an account* is inadequate since it is clear that a headmaster who harangues his assembled school with political propaganda for half an hour every morning and is happy to describe or explain his actions to anyone who requires him to do so will not have fulfilled the requirements of accountability. Educational accountability also involves *taking into account* the requirements of the law, the values of the broader society, the guidelines of the local authority, the professional code of conduct, the rights of the parents, the interests of the children and so on. In addition, accountability implies that the educators' account of their actions should (implicitly if not explicitly) be judged to be satisfactory by those who have a legitimate stake in the educational process. Accountability thus inevitably raises questions about who should have a stake in the educational process, and is never far removed from questions about power and control. As Bridges points out,

> an explanation of educational accountability couched simply in terms of a school's concern to communicate what it is doing to an outside audience fails to tell us enough about educational accountability as a political concept located among discussions about the control of education.
>
> (1981, p. 224)

The equation of accountability with responsibility involves different problems, not least that it provides too easy a justification for the claim that teachers should be accountable in the main to their own informed conception of the role of the general educator. Bailey argues that

> the more I am morally responsible or accountable for my own actions, the less it is reasonable to expect me to be responsible or accountable to anyone else in the sense of simply obeying them; though it might indeed be reasonable to expect me to give an account of, explain or justify my actions, if only to show publicly that I am acting in a morally responsible way.
>
> (1983, p. 14)

The trouble with this argument is that 'responsibility' is a much broader concept than 'accountability', and one cannot therefore make distinctions that relate to the former and apply them uncritically to the latter (cf. Gaden, 1990, pp. 28–9). The primary force of the sentence 'Kitty is responsible for her own actions' is that the origin of her actions can be traced back to Kitty herself. This implies (a) that she is capable of rational conduct; and (b) that she is free to choose between courses of action. It may also, but need not, imply that she is liable to be called on to answer for her actions. Accountability, however, means responsibility only in this latter, narrower sense of answerability. But to be answerable implies an audience (whether explicitly referred to or merely understood) in a way which acting in a morally responsible manner does not, and so it is not possible to discuss educational accountability without asking to whom the educator is to be accountable. It may be possible under certain conditions to justify a professional model of accountability which lays stress on the teacher's autonomy, as I shall argue later, but a justification that is based on too broad an understanding of the concept will not do.

An adequate account of educational accountability must therefore steer a middle path between control and autonomy. The autonomy of educators will be

147

tempered by the fact that they are answerable to those they serve, and that those they serve have legitimate expectations and requirements which should be satisifed. On the other hand, the control of education can never be so tight that educators are reduced to the status of conveyer belts carrying precious nuggets from the mines of knowledge to the railway track where rows of empty minds are waiting to be filled. From what has been said so far, it appears that there are six conditions which any case of educational accountability must satisfy:

1. The person who is accountable is the holder of a defined role.
2. The role-holder's accountability relates to actions carried out in connection with the requirements of the role, actions for which the role-holder carries responsibility.
3. The role-holder's accountability is to one or more specific audiences – those who have delegated the responsibilities of his role to him, and/or those who are on the receiving end of his actions.
4. The audience has certain legitimate expectations which the role-holder should take into account, and has grounds for insisting that those expectations be satisfied.
5. The role-holder should be willing to accept that some account, explanation or justification of how the expectations are being satisfied should be prepared if the audience requires it, or at least that evidence should be made available to the audience so that some assessment of how the expectations are being satisfied can be made.
6. Sanctions or other forms of appropriate action (including professional advice, remedial help, further feedback) are available if the account or assessment indicate that the legitimate expectations are not being satisfied. (cf. Whitfield, 1976, p. 6).

Two main types of question emerge from these six conditions. The first concerns who defines the responsibilities of the specific role: it may be the role-holder herself relying on her own professional expertise or acting in conjunction with her professional colleagues; or it may be the audience. If it is the latter, this may refer to those who foot the bill, or to those who receive the service. The second question concerns the level of control implicit in the notion of accountability to a specific audience. Should the role-holder merely be responsive to the expectations and requirements of those she serves, or is she answerable to them in the sense of being legally or morally obliged to demonstrate that she is carrying out their requirements? The way in which educational accountability is understood in practice depends on the answers given to these two questions. Let us look at the two questions in more detail.

Accountability is usually invoked when there are three parties to an agreement rather than just two, i.e. when the role-holder is engaged to provide a service but is paid by someone other than the person who receives the service. In other words, a is paid by b to provide a service for c, and a is accountable to both b and c for providing that service. Thus a bus driver is accountable both to the bus company which hires him and to the passengers he serves, though on some occasions he might allow his own claims to expertise to override the requirements of the other two parties ('I've been driving buses for fifteen years, and I know what I'm doing'). Accountability procedures are less likely to be invoked in a situation where *b* pays for a service which she herself receives from *a*, since the direct control she can exert (for example by refusing to pay for the service) normally obviates the need for a more time-consuming and less clear-cut calling to account. In education, there is some uncertainty about who *b* actually is (the local government, the national government, the taxpayer or the rate-payer), about who *c* actually is (the child, the parent, the local community or society as a whole: cf. Maden, 1990, p. 22) and about the legitimacy of the claims of other groups (employers, unions, universities and so on) to have a say in the process. The situation is further complicated by the fact that parents may well pay for education as taxpayers as well as being on the receiving end as consumers. Nevertheless, the crude distinction between *a* (the educator), *b* (those who employ him) and *c* (those for whom he carries out a service) still has some validity. The question of which of these should have the greatest say in determining the responsibilities of educators lies at the heart of the debate about accountability.

The second question requires a distinction between on the one hand the answerability of educators, their responsibility to demonstrate that they are satisfying the expectations of the audience and that, for example, pupils are in fact learning what they are supposed to learn (which I shall call 'contractual accountability'), and on the other the process of taking into account the requirements of all interested parties when making educational decisions (which I shall call 'responsive accountability'). The former category is exemplified in the question whether we are getting value for money from our educational service, the latter in the question which figured highly in Callaghan's Great Debate launched in 1976, whether education should be more accountable to industry and to society as a whole (see Jonathan, 1989, p. 332). Contractual accountability is primarily concerned with educational outcomes and results, whereas responsive accountability, while not ignoring these, puts more emphasis on educational processes and decision-making. Contractual accountability is directed more towards control (though, as we shall see, self-accounting procedures are an attempt to fulfil the requirements of contractual accountability while playing down the element of control); responsive accountability is directed more towards involvement and interaction between the decision-makers and those whom the decisions affect. In contractual accountability, the requirement for educators to give an account of their actions means no more than that they should give a description of them; in responsive accountability, on the other hand, giving an account of one's actions involves explaining and justifying them.

SIX MODELS OF EDUCATIONAL ACCOUNTABILITY

An analysis which combines the distinction between contractual and responsive accountability with the dominance of one of the three main parties to the accountability process – the employer (i.e. the LEA, the governing body or other employer), the autonomous professional and the consumer – produces six possible models of educational accountability. These are:

1. the Central Control Model (contractual, employer dominant);

1. the Central Control Model (contractual, employer dominant);
2. the Self-Accounting Model (contractual, professional dominant);
3. the Consumerist Model (contractual, consumer dominant);
4. the Chain of Responsibility Model (responsive, employer dominant);
5. the Professional Model (responsive, professional dominant);
6. the Partnership Model (responsive, consumer dominant).

These models are, of course, ideal types, but it is hoped that, in spite of the inevitable oversimplification, a brief examination of each will contribute to our understanding of the nature of accountability.

The Central Control Model lays stress on teachers' status as employees with a contract of employment (at least in some sense), who are under the obligation to demonstrate that they are in fact doing what they are paid to do (see Gibson, 1980). Since 1988, the National Curriculum in Britain has enabled teachers to be more accountable by formalizing and clarifying what they are being paid to do. But the model has a much longer history. Even after payment by results was abandoned, the accountability of educators was for many years judged primarily in terms of their students' success in public examinations. The requirement of the 1980 Education Act that schools should publish a detailed analysis of their examination results for the benefit of prospective parents, and the requirement of the 1988 Education Reform Act that pupils should be tested at the ages of 7, 11, 14 and 16, both reflect this view of accountability. A similar approach has been much in vogue in the USA since the 1960s: educators are accountable to the general public (who pay for the education through taxes) for the achievement of pre-specified objectives by the children they teach, and this achievement is assessed on the basis of the test scores gained by the children. Test results thus loom large in the accountability process, and the question of whether the taxpayer is getting value for money from the educational system can be answered in terms of what results are achieved from what outlay of resources. In performance contracting, the educator agrees to achieve a predetermined level of performance with selected groups of children for a designated sum, and payment may be withheld if student performance fails to reach the agreed standard. The main objections to this approach to accountability have been set out by Sockett (1980, pp. 17–19). A much less crude approach to central control, which takes account of the fact that the success of a school can never more than partly be judged by test or examination results, is seen in the external monitoring of schools carried out by representatives of the teachers' employers (HMI at the national level and LEA advisers or inspectors at the local level – see Nixon and Rudduck, Chapter 8, and Fitz and Lee, Chapter 7 in this volume) or, since the 1992 Education (Schools) Act, by inspection teams led by registered inspectors.

The Self-Accounting Model involves schools and teachers monitoring their own activities in an attempt to satisfy the requirements of contractual accountability while holding on to as much professional autonomy as possible and avoiding increased bureaucratic control of education. The Cambridge Accountability Project (Elliott et al., 1981a, b) was mainly concerned with investigating schools that were committed to the Self-Accounting Model. Both Scrimshaw (1980) and Becher, Eraut and Knight (1981, p. 75ff.) offer a number of arguments in favour of a school offering an account of its activities rather than being called to account by an external body.

Sockett (1982, p. 544), on the other hand, questions whether self-accounting is a credible alternative to the bureaucratic centralism of the first model, since 'accountability without redress is empty'. The Self-Accounting Model may also be open to the criticism that it is dominated by self-interest (cf. Sallis, 1988, p. 11; Ball, 1993, p. 4). Where self-accounting exists, as in the recently developed quality assurance mechanisms in higher education, it is usually subject to some form of external monitoring.

The Consumerist Model, much beloved by the Conservative Party in recent years, introduces the mechanisms of the free market in place of central or professional control as the primary means of enforcing educational accountability (see Kogan, 1986, p. 51ff.). The model is based on the belief that if schools or LEAs no longer have a guaranteed clientele, they will have an incentive to compete which will in turn push up educational standards (cf. Cox and Marks, 1989). The model is exemplified in proposals for a voucher system such as that advocated by Coons and Sugarman (1978) and Seldon (1986), whereby parents' influence on the character of the school would be strengthened by their freedom to spend their vouchers at the school of their choice. Of course, individual parents who are dissatisfied with the educational provision at one school have always had the right to transfer their children to another. The William Tyndale affair, for example, started with a considerable number of parents transferring their children to other schools before the ILEA began to investigate what was going on at the school. But the Consumerist Model goes beyond this in that it involves a radical redistribution of power and authority in educational matters (see Johnson, 1990, ch. 6). The model clearly lies behind the provisions of the 1988 Education Reform Act which allow the governing bodies of schools to opt out of local authority control and give parents greater freedom to send their children to the school of their choice. The 1992 Education (Schools) Act further extends this consumerist philosophy by increasing the information given to parents about schools in an attempt to facilitate the exercise of informed consumer choice, in line with the principles of the *Citizen's Charter*, which had been published a year earlier (Harris, 1992). The ideological underpinnings of the Consumerist Model have been strongly criticized in recent years because of the social and economic inequality it is said to generate (Sallis, 1988, ch. 2; Jonathan, 1989; Edwards and Whitty, 1992; Ball, 1993; Brown, 1994; White, 1994).

The Chain of Responsibility Model (see Figure 11.1) is a form of responsive accountability based on an acknowledgement of the complexity of the relationship between employer, practitioner and client in the field of education, and an acknowledgement that different types of educational decisions may reasonably be considered the domain of different groups. The model has three main features. The first is that an initial distinction is made between those who make educational decisions and those whose wishes, interests, requirements or opinions are merely taken into account by the decision-makers. The second is that the various groups of decision-makers, who consist of different categories of elected representatives and their employees, are ranked in a chain which extends from Parliament and the DES, to local councils and LEAs, to school governors, to headteachers, to senior staff and finally to assistant teachers. School governors, for example, who find themselves in the middle of the chain, have a monitoring role over the individual school's performance, but are themselves accountable for certain duties such as the

151

The chain	responsive to . . .	The interest groups
Parliament/DES	. . .	General public, CBI, TUC, universities, national pressure groups
Local government/LEA	. . .	Rate-payers, local electorate, employees, local industry
Governors	. . .	Parents and local community
Head	. . .	Parents, higher education, colleagues
Senior staff	. . .	Parents, pupils, colleagues, unions, other educational institutions
Assistant teachers	. . .	Parents, pupils, colleagues, unions, other educational institutions

Figure 11.1 The Chain of Responsibility Model.

production of a prospectus and the publication of examination results (Golby, 1992, pp. 166–7). In some respects the relationship between the links in the chain is hierarchical, in that each link can control, to a greater or less extent, the practice of subsequent links, and the autonomy of any given link is subject to the constraints which may be placed upon its freedom of action by the preceding links. However, to describe the relationship as hierarchical or as one of control is to oversimplify it. Maden (1990, p. 23) discusses the *mutual* accountability of schools and LEAs. In any case, the elected representatives are unlikely to act without at least seeking the professional advice of their employees, and those at the teaching end of the chain have a variety of means open to them for diminishing the effectiveness of policies initiated without their approval. These include tacitly ignoring the policy, going through the motions of compliance, campaigning against the policy through their unions, working to rule and so on. The third characteristic feature of the model is that each link in the chain has a special responsibility to particular interest groups. Each link demonstrates its responsiveness to its interest groups in two ways: sounding out opinion and engaging in dialogue on the specific educational decisions for which it has responsibility, and delivering an account of the decisions it has made. One disadvantage of the Chain of Responsibility Model is that it might lead both to a growth of bureaucracy and to power struggles between different links in the chain. An extreme example of such power struggles is the conflict between head and governors at Stratford School in Newham in 1992, where the situation may have been further exacerbated by a general confusion and blurring of lines of accountability in the grant-maintained schools once the LEA link in the chain has been removed. Another disadvantage of this model is the implicit hierarchy of interests which results from the more or less explicit hierarchy of educational decision-making and control. Thus the interests of the parent *qua* parent rank lower than the interests of the parent *qua* rate-payer, and both rank lower than the interests of national industry. An interest group may appeal to a higher link in the chain if it believes the response to its wishes and demands has been unsatisfactory, but has no guarantee of a sympathetic hearing. Sir Keith Joseph, the then Secretary of State for Education, for example, was very responsive to a small number of complaints from parents about peace studies in schools, but refused to get involved in the Honeyford affair.

The Professional Model avoids the problem of a hierarchy of interests by leaving educational decisions (except on matters on which they are contractually accountable) to the judgement of the professional educators – or of the school, though I tend to agree with Sockett (1980, p. 13) that school accountability is reducible to the accountability of the head and other teachers. On this model, which is set out in more detail by Bailey (1980, 1983), professional educators seek to retain control over educational decisions which affect themselves, and see themselves as the arbiter when they are faced with conflicting demands from different interested parties. Their professional status requires them to take account of all the expectations, wishes and criticisms emanating from those with a legitimate interest in the education they are providing, but as they are ultimately responsible for educational practice, so they claim the right to make final judgements and to define the boundaries of their own accountability. This right is based on their professional training and expertise, on the standards they have implicitly committed themselves to when entering the profession, and on the professional autonomy that teachers have traditionally been allowed in this country. The 1988 Education Reform Act introduced one move in the direction of the Professional Model and greater autonomy for schools with the introduction of the local management of schools (LMS), by which part of the LEA budget was transferred directly to the schools (Lawton, 1992, p. 127).

The Partnership Model combines two main principles. The first is that the responsibility for educational decisions should not lie with one dominant group, but with a partnership of all those directly affected by a particular decision or with a legitimate interest in it. One small step in this direction is the requirement in the 1992 Education (Schools) Act that each inspection team must include at least one lay member. The second principle is that all the parties to the partnership are not merely consulted before the decisions are taken, but have a share in the actual decision-making, either directly or through their representatives (the distinction between representation and direct participation, which Pateman (1970) makes much of, is not central to the argument here). There are likely to be three stages in decision-making on this model: (a) the pooling of ideas and the critical discussion of options; (b) 'the negotiation through argument and compromise of whatever can satisfy most people as being the most rational, or, failing that, the most reasonable solution' (Bridges, 1978, p. 118); and (c) the acceptance of the obligation to abide by and help carry through the decisions which have been reached in this democratic manner. This model therefore provides a quite different approach to accountability from the Chain of Responsibility and Professional Models. Each member of the partnership is accountable to the other members in the sense of being under an obligation to take their views and interests into account, but is not accountable to any outside interest group (unless of course a member has been elected as a representative of a broader group, in which case he or she will be answerable to them for the way in which he or she represents their interests).

A major obstacle facing the Partnership Model is the difficulty of gathering all the parties with a legitimate interest into a single manageable committee which can actually make decisions. Usually in practice only some of the main interested parties are brought together on a decision-making body. The Schools Council was one such attempt, but was perhaps too dominated by teachers. Prior to the 1986 Education

153

(No. 2) Act, governing bodies were often dominated by political nominees. The theory behind the encouragement of greater extra-professional participation in educational planning and decision-making is set out in the Taylor Report, to which the roots of the 1986 Act can be traced:

> The Secretaries of State have pointed out that curricula must meet, and be responsive to the needs of society.... If ordinary people do not, as some teachers suggest, understand what schools are trying to do, it is in part because they have traditionally not taken an active part in determining the educational policy of the schools.
>
> (DES, 1977, p. 32)

Elliott (1980, p. 82), however, has argued against the participation of non-professional bodies in final decisions about educational policy, and in any case it has been suggested (Bridges, 1982, p. 14) that many parents do not see PTA committees and parent governors as a genuine vehicle for the expression of their concerns.

EDUCATIONAL ACCOUNTABILITY AND THE HONEYFORD AFFAIR

It may be helpful at this stage to look at a practical example to illustrate the distinctions that have been made. The Honeyford affair (cf. Halstead, 1988) provides probably the most important single case study in educational accountability and control, as Honeyford was called to account both by the LEA and by his parents and local community after the publication of his provocative article 'Education and race – an alternative view' (Honeyford, 1984) and a protracted campaign was launched against him, calling for his dismissal from his post as headteacher in Bradford.

The progressive multi-cultural policies which were being introduced in Bradford in the four years prior to the Honeyford affair provide an archetypal example of the Chain of Responsibility Model. A number of features of the policy make this clear. First, the Council and LEA were attempting to respond to the perceived needs and wishes of the particular interest groups to which they were responsible. The Chairman of the Educational Services Committee at the time said: 'One in six of our children come from Asian families.... It is the simple duty of the Council to try to satisfy their needs' (quoted in *The Times Educational Supplement*, 25 May 1984). Secondly, though they took care to engage in dialogue with the minority communities, the Council and LEA emphasized their own right to interpret and evaluate the requirements of those communities. Thirdly, the Council and LEA drew attention to the fact that they were acting within the guidelines defined by the government or the DES; usually, they claimed to be 'clarifying' or 'interpreting' or 'acting within the spirit of' the 1944 Education Act. Fourthly, the Council and LEA expected subsequent links in the chain of responsibility (that is, heads and teachers) to take account of their guidelines and definitions of good practice and to act in accordance with them.

Honeyford's stance, on the other hand, provides an equally clear example of the Professional Model. Where LEA guidelines were specific, he took these to form part of his contractual obligations and carried them out to the letter. But where LEA guidelines were expressed in general terms as recommendations for good practice, he considered these as advice which he as an autonomous professional could weigh alongside other considerations before making decisions about educational practice within his own school. The high value which Honeyford put on professional autonomy is made clear in his guide for probationary teachers (1982, p. 158) as well as in the reports he prepared for the Schools (Education) Sub-Committee.

The view of accountability which emerges from the protests against Honeyford, however, is much less straightforward. The protest may be divided into three stages. The first stage involved the two logical courses of action open to parents according to the analysis of responsive accountability which has been offered: organizing a protest group, the Drummond Parents' Action Committee (DPAC), to co-ordinate action against Honeyford and to put pressure on the LEA to respond to their demands (in keeping with the Chain of Responsibility Model); and urging the school's parent governor to press the claims of the DPAC on the governing body as a whole (in keeping with the Partnership Model). In the event, the existing parent governor could not handle the demands and resigned, and the election of the DPAC chairperson as the new parent governor by a large majority put her in a strong position to urge both governors and LEA to call Honeyford to account. The LEA's response to this first stage of the protest appeared to miss the point, however; the DPAC were objecting to Honeyford's failure to be responsive to their wishes and needs, but the LEA sent in a team of inspectors to Honeyford's school to check that its educational provision was in line with LEA policies. In other words, complaints about a lack of responsive accountability were being met in terms of the contractual accountability of the Central Control Model.

In the second stage of the protest, the DPAC began to call the LEA to account. They claimed to be supporting LEA policies on race relations, and called on the LEA to take what was in their eyes the necessary step of dismissing a head who was contravening these policies. The Council's response this time was to require Honeyford to prepare six reviews of aspects of his school's provision – a requirement closely in line with the Self-Accounting Model, except that there were still a strong element of central control in the advisers' evaluation of these reports. The main complaints against Honeyford in the second report by the advisers were that he had not changed his attitude in any way and that he was not sufficiently responsive to the requirements of the interest groups that according to the Chain of Responsibility Model were primarily his responsibility – the parents and the local community. As a result of this report he was suspended.

The final stage of the protest, after Honeyford had been reinstated, had much more in common with the Consumerist Model. This stage was marked by direct action aimed at making his school unworkable and thus his departure inevitable. The justification for this action was based on the claim that the parents had the right, as the representatives and trustees of the children at the school, to call a head directly to account themselves. This of course raises the question of whether the wishes and judgements of parents should be paramount in the education of their children, a question which has been much debated in recent years (cf. Coons and Sugarman, 1978; O'Neill and Ruddick, 1979; McLaughlin, 1984; Crittenden, 1988; Tamir, 1990). The mode of Honeyford's actual departure, however, was such that he could claim it was an autonomous decision on his part, in line with the Professional Model; although he was willing and able to carry on as head, he weighed the effect the dispute was having on his wife's health, the morale of the staff and the education of

155

the pupils and decided that the best course of action was to accept early retirement.

The fact that all six models were operating in the Honeyford affair highlights the danger of adopting too simplistic an approach to the concept in any discussion of accountability. It also draws attention to the difficulty of taking account of the conflicting wishes of the various parties with a legitimate interest in education in a pluralist society. A number of crucial questions are involved here. How should educational decisions be reached? How much account should be taken of the wishes of interested parties? Is it in fact possible to take account of conflicting wishes, and, if not, whose interests are to take priority? Are there basic criteria according to which educational problems should be resolved irrespective of the wishes of interested parties? If there are, are teachers in the best position to understand these criteria and should they therefore have the final responsibility for decisions relating to educational policy and practice? The remainder of this chapter briefly examines the kinds of answers provided to these questions by the three models of responsive accountability.

THE PROFESSIONAL MODEL

Accountability according to this model involves professional responsibility, plus a willingness to offer an account of one's actions when this is required of one (for example, by a school's governors). It stresses a relationship of trust between the various parties involved in the educational enterprise, rather than one of compulsion, and stresses the professional judgement of the individual teacher rather than the following of externally imposed rules and guidelines. Bailey (1980) argues that it is based on the principle of teacher autonomy:

> An autonomous teacher does not ignore the wishes and interests of others
> – parents, pupils, governments and employers – but such a teacher does
> reserve the right to consider such wishes and interests in the light of
> appropriate criteria. The wants and wishes cannot simply be taken as
> given starting points. An autonomous teacher does not necessarily refuse
> to submit to the judgment of others, but again such a teacher would need
> to satisfy himself concerning the criteria of judgment and the procedures
> by which he is asked to accept the judgments of others. In particular he
> might consider it proper to be subject in some matters to the judgment of
> his professional associates.
>
> (1980, p. 99)

Bailey offers three main justifications for linking accountability to professional autonomy. First, he argues that accountability necessarily involves autonomy and that accounts of moral and professional action make sense only where the agent is considered to be autonomous (although he points out that autonomy is always a matter of degree: cf. 1980, p. 104; 1983, pp. 11, 15). If the agent is merely responsible to his superiors in the sense of working strictly to their orders, then it is they, not he, who should provide the explanation and justification of his actions. The second argument is a refinement of the assumption held in some quarters that teachers' professional knowledge and expertise justifies them in holding themselves aloof from non-expert interference and criticism, or at least that if their actions are questioned by parents, for example, the appropriate response is for teachers to attempt to 'educate' the parents (see Nias, 1981, p. 202) by patiently explaining what they are seeking to do and why. Bailey (1983, pp. 13–14) argues that teachers' professional expertise consists not in the possession of specialized packages of information and skills but in the capacity to apply broadly generalizable knowledge, skills and attitudes to whatever situations they find themselves in. The capacity to make autonomous decisions is thus a major part of teachers' expertise, and to instil that capacity in their pupils is one of their major goals; but it is because their decisions are autonomous ones that they have a duty to explain them or give an account of them to all interested parties. The third argument is that teachers in fact have to be accountable within considerably diverse contexts, and that the best way to help teachers to fulfil their role satisfactorily in these differing school conditions and arrangements is to encourage them to develop the capacity to reflect critically on the possible ways of applying general educational principles to specific situations and to act on the basis of this rational reflection. Only if teachers are professionally autonomous will there be a system of decision-making flexible enough to take into account the needs of individual children and the requirements of specific contexts: a centrally imposed system could not be sufficiently adaptable.

The first of these arguments is broadly acceptable, so long as it is acknowledged that accountability involves, in addition to autonomy, at least a minimal sense of responding to, or being constrained by the legitimate claims of, interested parties. Indeed, it is this very tension between autonomous action and legitimate constraint that is picked out by the term 'accountability'.

Bailey's second argument, which defines teachers' professional expertise in terms of the ability to make autonomous decisions about what and how to teach children, is more problematic. Clearly teachers cannot exercise their professional autonomy in total isolation and independence from their professional colleagues. But as soon as Bailey concedes that professional autonomy includes 'the right to participate in the formation of policy to be collectively implemented' (1980, p. 107), we are forced to ask why this right to participate is restricted to professional educators. If the parents (or politicians, employers, trade unionists, social workers or other interested parties) share the fundamental knowledge and commitment to autonomy which in Bailey's view form the basis of teachers' professional expertise, on what grounds are they to be excluded from participation in decisions affecting the future generation? Even if parents do not share this knowledge and commitment, to exclude them from the decision-making process has every appearance of oppression and a lack of respect for the rights and opinions of others.

If the second argument relates primarily to questions of practical detail requiring immediate resolution, then few would dispute that these are best dealt with by the person on the spot; and much educational decision-making belongs to this category. But Bailey appears to argue that more fundamental decisions, such as educational aims and priorities, should also be the exclusive domain of the professionally autonomous teacher. This does not mean that the wishes and requirements of interested parties would be ignored, but simply that they would be put through the filter of the teacher's own rationality, expertise and professional judgement. On Bailey's view, the teacher, who has an informed and rational conception of what education is and where it should be leading, fights for education as he sees it and tries to stop it being domesticated to other ends. The resulting decisions and actions would thus inevitably be dependent on the teacher's perception and understanding of the situation. It is clear that if a system of autonomous decision-making by professional teachers is to be found acceptable, there has to be a high level of trust in the teacher's perception and understanding of the situation and an agreement on the basic criteria according to which the autonomous decisions should be made. Significantly, total quality management (TQM) takes as its starting point the same basic agreement on values and a common purpose (Horwitz, 1990, p. 57). Our contemporary multi-cultural context underlines the difficulties in achieving either of these conditions. Teachers' perceptions, preconceptions and tacit cultural assumptions are no longer universally shared (if they were ever), and teachers themselves are in any case notoriously divided on many issues, including the aims of education. It is doubtful if there is sufficient agreement on the values which are basic to our shared form of life to provide a framework of basic educational criteria.

Teachers can count on public and parental support most readily when they are perceived to be doing their best to achieve educational goals which are shared by all interested parties. Such trust is clearly much more readily achieved in a mono-cultural than in a multi-cultural context. Nias comes to more or less the same conclusion when she argues that trust, at least in an educational context, involves (a) predictability of personal and institutional behaviour; and (b) agreement on ends (1981, p. 211ff.). Where these two conditions prevail, parents and the general public appear happy to leave educational decision-making to the autonomous professional, confident 'that the school was doing what they would broadly wish it to do and that it could apparently be trusted to get on with the job' (Bridges, 1982, p. 14). In the absense of such predictability and agreement, however, the claim of teachers to professional autonomy is likely to be seen as a barrier to, rather than as a way of facilitating, accountability. A common educational system in a pluralist context is bound to produce conflict over the aims of the education provided, and thus over educational practice, and there will be increasing dissatisfaction with the policy of leaving the decisions to the teachers.

To sum up, it seems almost impossible to have (a) the professional autonomy of teachers; (b) the common school; and (c) a pluralist society at the same time: any two of these conditions precludes the third. Perhaps (a) and (b) are compatible only in a homogeneous, mono-cultural society where there is a broadly shared framework of educational assumptions; they are likely thus to be able to continue in those parts of the UK which have so far been untouched by cultural and ethnic diversity; while (a) and (c) can exist together only when two conditions prevail: first, that 'virtually everyone in the school knows what [its educational] assumptions are before joining it and has some fair measure of sympathy with them' (Scrimshaw, 1980, p. 52ff.); and secondly, that parents have some measure of free choice between schools so that they can in fact find a school with whose goals they are in sympathy (Almond, 1994). Although parental choice has become a slogan of Conservative educational policy in recent years, it seems likely that there are still many minority groups in the UK which do not yet have the freedom to choose a school for their children that is in harmony with their own educational beliefs and values. Whether this forms an argument for the establishment of Muslim voluntary-aided schools is a matter for debate. If (b) and (c) are to be combined, however, Nias (1981) suggests that the professional autonomy of teachers will have to be tempered with what she calls 'formal procedures' of accountability, by which she appears to mean forms of organization that structuralize relationships, responsibilities and roles within the school and that make explicit the criteria according to which decisions are made. This is because in a pluralist society, groups such as Muslims are likely not to share all the tacit assumptions or stated educational goals of the common school, and therefore parental rights may be invoked which are ignored when there is a consensus of values, and teachers' actions are likely to come under much closer scrutiny. 'Formal procedures' may well involve increased central control, but may also open up greater participation in decision-making by all the parties involved. The Chain of Responsibility Model is an approach to accountability which takes account of the need for 'formal procedures' and which perhaps has more potential for coping with the fundamentally conflicting educational values, goals and assumptions held by different groups in our society than does the Professional Model. Indeed, in so far as he acknowledges the need for 'a structural framework for policy-forming discussion', Bailey (1980, p. 107) concedes the existence of constraints on teachers' professional autonomy.

THE CHAIN OF RESPONSIBILITY MODEL

Two main arguments can be marshalled in support of the Chain of Responsibility Model of accountability. The first is that it is a workable and bureaucratically efficient model which succeeds in balancing the rival claims of a number of different parties with an interest in educational decision-making. Of all the models under discussion, it comes the nearest to current practice in the UK. It seeks to maximize efficiency by opting for central planning where this would avoid overlapping or duplication in educational decision-making (the National Curriculum is an example of this), but a balance is sought between public, national interests and the interests of the individual. There are clear-cut channels for parents and other interested parties to make their influence felt. It even allows for a certain amount of jockeying for position among the various groups, for example between headteacher and governors or between LEA and DES. The state in fact has some trump cards; it has the financial clout, for example, to impose some decisions (such as the introduction of TVEI, Technical and Vocational Education Initiative) which have been reached with the minimum of consultation. However, teachers can sometimes command a virtual veto of some state policies by refusing to co-operate in their implementation; the boycott of testing of 14-year-olds in 1993 illustrates this. The Chain of Responsibility Model thus allows both for centralizing tendencies and for the inevitable opposition to them.

The second main argument in support of the Chain of Responsibility Model is that there is greater legitimation for the decisions being made since they are made not by autonomous professionals but by democratically elected representatives (MPs, local councillors, some governors) or by their employees who are directly answerable to them. Bridges (1979, p. 161ff.) and White (1980, p. 27ff.) take this point further and argue that decisions about what to teach in school are dependent on conceptions of the good life and the good society, and that teachers cannot claim any special expertise which would justify leaving such decisions in their hands. The Chain of

Responsibility Model seems to be capable of taking into account a wider variety of conceptions of the good life and is more amenable to the principles of distributive justice and to the values of our contemporary pluralist society than the Professional Model.

Some of the disadvantages of the Chain of Responsibility Model have already been mentioned: its tendency to encourage bureaucracy and to increase power struggles between groups and the implicit hierarchy of interests which it entails. The argument that greater legitimation is given to the educational decisions according to this model because some of those making the decisions have been elected democratically depends on one's understanding of representation. On one view, representatives are elected to carry out the wishes of the electorate; but in practice there is rarely, if ever, any clear electoral mandate on education matters from the electorate as a whole. As Becher, Eraut and Knight point out,

> It is seldom given to education ministers to be able to quote the backing of electoral authority for what they do, because education rarely – perhaps more rarely than other areas of government – gives rise to any clear mandate for reform.
>
> (1981, p. 151)

On another view, representatives are elected, not to carry out the specific wishes of the electorate, but because they broadly share the same framework of values and can therefore be trusted on the whole to make decisions that are in the best interests of those they represent. But the particular form that parliamentary democracy takes in the UK currently ensures that no one is elected to Parliament who shares the framework of values of the country's one million Muslims. This does not mean that their interests are not represented in the sense of being taken into account in the decision-making process at the national level; but it does mean that the terms of reference by which those interests are expressed and judged are defined by people who do not share their framework of values and who may indeed hold incompatible beliefs and assumptions. The problem is that the agreement of the majority is all that is needed to make the Chain of Responsibility Model workable, but in a pluralist context, simple majoritarianism is likely to leave some minority groups dissatisfied and anxious to opt out of the current system. No doubt the establishment of the Muslim Parliament of Great Britain in January 1992 arose precisely out of this dissatisfaction (see Modood, 1993). One solution to the problem of the apparent oppression of minority groups would appear to be to encourage greater participation in actual decision-making by all the parties affected by the decisions, as allowed for in the Partnership Model.

THE PARTNERSHIP MODEL

The arguments in support of the Partnership Model fall into two main sections: those relating to the rights of individuals to protect their own interests, and those relating to the intrinsic value of collective decision-making. The first set of arguments sees the primary aim of the partnership as giving an interested party, either individually or in alliance with others, the opportunity to protect or defend his own interests, values, wishes and points of view against competing claims which are put forward by others. Mill justifies democracy in such terms:

> The rights and interests of every or any person are only secure from being disregarded when the person interested is himself able, and habitually disposed, to stand up for them . . . . Human beings are only secure from evil at the hands of others in proportion as they have the power of being, and are, self-protecting.
>
> (1972, p. 186)

Free and fair discussion between the partners would give each the chance to put forward his case and would set in motion negotiations about the best way to accommodate the different interests. The final decision would ideally represent some kind of balance of individual interests, settled amicably if possible by mutual consent after free and open discussion, but settled by a vote if disagreements remain too strong to do otherwise. This argument is clearly based on the fundamental liberal values of justice, equality and rationality. The second set of arguments have been developed recently by Bridges (1979), White (1987) and Haydon (1987), who emphasize the value of the democratic process *per se*, according to which all interested parties have a share in the actual decision-making. Drawing heavily on Mill (1972), Bridges argues that co-operation in a common cause is a value in itself (1980, p. 67) and that participatory democracy enhances the quality of life (1979, p. 164) both for the community as a whole and for the individual participants (1978, pp. 118–21).

There are a number of practical difficulties with this Partnership Model, however: how to decide whose interests in educational decision-making are legitimate; how to balance the partnership between numerically uneven parties such as parents, teachers, the general public, LEAs and industry; how to justify the extensive demands participation makes on the time, effort and commitment of those involved; how to avoid conflict and divisiveness as groups realize that their chances of gaining concessions increase with the intensity of feeling with which they express their views; and how to ensure that the decisions reached through democratic participation are actually good ones. There is a danger that democratic participation may become more of a power struggle between rival factions than an impartial way of resolving disagreements in a spirit of co-operation. Dunlop (1979, p. 48) juxtaposes a different type of co-operation in which identity with the community is achieved through the sharing of customs, traditions, values and tacit assumptions, and sees this identity with the community as taking the sting out of any disagreements that might arise and enabling a common mind to emerge. Within a homogeneous, mono-cultural society, such a spirit of co-operation is quite compatible with the autonomy associated with the Professional Model. In a multi-cultural society, however, it is only likely to be achieved within separate cultural groups, or else under a system whereby parents are genuinely free to choose schools which share their own fundamental values and beliefs. Again, this raises the question of the establishment of separate Muslim voluntary-aided schools.

Bonnett (1979, p. 166) reminds us that there is a danger in what I have called the Partnership Model of losing sight of the fact that there are objective criteria that provide 'a firm and limiting framework' within which democratic decisions can be made. He points out that 'consistency with the values upon which the idea of democracy rests would seem to demand set limits upon the content' of decisions reached by participatory democracy. If Parliament were to push through a law requiring boys to have two years' more compulsory schooling than girls, this would be unjust whatever democratic procedures were involved in passing the legislation. It would be unjust because it did not meet certain criteria of justice, and these criteria of justice are a matter of rational appraisal rather than democratic decision (cf. Gutmann, 1980, p. 176). A corollary of this (and here I am extending Bonnett's argument) is that a dissenting minority need not consider itself bound by a democratic decision unless that decision satisfies such objective criteria as the demands of justice; otherwise, as Bridges, (1980, p. 69) concedes, corporate decision-making would be oppressive of individual freedom and smack of totalitarianism. This highlights the need, before democratic decision-making can even start, to endeavour to establish the criteria according to which those decisions can be made, criteria which are consistent with our fundamental shared beliefs and values. Bonnett goes on to suggest that establishing such criteria might resolve most of the fundamental problems about educational provision, 'such that matters remaining to be resolved are predominantly technical and therefore more appropriately the domain of relevant experts'. If this is so it will be necessary, before any decisions can be made about educational provision for minority groups in our society, to establish the criteria (such as the rights of parents and the rights of minorities) by which those decisions will be made, and to set out the fundamental values (such as freedom, equality and justice) according to which those criteria are established.

CONCLUSION

All this, however, presupposes the acceptance of a basic liberal framework of values (see Whitfield, 1976, pp. 24–5). Indeed, liberal values are the only thing which the three models of responsive accountability examined in the present chapter have in common. The Professional Model lays particular stress on autonomy, the Chain of Responsibility Model on distributive justice, and the Partnership Model on democratic participation. But these values are far from being generally accepted by the Muslim community, for example. The question therefore arises whether liberal values can actually provide a framework within which the question of educational provision for minorities can be resolved to the satisfaction of the minorities themselves. The arguments of the present chapter have suggested, somewhat pessimistically, that all forms of responsive accountability work best in situations where such accountability is least likely to be called for; that is, in situations of trust where there is broad agreement on fundamental values. What is perhaps needed most urgently now is research to explore whether there is in fact a sufficient basis of shared values to enable all the world views represented within our culturally diverse society to work together within a common educational system.

NOTE

I am grateful to Falmer Press for permission to draw substantially on the first part of Chapter 7 of my book *Education, Justice and Cultural Diversity* (1988) in the preparation of this chapter.

REFERENCES

Almond, B. (1994) In defence of choice in Education. In Halstead, J.M. (ed.) *Parental Choice and Education*. London: Kogan Page.

Bailey, C. (1980) The autonomous teacher. In Sockett, H. (ed.) *Accountability in the English Educational System*. Sevenoaks: Hodder & Stoughton.

Bailey, C. (1983) Education, accountability and the preparation of teachers. *Cambridge Journal of Education* 13 (2), 10–19.

Ball, S. (1993) Education markets, choice and social class: the market as a class strategy in the UK and the USA. *British Journal of Sociology of Education* 14 (1), 3–19.

Becher, A., Eraut, M. and Knight, J. (1981) *Policies for Educational Accountability*. London: Heinemann.

Bonnett, M. (1979) Reply to David Bridges. *Journal of Philosophy of Education* 13 (2), 165–8.

Bridges, D. (1978) Participation and political education. *Cambridge Journal of Education* 8 (2–3), 117–30.

Bridges, D. (1979) Some reasons why curriculum planning should not be 'left to the experts'. *Journal of Philosophy of Education* 13 (2), 159–64.

Bridges, D. (1980) Accountability and the politics of the staffroom. In Sockett, H. (ed.) *Accountability in the English Educational System*. Sevenoaks: Hodder & Stoughton.

Bridges, D. (1981) Accountability, communication and control. In Elliott, J., Bridges, D., Ebbutt, D., Gibson, R. and Nias, J. (eds.) *School Accountability: The SSRC Accountability Project*. London: Grant McIntyre.

Bridges, D. (1982) Accountability and schools. *Where*, July/August, 12–14.

Brown, P. (1994) Education and the ideology of parentocracy. In Halstead, J.M. (ed.) *Parental Choice and Education*. London: Kogan Page.

Coons, J.E. and Sugarman, S.D. (1978) *Education by Choice: The Case for Family Control*. Berkeley: University of California Press.

Cox, C. and Marks, J. (1989) *The Insolence of Office*. London: Claridge Press.

Crittenden, B. (1988) *Parents, the State and the Right to Educate*. Carlton, Victoria: Melbourne University Press.

Department of Education and Science (DES) (1977) *A New Partnership for Our Schools* (The Taylor Report). London: HMSO.

Dunlop, F. (1979) On the democratic organisation of schools. *Cambridge Journal of Education* 9 (1), 43–54.

Edwards, A. and Whitty, G. (1992) Parental choice and educational reform in Britain and the United States. *British Journal of Educational Studies* 40 (2), 101–17.

Elliott, J. (1980) Who should monitor performance in schools? In Sockett, H. (ed.) *Accountability in the English Educational System*. Sevenoaks: Hodder & Stoughton.

Elliott, J., Bridges, D., Ebbutt, D., Gibson, R. and Nias, J. (1981a) *School Accountability: The SSRC Accountability Project.* London: Grant McIntyre.

Elliott, J., Bridges, D., Ebbutt, D., Gibson, R. and Nias, J. (1981b) *Case Studies in School Accountability,* Vols I, II and III. Cambridge: Institute of Education.

Gaden, G. (1990) Rehabilitating responsibility. *Journal of Philosophy of Education* 24 (1), 27–38.

Gibson, R. (1980) Teachers as employees. In Sockett, H. (ed.) *Accountability in the English Educational System.* Sevenoaks: Hodder & Stoughton.

Golby, M. (1992) School governors: conceptual and practical problems. *Journal of Philosophy of Education* 26 (2), 165–72.

Gutmann, A. (1980) *Liberal Equality.* Cambridge: Cambridge University Press.

Halstead, J.M. (1988) *Education, Justice and Cultural Diversity: An Examination of the Honeyford Affair, 1984–85.* London: Falmer Press.

Harris, N.S. (1992) Quality control and accountability to the consumer: an evaluation of the Education (Schools) Act 1992. *Education and the Law* 4 (3), 109–21.

Haydon, G. (1987) Towards a framework of commonly accepted values. In Haydon, G. (ed.) *Education for a Pluralist Society: Philosophical Perspectives on the Swann Report* (Bedford Way Paper 30). London: University of London Institute of Education.

Honeyford, R. (1982) *Starting Teaching.* London: Croom Helm.

Honeyford, R. (1984) Education and race – an alternative view. *Salisbury Review* 6, Winter, 30–2.

Horwitz, C. (1990) Total quality management: an approach for education. *Educational Management and Administration* 18 (2), 55–8.

Johnson, D. (1990) *Parental Choice in Education.* London: Unwin Hyman.

Jonathan, R. (1989) Choice and control in education: parental rights, individual liberties and social justice. *British Journal of Educational Studies* 37, (4), 321–38.

Kogan, M. (1986) *Educational Accountability: An Analytical Overview.* London: Hutchinson.

Lawton, D. (1992) *Education and Politics in the 1990s: Conflict or Consensus?* London: Falmer Press.

McLaughlin, T.H. (1984) Parental rights and the religious upbringing of children. *Journal of Philosophy of Education* 18 (1), 75–83.

Maden, M. (1990) Quality, accountability and the LEA. *Educational Management and Administration* 18 (2), 21–6.

Mill, J.S. (1972) *Considerations on Representative Government* (1861). London: Dent.

Modood, T. (1993) Muslim views on religious identity and racial equality. *New Community* 19 (3), 513–19.

Nias, J. (1981) The nature of trust. In Elliott, J. *et al.* (eds) *School Accountability: The SSRC Accountability Project.* London: Grant McIntyre.

O'Neill, O. and Ruddick, W. (eds) (1979) *Having Children: Philosophical and Legal Reflections on Parenthood.* New York: Oxford University Press.

Pateman, C. (1970) *Participation and Democratic Theory.* Cambridge: Cambridge University Press.

Sallis, J. (1988) *Schools, Parents and Governors: A New Approach to Accountability.* London: Routledge.

Scrimshaw, P. (1980) Making schools responsible. In Sockett, H. (ed.) *Accountability in the English Educational System*. London: Hodder & Stoughton.

Seldon, A. (1986) *The Riddle of the Voucher*. London: Institute of Economic Affairs.

Sockett, H. (1980) Accountability: the contemporary issues. In Sockett, H. (ed.) *Accountability in the English Educational System*. London: Hodder & Stoughton.

Sockett, H. (1982) Accountability. In Cohen, L., Thomas, J. and Marian, L. (eds) *Educational Research and Development in Britain 1979–1980*. Windsor: NFER–Nelson.

Tamir, Y. (1990) Whose education is it anyway? *Journal of Philosophy of Education* 24 (2), 161–70.

Wagner, R.B. (1989) *Accountability in Education: A Philosophical Enquiry*. New York: Routledge.

White, J. (1980) Should schools determine their own curricula? In Sockett, H. (ed.) *Accountability in the English Educational System*. London: Hodder & Stoughton.

White, J. (1987) The quest for common values. In Haydon, G. (ed.) *Education for a Pluralist Society: Philosophical Perspectives on the Swann Report* (Bedford Way Paper 30). London: University of London Institute of Education.

White, P. (1994) Parental choice and education for citizenship. In Halstead, J.M. (ed.) *Parental Choice and Education*. London: Kogan Page.

Whitfield, R.C. (1976) *Curriculum Planning, Teaching and Educational Accountability*. Birmingham: University of Aston.

Chapter 12

Afterword

David Scott

Three questions were asked in the Introduction to this book: Who are the appropriate partners in accountability relationships? How should the one exercise control over the other? How do the various accountability models operate in practice? Contributors have discussed and debated answers to these questions, paying particular attention to recent legislation in the United Kingdom such as the 1988 Education Reform Act. In doing this, they have sought to understand how policy processes work and to develop models to account for their empirical observations. In some cases, this has meant making refinements to existing theories and conceptual frameworks. Thus Walford in Chapter 6 shows how market and consumerist accountability models, which understand the parent as a consumer who chooses between schools in terms of published examination and Key Stage test results, are flawed. Again, Scott in Chapter 4 provides evidence to show that state control models of curriculum change, which suggest either that the policy flow from centre to periphery is unimpeded and uncontested, or that, in the last resort, the central authority always has control of sufficient resources to achieve its ends, need further refinement.

Authors have also pointed to significant tensions in the arrangements made as a result of the Act, and subsequent legislation. Deem in Chapter 5, for example, identifies two school governor ideologies, though she is careful not to tie them to specific types of individual. In so far as governing bodies are able to exert an influence over the way schools organize teaching and learning experiences for pupils, they are now more likely to do so with regard to that one school and not the system as a whole. Collective concern ideologies are in part being replaced by consumer interest ideologies. Two consequences follow: the system is more competitive and there is less equality of the different parts. This tension, it should be said, operates at individual and systemic levels.

Another example chronicled in this book is the evolving arrangements for assessing the National Curriculum. Two contrasting assessment agendas were identified, the one emphasizing contextualized, positive and non-competitive means for collecting data about pupils, the other stressing decontextualized, formal and standardized methods to allow comparisons to be made between schools and pupils. Scott in Chapter 4 shows that, even with the latest suggestions for assessment arrangements in the National Curriculum (Dearing, 1993), the latter is still in the ascendancy.

A further source of tension, identified by Nixon and Rudduck in Chapter 8, focuses on the question of whether inspection should operate with implicit or explicit criteria. They suggest that there are dangers in relying too much on the latter, because to undervalue or circumscribe the tacit and inferential element in the judgements made by inspectors is to weaken and in some cases damage the whole process of inspection. This tension between implicit and explicit criteria for judgement points to the central dilemma in accountability relationships, which is that data collected about schools and education systems can be useful only if they accurately represent how schools and systems actually function. The text, whether an OFSTED inspector's report, a league table of examination results or an academic researcher's account of education processes, needs to be interrogated, as well as taken account of, if genuine improvements are to be made to schools and systems. In this context, this Afterword will examine four methods for collecting data about schools, which result in texts and which are central to accounting processes.

The first method concerns the new arrangements for inspecting schools, which combine elements of previous HMI and LEA practice. Under OFSTED control, inspectors visit the school to be inspected and collect data over a relatively short period of time. A report is then compiled and the governors are required to draw up an action plan, though it is as yet unclear who has responsibility for implementing it. The procedure is hierarchical – in the first instance the report is presented to the school's senior management team – and distrustful of professional manipulation – the registered inspector, her deputy and the lay member of the team meet with parents. The headteacher and his or her staff are allowed to attend only if they have a child at the school.

The model departs from previous inspection models in three highly significant ways: first, criteria for judging organizational, curricular and pedagogic arrangements in schools have been made more explicit (OFSTED, 1993). Second, inspection now occurs at more regular moments in the lifetimes of schools. Third, data will be collected from a wider range of sources, with parental views and opinions given greater prominence. What is proposed here has elements both of state control models of accountability – clearer and more obvious lines of control with explicit descriptions of the type of data to be collected, and thus of appropriate ways for a school to organize itself – and of consumerist models – data are collected from parents. The intention is to make schools more responsive, the calculation being that parents will wish to see the school operate in ways with which they are familiar. The impulsion here is towards tradition, order, differentiation and control.

A number of problems present themselves with this model of inspection. First, the data that the team gathers will be highly selective (even if criteria for that selection are set out beforehand), and more importantly, the data will be open to deliberate manipulation by teachers and governors within the school. HMI inspectors have always accepted that, as inspectors, they are positioned both within their own frameworks of beliefs, norms and values, and within a situation to which they can gain only partial access. This is acknowledged by Sheila Browne, herself an ex-inspector, when she accepts that: 'HMIs have always to remember that their selective observation can never match the collective knowledge of the Head and teachers' (Browne, 1979, p. 37). Second, the data will inevitably be restricted since the collection period is short, so conclusions reached are more likely to be framed within those inspectors' understandings of how this particular type of school and schools in

167

general operate. Third, data collected from parents will be given a high priority, even though they are likely to be anecdotal and fragmentary. Fourth, inspection which operates with explicit and normative pedagogic and organizational models is less responsive to local ways of organizing teaching and learning experiences. Finally, the production of the report excludes significant amendments being made on the basis of representations by the headteacher and staff in that school:

> Where there are serious errors of factual accuracy which have a significant bearing on the findings of the inspector, inspectors will reconsider the relevant judgements. In other cases there can be no modification of the judgements to be included in the report.
>
> (OFSTED, 1993, p. 12)

In practice, this may be interpreted loosely, but it does suggest that the evaluation style is likely to be more autocratic than democratic (Macdonald, 1974).

Consumerist accountability models, on the other hand, work by positioning schools in the market-place, with improvement driven by comparison between schools and action taken by parents as a result. This may take two forms. First, there is exit (Hirschman, 1970), in which the consumer withdraws from the exchange; the child is moved from one school to another. Second, there is voice (Hirschman, 1970), in which the parents allow their child to remain at the school, but by various means seek to influence and improve the educational provision offered to the child. In order for the parents to make judgements between schools, to exercise either voice or exit, there must be some form of credible currency by which they can make those judgements. Three models have been suggested, though proponents of the third may reject market models of school improvement. The first proposes publication of 'raw' data about students and schools in alphabetically arranged or league tables. The second proposes a modified version of this with those data adjusted to take account of socio-economic factors because this is considered to be a fairer way of judging school effectiveness. The third proposal is to use these techniques to identify those factors which relate to good schools, and then to persuade schools to follow these models of good practice.

The arguments against publication of 'raw' examination or Key Stage results have been well rehearsed (see Goldstein, 1990). Unadjusted test results tell us something about the performance of students, but little about the effectiveness of the teaching and learning programmes in each school. Furthermore, care needs to be taken that any performance measures do in fact show what they purport to. Wood (1987), for instance, suggests that for each student there is a broad theoretical notion of capability. He goes on to argue that there is always a gap between this theoretical capability and its description by the use of testing devices. Wood and Power (1987) provide examples of that gap. They distinguish between false negative and false positive experiences of assessing performances. In the former, owing to anxiety, nerves and a host of other reasons, students do not perform as well as they can. In the latter, the test records high success at a specific task, and yet in reality the student is not able to perform in this way. GCSE coursework arrangements, and the arrangements for their assessment, are clearly attempts at closing this gap. If unadjusted data are used it is difficult to make proper comparisons between schools in terms of their effectiveness.

Various value-added approaches have been developed (Goldstein, 1987). Academic researchers working in the school effectiveness field (Mortimore *et al.*, 1988; Smith and Tomlinson, 1989; Rutter *et al.*, 1979; Sanday, 1990) argue that schools can and do make a difference, so it is important to look at improvements pupils in a particular school make between entry and some fixed point (school-leaving age in the case of secondary schools). The difficulty is to judge how much differences in performance between schools are due to teaching and learning programmes and how much to factors outside the school. Multi-level data analysis (Goldstein, 1987) enables researchers to make allowance for these social factors, so in effect like student is being compared with like student, and here some measure of pupil progress can be abstracted free from socio-economic variables.

But these socio-economic variables have differential impacts on individual student performances and cannot be treated as equally influential measures, as school effectiveness researchers are bound to treat them. Value-added data reflect performance between two set points in time (entering and leaving school, for example). Some of those socio-economic factors (lack of space to do homework; lack of parental support) impact upon performance after they have been taken into account at the point of entry. Furthermore, they are influential in different ways and to different degrees before and after entry to secondary school. Thus value-added measures, though much better descriptors of school effectiveness, are still problematic.

There are also basic problems with displaying such results in league or alphabetically arranged tables. Quite small adjustments in criteria for ranking them could result in large changes to the ranking order (Goldstein, 1990). Furthermore, as Gipps suggests, league tables produce 'a top and a bottom, with little indication of what these mean in terms of performance' (1990, p. 60). Value-added approaches control for differences of intake, mainly ability and socio-economic factors. Goldstein and Woodhouse (1988) have demonstrated the weakness of comparing aggregate examination scores with aggregate test scores at entry as a statistical procedure. They suggest that aggregation between the two should occur at the individual-pupil level, but this is expensive and difficult. There is a more general problem with aggregating at any level, which is that you lose meaning about specific areas. English departmental examination results may be good, but do not show up if the whole school is being judged using aggregated data.

Two types of factor (those which are 'internal' and those which are 'external' to the school) which impact upon performance have been identified, and it has been suggested how difficult it is to separate the one from the other, even using complicated statistical techniques. However, it is generally believed that schools do make a difference. Rutter *et al.* (1979) argued that the best schools had four times as many examination successes as the worst. Mortimore *et al.* (1988) attributed 9 per cent of differences in reading progress and 11 per cent of progress in mathematics to school processes. Smith and Tomlinson (1989, p. 163) have maintained that: 'in fact, if schools were improved only within the current range of performance of urban comprehensive schools, this would be enough to transform the standards of secondary schools'. Research of this sort can be put to use in a number of ways.

169

Proponents of market accountability models argue that even the creation of a limited market will unleash entrepreneurial talents, improve teacher productivity and creativity, and contribute to improved standards. But such research can also be used to produce models which can then contribute to the stock of knowledge that schools have about effective practice.

Mortimore *et al.* (1988), for instance, argued that schools which performed the best according to analysis of test data adjusted for socio-economic factors had twelve distinguishing features: purposeful leadership of the staff by the headteacher; involvement by the deputy head; involvement in the running of the school by teachers; a consistent approach; structured teaching sessions; intellectually challenging teaching; the creation of a work-centred environment; a limited focus within teaching sessions; maximum communication between teachers and pupils; effective record-keeping; parental involvement; and the creation of a positive climate for teachers and pupils.

A number of problems with this approach have been suggested. First, it is difficult to identify appropriate measures by which classrooms and schools can be compared. Even if there is a wide range of ability in any particular classroom, this does not necessarily mean that the method of instruction is mixed ability. Again, behaviour measures are problematic because good and bad behaviour are always contextualized. Second, it is difficult to know whether such factors are necessary or sufficient. Sanday (1990) asks three questions about Mortimore *et al.*'s (1988) first feature: does an effective school have to have purposeful leadership by the head? Can a school function effectively without such leadership? Even if the head does show purposeful leadership, could the school still be ineffective? Third, as was suggested above, as soon as you aggregate anything you lose information and detail. Fourth, such an approach assumes a divide between means and ends, those ends having been determined by research. Teachers are then characterized merely as technicians. This is opposed to the Aristotelian notion of teaching as a moral and deliberative activity. Fifth, this approach operates with the assumption that notions of school effectiveness are unproblematic, whereas in fact they are not, and cannot be, ideologically neutral, so they always assume particular views of teaching, learning and child development. Finally, there are problems with linking these findings to the improvement of schools. Rudduck argues that 'we are beginning to see change not simply as a technical problem but as the creation of shared meanings' (1992, p. 38). Technicist approaches to change in schools limit and circumscribe the degree and level of involvement and ownership by teachers in that process of change.

Other contributors to this book have examined different texts. Sealey in Chapter 9 interrogates media representations of educational processes. Burgess in Chapter 10 looks closely at the ethical and political problems of producing 'academic' texts. By examining the way these texts are produced, we can begin the process of understanding how accountability relationships work, and how the various models can be distinguished. So, for example, proponents of self-evaluating models of accountability produce texts to satisfy different audiences and to create effects different from those produced by the media. Government education reforms over the last decade and a half have allowed researchers and practitioners to examine these different models, in particular those which emphasize the importance of market mechanisms. The different accounts presented here are the consequences of that deliberation and research.

REFERENCES

Browne, S. (1979) The accountability of HM Inspectorate. In Lello, J. (ed.) *Accountability in Education*. London: Ward Lock.

Dearing, R. (1993) *The National Curriculum and Its Assessment*. London and York: SEAC and NCC.

Gipps, C. (1990) *Assessment: A Teachers' Guide to the Issues*. Sevenoaks: Hodder & Stoughton.

Goldstein, H. (1987) *Multilevel Models in Education and Social Research*. Oxford: Clarendon Press.

Goldstein, H. (1990) The fundamental assumptions of national assessment. In Dowling, P. and Noss, R. (eds) *Mathematics versus the National Curriculum*. Lewes: Falmer Press.

Goldstein, H. and Woodhouse, G. (1988) Education performance indicators and LEA league tables. *Oxford Review of Education* 14 (3), 301–17.

Hirschman, A.O. (1970) *Exit, Voice and Loyalty: Response to Decline in Firms, Organizations and States*. Cambridge, MA: Harvard University Press.

Macdonald, B. (1974) Evaluation and the control of education. In Macdonald, B. and Walker, R. (eds) *SAFARI: Innovation, Evaluation, Research and the Problem of Control*. Norwich: University of East Anglia Centre for Applied Research in Education.

Mortimore, P., Sammons, P., Stoll, L., Lewis, D. and Ecob, R. (1988) *School Matters*. London: Open Books.

Office for Standards in Education (OFSTED) (1993) *Handbook for the Inspection of Schools*. London: HMSO.

Rudduck, J. (1992) *Innovation and Change*. Milton Keynes: Open University Press.

Rutter, M., Maughan, B., Mortimore, P. and Ouston, J. (1979) *Fifteen Thousand Hours*. London: Open Books.

Sanday, A. (1990) *Making Schools More Effective* (CEDAR Papers 2). Centre for Educational Development, Appraisal and Research, University of Warwick.

Smith, D. and Tomlinson, S. (1989) *The School Effect: A Study of Multiracial Comprehensives*. London: Policy Studies Institute.

Wood, R. (1987) *Measurement and Assessment in Education and Psychology*. Lewes: Falmer Press.

Wood, R. and Power, C. (1987) Aspects of the competence–performance distinction: educational, psychological and measurement issues. *Journal of Curriculum Studies* 19 (5), 409–24.

Name Index

Abbot, D.M. 88, 103
Adler, M. 74, 75, 80, 81, 85
Ahier, J. 29
Alexander, R. 3–4, 6, 100
Alexander, Sir W. 9
Allen, D. 125, 135
Almond, B. 158, 163
Alston, C. 81, 85
Apple, M.W. 43, 44, 45, 56
Arnold, Matthew 90, 124, 125

Bailey, C. 147, 153, 156, 157, 159, 163
Baker, Kenneth 22, 24, 28, 121, 124
Ball, S.J. 35, 39, 42, 44, 56, 61, 62, 65, 71, 82, 85,
    88, 91, 92, 103, 123, 135, 151, 163
Barthes, R. 42, 53, 56
Bash, L. 2, 6
Beattie, A. 52, 56
Becher, A. 137, 138, 145, 150, 160, 163
Belsey, A. 23, 28
Benn, C. 10, 28
Benn, Tony 9, 28
Bernstein, B. 36, 39, 56
Bhaskar, R. 44, 45
Biggs, E. 90
Blackstone (Lady) T. 28
Blair, M. 71
Bogdanor, V. 8–9, 28
Bolton, Eric 25, 28, 91, 93, 103
Bonnett, B. 161, 162, 163
Booth, J. 145
Boulton, P. 82, 85
Bourne, J. 136
Bowe, R. 35, 39, 42, 56, 62, 71, 82, 85
Boyle, Sir Edward 9, 10, 11
Boyson, Sir Rhodes 12, 14, 15, 28
Brehony, K.J. 58, 59, 63, 64, 68, 69, 70, 71, 72
Bridges, D. 147, 153, 154, 158, 159, 161, 162, 163,
    164
Brigley, S. 60, 71
Broadfoot, P. 57
Brown, M. 51, 53, 56
Brown, P. 151, 163
Browne, S. 167, 170
Bryant, A. 33, 38, 40
Burchill, J. 92, 93, 101, 103
Burgess, R.G. 5, 72, 137, 139, 140, 142, 145, 170
Butler, R.A. 26, 28

Callaghan, James 12, 16, 17, 18, 28, 87, 91, 94,
    149
Campbell, R.J. 88, 94, 103
Cameron, D. 136
Candappa, M. 145
Canning, T. 145
Carter, R. 123, 129, 131, 135
Chequer, N. 27, 30
Cherryholmes, C. 42, 56
Chitty, C. 2, 3, 8, 23, 24, 32, 39
Clanchy, J. 134
Clare, J. 132, 135
Clark, L. 89, 90, 91, 93, 104
Clarke, Kenneth 53, 54, 56, 133, 134
Cohen, L. 165
Coldron, J. 82, 85
Coons, J.E. 151, 155, 163
Corbett, A. 11
Cordingley, P. 24, 29, 105, 117, 119
Coulby, D. 2, 6
Cox, C. 22, 151, 163
Cox, C.B. 11, 12, 14, 29, 122, 123, 135
Crequer, N. 27, 30
Crittenden, B. 155, 163
Crome, D. 86
Crossman, R. 42, 56
Crowley, R. 135

Dale, R. 9, 26, 29, 60, 71
Daley, J. 128, 129, 132, 135
Davies, B. 33, 39, 40
Dearing, Sir Ron 25, 41, 42, 48–9, 51, 54, 55, 56,
    166, 171
Deem, R. 3, 4, 47, 58, 59, 61, 63, 64, 67, 68, 69,
    71, 72, 166
Dennison, B. 83, 86
Dent, H.C. 8, 29
Donoughue, Bernard 15, 16, 17, 18, 19, 27, 29
Dougill, P. 135
Douglas-Home, J. 22
Dowding, K. 119
Dowling, P. 171
Dunleavy, P. 119
Dunlop, F. 161, 163
Dyson, A.E. 12, 29

Eagleton, T. 124, 132, 135
Ebbutt, D. 163, 164

Eccles, Sir David 9
Echols, F. 76, 85, 86
Eco, V. 42, 57
Ecob, R. 171
Edwards, T. 4, 6, 77, 82, 85, 151, 163
Eggar, Tim 123, 126, 131, 132, 133, 135
Elliott, J. 57, 150, 154, 163, 164
Eraut, M.R. 137, 138, 145, 150, 160, 163
Esland, G. 71
Evans, J. 3, 32, 33, 35, 36, 38, 39, 40, 41, 42
Evans, K. 8, 29

Fenwick, I. 10, 29
Fergusson, R. 71
Fernandes, C. 63, 72
Fitz, J. 4, 5, 6, 77, 80, 82, 85, 86, 87, 150
Flower, D. 30
Flude, M. 29, 71
Fookes, Dame Janet 27
Fox, I. 80, 85

Gaden, G. 147, 164
Galloway, S. 145
Gamble, A. 23, 29
Gardiner, D. 123, 135
Gardiner, H. 90
Gewirtz, S. 82, 85
Gibson, R. 163, 164
Giddens, A. 35, 40, 43, 44, 45, 46, 57, 113, 119
Gill, D. 71
Gipps, C. 5, 6, 54, 55, 56, 57, 171
Giroux, H. 42, 57
Glatter, R. 71, 72
Goddard, R. 123, 127, 135
Golby, M. 71, 152, 164
Gold, A. 35, 39, 42, 56, 62, 71
Goldstein, H. 50, 51, 57, 168, 169, 171
Goodson, I. 44, 57, 135
Gould, Sir R. 9
Gow, D. 21, 28, 29
Graham, C. 131, 132, 133, 135
Graham, D. 3, 7
Gramsci, A. 135
Grant, M. 108, 120
Green, B. 125, 135
Griffiths, B. 20, 21, 22, 25, 27
Griggs, C. 22, 29
Gutman, A. 162, 164

Halliday, M. 127, 128, 135
Halpin, D. 80, 86
Halsey, A.H. 73, 86
Halsey, C. 47, 57
Halsey, P. 27
Halstead, J.M. 5, 6, 146, 154, 163, 164, 165
Hamilton, James 17, 18, 19, 27
Hammer, M. 71
Hammersley, M. 59, 72
Hargreaves, D. 110, 116, 119

Harris, N.S. 151, 164
Haydon, G. 161, 164, 165
Heath, A. 73, 86
Heath, Edward 12, 16, 20
Hemmings, S. 58, 68, 70, 71
Hennessy, P. 15, 20, 28, 29
Hiley, K. 115, 120
Hill, M. 34–5, 36, 37, 40
Hirschman, A.O. 168, 171
Hockey, J. 142
Holland, Sir Geoffrey 25
Honeyford, R. 129, 130, 131, 132, 133, 135, 154, . 155, 164
Horwitz, C. 158, 164
Hoskyns, Sir John 20, 27
House, E.R. 113, 120
Hoyles, C. 51, 57
Hughes, C. 139, 145
Hunter, J. 81, 86
Hymas, C. 131, 132, 135

Jeffries, G. 63, 72
Johnson, D. 72, 80, 81, 86, 151, 164
Johnson, R. 130, 135
Jonathan, R. 149, 164
Jones, G.W. 20, 29
Jones, K. 2, 6, 23, 30, 130, 135
Jones, M. 136
Joseph, Sir Keith 13, 23, 26, 28, 30, 87, 91, 118, 120, 152
Judd, J. 27, 30

Kelly, A.V. 33, 40
Kenney, A. 123, 135
Keys, W. 63, 72
King, A. 20, 30
King, D. 119
Kingman, Sir J. 122, 123, 135
Kirk, D. 34, 38, 40
Knight, C. 11, 14, 27, 30
Knight, J. 137, 145, 150, 160, 163
Kogan, M. 1, 5–6, 7, 51, 55, 57, 59, 63, 72, 105, 106, 117, 120, 137, 145, 150, 164

Lawlor, S. 28, 30, 101, 134, 135
Lawrence, I. 27, 30
Lawton, D. 51, 57, 153, 164
Lee, J. 5, 87, 150
Lello, J. 171
Leracic, R. 71
Levitas, R. 28
Lewis, D. 171
Lyotard, J–F. 115, 120

Macaulay, C. 75, 81, 86
Macbeth, A. 75, 81, 86
Macdonald, B. 168, 171
Macdonald, M. 71
McFee, G. 40

Tapper, T. 88, 104
Telfer, B. 132, 136
Thatcher, Margaret 12, 13, 14, 20, 21, 22, 24, 25,
    26, 28, 97
Thomas, A. 83, 86
Thomas, J. 165
Thomas, S. 34, 40
Tomlinson, A. 40
Tomlinson, S. 169, 171
Torrance, H. 57
Troyna, B. 71
Tweddie, J. 74, 75, 80, 81, 85
Tytler, D. 7

Van der Eyken, W. 72
Varlaam, R. 81, 84, 86

Wagner, R. 165
Walden, G. 129, 130, 131, 132, 133, 136
Walford, G. 4, 68, 72, 73, 78, 79, 80, 83, 86, 137,
    145, 166
Walker, R. 120, 171
Wallace, G. 71
Webb, S. 59, 61, 72

Webster, A. 83, 86
West, A. 81, 84, 86, 136
Westoby, A. 2, 7, 61, 62, 72
White, J. 151, 159, 161, 165
White, P. 165
Whitfield, R.C. 148, 162, 165
Whittaker, T. 72
Whitty, G. 2, 3, 4, 6, 7, 44, 57, 77, 82, 85, 151, 163
Wilby, P. 22, 24, 29, 31
Wilcox, B. 118, 120
Willetts, David 20–1, 27, 31
Willis, P. 44, 57
Willms, J.D. 76, 85, 86
Wilson, Harold 12, 15, 16
Winkley, D. 115, 120
Wood, R. 168, 171
Woodhead, C. 3–4, 6, 100
Woodhouse, G. 169, 171
Woods, P. 61, 62, 66, 72
Worthen, J. 53, 57
Wright, A. 30

Young, H. 12, 26, 31
Young, M. 57

Subject Index

accountability 1, 3, 4, 5, 19, 53, 54, 55, 137–45,
 146–62
 audiences for 138
 central control model of 1, 19, 41, 53, 149,
 150, 155
 chain of responsibility model of 150, 151, 152,
 153, 154, 155, 159–60
 consumerist model of 1, 53, 55, 63, 150, 151,
 155, 168
 contractual 143–4, 149
 market mechanism model of 1, 53, 55
 moral 138–41
 partnership consumerist model of 1, 115, 150,
 153, 155, 160–2
 professional control model of 1, 5, 55, 141–3,
 147, 150, 153, 155–9
 self-reporting evaluation model of 1, 150, 155
agency, in the policy process 35, 43, 44, 46
art 79, 90
assessment 32, 41–57, 99, 166
 comparability of 48, 54
 competitive 51
 connected 50
 contextualized 51, 166
 coursework 53
 decontextualized 3, 51, 166
 evaluative 4, 49, 54
 false negative 168
 false positive 168
 formative 3, 49, 53, 54
 ipsative 51
 non-competitive 51, 166
 norm-referenced 50
 phases of 49–55
 reliability of 48, 53, 54
 separated 50
 summative 3, 4, 48, 49, 54
 teacher 48, 49
 terminal 48
 validity of 53, 54
assisted places scheme 4, 73, 77, 82
Attainment Targets 32, 48, 52, 53
Audit Commission Report (1989) 106–7
autonomy 36, 147

balance 33, 34, 96, 98, 99
biography 44, 45
Black Papers 11, 12, 14

breadth 33, 34, 95, 96, 97, 98, 99
British Educational Research Association
 (BERA) 144
British Sociological Association (BSA) 141, 143,
 144

Campaign for Real Education 25
Central Policy Review Staff 20
Centre for Contemporary Cultural Studies
 (CCCS) 92
Centre for Educational Development, Appraisal
 and Research (CEDAR) 70
Centre for Policy Studies (CPS) 13, 21, 22, 27,
 101
chief education officers 59
Circular 10/65 9
city technology colleges 4, 73, 78, 83, 84
civil service 27
class 62, 63, 75, 77, 82, 83, 84, 169
compulsory competitive tendering 38
Conservative Party 2, 9, 10, 11, 12, 13, 14, 22, 24
content in policy-making 35
context in policy-making 33, 35, 42, 43, 45, 48
Coopers & Lybrand Deloitte 117
Council for the Accreditation of Teacher
 Education (CATE) 88, 95, 99, 100–1
Cox Report 122, 123
Croydon Education Committee 28
curriculum 3, 19, 24, 32, 41, 95–8, 110
Curriculum Matters service 95–8

dance 33
Department for Education (DfE) 5, 36, 66
Department of Education and Science (DES) 5,
 9, 16, 17, 18, 19, 27, 52, 88, 132
differentiation 2, 4, 96, 97, 98, 99
Downing Street 2, 15, 17, 19, 21, 22, 27
Drummond Parents' Action Committee 155

Economic and Social Research Council
 (ESRC) 70, 140, 142–3
Education Act (1944) 2, 8, 26, 73, 89
Education Act (1980) 59, 60, 73, 74, 77, 80
Education Act (1981) 73
Education Act (1993) 5, 48, 58, 61
Education Act (no. 2) (1986) 47, 58, 59, 60, 63,
 153–4
Education Reform Act (1989) 2–4, 5, 6, 24–5,